THE
Insightful
Sportsman

Ted Williams

THE Insightful Sportsman

Thoughts on Fish, Wildlife and What Ails the Earth

TED WILLIAMS

THE SILVER QUILL PRESS
an imprint of
Down East Books • Camden, Maine

ISBN 0-89272-383-1

Text and cover design by Kat Rosard
Cover photograph by Jim Butler
Color separation by Roxmont Graphics
Printed and Bound at Bookcrafters, Inc., Fredericksburg, Va.

1   3   5   4   2

Down East Books
Camden, Maine

Library of Congress Cataloging-in-Publication Data

Williams, Ted, 1946-
    The insightful sportsman : thoughts on fish, wildlife and what
ails the earth / Ted Williams ; edited by James E. Butler.
        p.   cm.
    ISBN 0-89272-383-1 (pbk.)
    1. Wildlife management--United States. 2. Wildlife conservation-
-United States. 3. Hunting--United States. 4. Fishing--United
States.   I. Butler, James E.   II. Title.
SK355.W735   1996
333.7--dc20
                                                    96-1947
                                                    CIP

For Scott and Beth,

whom I have tried to infuse with this

philosophy. And for Mace,

who now infuses me.

Acknowledgments

THE HARD THING ABOUT WRITING real conservation pieces is not finding material but finding editors who dare to publish it consistently. I've been lucky to have found Roxanna Sayre (whose brave, generous spirit lives in all the writers she helped make) and Les Line, formerly of *Audubon*; Roger Cohn and Mike Robbins, currently of *Audubon*; Silvio Calabi and Jim Butler, of *Fly Rod & Reel*; Pete Rafle, of *Trout*, and his environmentalist boss Charles Gauvin, who saved Trout Unlimited; Harry Bruce, of the *Atlantic Salmon Journal*, and his boss Bill Taylor, the young knight the Atlantic Salmon Federation so desperately needed to lead it into the 21st Century; Debbie Behler, of *Wildlife Conservation*; and Cindy Berger, of *Living Bird*.

These smart, dedicated professionals have encouraged me, stood by me, pampered me, pushed me and done what so few editors are capable of—helped a writer do better work. My heartfelt thanks.

Contents

Introduction

THERE HAS NEVER BEEN A WRITER quite like Ted Williams. Surely, there are nature writers who can match his lyrical descriptions of the natural world and fishing scribes whose prose can equal his gripping accounts of angling for Arctic charr in Canada or bonefish in the Caribbean. And unquestionably, there are journalists who can probe as deeply and produce hard-hitting stories that have real impact on national policy.

But until Ted Williams emerged on the scene, there simply was no one who put all these skills together and thus forged a new kind of environmental journalism—rich in its detailed, relentless reporting, its uncompromising toughness and its love of the outdoors.

Some of the best of Williams' work is here in this collection of pieces, from *Audubon*, *Fly Rod & Reel* and other publications, dating back to 1981. In this volume is a range of topics that shows the breadth and depth of his writing on everything from why he prefers "jiggering" to ordinary ice-fishing, to how fish-farm operators legally slaughter thousands of birds annually, to how Idaho cattle barons threatened to kill a US Forest Service official who sought to end abusive grazing practices on the public range.

This is the first collection of Williams' writing—a remarkable fact, considering the influence he has had on his fellow writers and so many critical environmental issues. In re-reading the stories here, I am struck by how well this work has stood the test of time. Though mostly tied to the events of the day and written with the immediacy and power of daily journalism, the writing has an enduring quality that transcends the shelf life of any magazine.

In many ways, Williams' growth as a writer—as reflected in these pages—parallels the maturation of the conservation movement. When he first started his career, in 1970, Ted was a writer for the Massachusetts Division of Fisheries and Wildlife—a Yankee kid who had grown up canoeing and fishing the waters of his native New England and hiking the backcountry of his beloved Maine. As his articles began appearing in national publications, he kept honing his craft and expanding his notions of what a wildlife or conservation story might be.

And so we have in this book some of Williams' earlier wildlife pieces, including a report on wild turkey restoration and a homage to flying squirrels, and more recent stories reflecting a broader view of environmental issues, such as the poisoning of Alaskan rivers by a new gold rush and the effects of pesticide abuses in Louisiana on both wildlife and the families living near the sugarcane fields.

In breaking new journalistic ground, Williams has kept his keen Yankee eye focused on nature. Consider this description of fishing for Atlantic salmon in New Brunswick: "With delicate swirls or savage boils they detoured to my barbless fly, then vaulted into the air, flashing sunlight." Or his report of flying in a bush plane over the Alaskan wilderness: "Even now, in high summer, snowdrifts persevered on the north faces of bald hilltops, deserted save for scattered caribou that tossed their heads and showed the whites of their eyes as we raced low over the summits."

Ted Williams was already a national institution by the time I arrived at *Audubon* five years ago. Though a newcomer to the magazine, I was handed the daunting assignment of editing Williams' regular Incite column—for me, a task almost akin to being asked to perfect the work of the Creator while he rested on the Seventh Day. Working with Ted has proven the maxim that the best writers are the easiest to edit—not just because his writing needs so little editing, but because he looks at every suggestion as an opportunity to cut and polish the gem he has produced.

He is doggedly loyal to his friends (who are classed in the Williams lexicon as "good shits") and fierce in his steadfast opposition to those who would sacrifice the natural world to their own vanity and the pursuit of profit. And behind the fearless journalist who delights in skewering environmental villains, there lies an utterly self-effacing, genuinely modest and throughly generous man.

This was brought home to me on my first fishing trip with Ted, a few years ago on Maine's Kennebec River. I had warned Ted that I was a novice angler, but he had not really taken me at my word. For most of the morning, he cheerfully brought in one gorgeous striped bass after another, admiring each fish with a respectful eye before gently releasing it. Finally I hooked one, its silver flank gleaming as I struggled to reel it in, when suddenly the line went slack. I'd lost my first fish.

Humiliated, I turned to Ted and asked what I'd done wrong. He looked at me with all the wisdom of his years of fishing, shrugged and said, "Bad luck."

Bad luck, indeed.

And all of us who have enjoyed his writing for years ought to be grateful for our truly good luck in having Ted Williams to keep us honest and to keep reminding us of the fragility and magnificence of the natural world.

Roger Cohn
Executive Editor, *Audubon* Magazine
February 1996

The Joe-Pye-Weed Is Always Taller in the Other Person's Yard

Taking sweet revenge on your lawn

Audubon, July 1981

BREATHES THERE a suburbanite who cannot empathize with Jack, the hero of Richard Brautigan's nonfictional short story "Revenge of the Lawn"? "Jack," writes Brautigan, "used to curse the front yard as if it were a living thing." Basically, it was not. And the reason it was not is that Jack refused to water it or to lavish upon it all the insecticides, herbicides and fertilizers that successful grass monocultures demand. The issue of mowing, like the grass, never came up. But if it had, Jack would have refused to do that, too.

To learn all the subtle and insidious ways the lawn got even with Jack, one must read the story, but the revenge of his lawn differs from the revenge of other lawns only in method, not degree. All lawns are, as Brautigan would say, bent on self-destruction and bitterly resentful of those who keep them from it. A lawn is a forced holding pattern in the natural progression of bare earth to forest or prairie. To maintain property in lawn, people must resist one of the most powerful and pervasive forces in nature, and they may resist only with monumental expenditure of energy. This expenditure and its attendant environmental degradation—not to mention numerous heart attacks, ulcers and severed toes—is the revenge that our lawns wreak upon us.

A relation of mine—Mort, we'll call him—recently moved from a house perched upon expansive grass to an apartment perched upon expansive cement. Mort's lawn ran him off his own land. For years he and it were drawn together in a perverse love-hate relationship where love, in terms of relative concentration, was the vermouth in a very dry martini. Whenever Mort was not sleeping, eating or selling insurance he was working on his lawn. He became a lawn fixture, nearly as permanent as the birdbath, a squatting Canute stabbing at the flooding tide of natural plant succession. He seeded, sprayed, mowed, raked, watered, limed, fertilized and reseeded. Every year he paid a company $400 to drench his turf with lawn elixirs and give it a once-over with a tooth-studded steamroller. He built a capacious shed to house his lawn equipment, but even that could not contain it all. In his garage an intimidating array of cans and bottles, sheathed in small-print labels stained yellow and brown, was piled nearly to the rafters. Mort seemed to have a chemical poison for every day of the week and every hour of the day. From this awesome stockpile he concocted the leprous distillation with which, out of consideration for his grass, he annually aborted his apple trees . . . along with Lord knows what else. Finally, Mort's health and money gave out. The lawn won.

Mort's effort on behalf of his lawn may sound a trifle excessive, but by the standards of the lawncare industry it was not. In *Horticulture* Magazine W.H. Daniel, who is identified as "a turf specialist and professor of turf management," has mapped March-through-November strategy in the eternal war against nature to preserve the lawn. It is the kind of article one reads over and over again until all hope that it is satire has vanished. Along with three pages of complicated instructions, Daniel offers a chart in which he unsmilingly sets forth 10 important treatments: "seeding," "mowing," "fertilizing," "killing weeds" (for this the reader is provided with a sketch of a dagger stuck in the ground), "irrigating," "reducing crab grass" (sketch of four tanks spewing herbicides), "preventing insect damage" (sketch of aerosol bomb zapping bug), "reducing thatch," "protecting against diseases" (sketch of six bottles, each labeled with skull and crossbones), and finally—or firstly, depending on how you look at it— "starting over" (sketch of two shovels stuck in ground). The title of the piece—conceived, one is tempted to conclude, by some smirking editorial assistant—is "The Thinking Man's Lawn."

Were I to enroll in Professor Daniel's class, I would promptly be awarded an F. The only piece of lawn equipment I own is a Hahn POW-R-PRO mower. Mort gave me the mower—spitefully, I've often thought—when he moved. In the two years that it has resided in my garage it has been cranked up but rarely and never by me. For the most part, the plant community on my property cannot honestly be called lawn.

My land is rife with what Mort and certain of my neighbors call deadwood, decadence and disorder. But my rebellion against the lawn is motivated by more than sloth alone. My land is also rife with wildlife. "Weeds" and wildflowers sustain nearly two dozen species of butterflies. Rabbits, flying squirrels, woodpeckers, hummingbirds and a host of songbirds abound. Sometimes there are hawks, owls and foxes. The meadow and vine-tangled woodlot teem with small mammals and provide food, cover and even nesting habitat for woodcock and killdeer. "Why," I asked Mort the other day, "would I want to exchange all this for an ordered, lifeless putting green?" I did not, I tactfully told him, wish to be mistaken for "Monoculture Man," described by Bill Mollison in his new book, *Permaculture Two*: "Monoculture Man (a pompous figure I often imagine to exist, sometimes fat and white like a consumer, sometimes stern and straight like a row crop farmer) cannot abide this complexity in his garden or his life."

But it is I, not Mort, who is out of step. Disparage the sacrosanct tradition of the American lawn, and people snicker and look at you as if you were a weird organic cultist plotting also, no doubt, against the wearing of clothing and the sanctity of the family unit. What is the purpose of a lawn, anyway? Why our national obsession with this odd ground cover? Like most of the grasses that make it up, the lawn is alien to North America and ill-adapted to most North American life zones. The tradition began in the wet, cool clime of England, where lawns succeed splendidly. There the wealth of a landowner was inverse to the length of his grass: even in the middle of town, horses were turned out to graze, and if your grass was close cropped, it meant you had a lot of horses. Thus the cultural heritage of the Kojak-coiffured grass monoculture as status symbol.

John H. Falk, of the Smithsonian Institution, who has conducted extensive research on his own lawn in Edgewater, Maryland, suggests that our lawn fetish has even deeper roots. "Could we be striving to create neosavannas in our own parks and front yards?" he asks. "Many anthropologists place the origins of Man in the shortgrass savannas of East Africa one to three million years ago. In any case, the majority of Man's development as a species has occurred in this habitat. Man, like most of the smaller savanna animals, probably restricted his movements to the shortgrass and avoided the tallgrass where predators could lurk undetected."

By best estimates, Americans spend around $12 billion a year to maintain a little more than 20 million acres of lawn. Mort never dared figure what it cost him to keep his lawn. But General Electric Medical Systems reports that it spends roughly $1,500 per acre per year to maintain a 23-acre lawn in Waukesha, Wisconsin. (Another 80 acres of GE's Waukesha property is maintained in natural prairie at an estimated annual cost of $25 per acre.)

Lawnowners now can contract with companies whose employees arrive by tank truck, periodically and unannounced, to fill up the lawn with chemical poisons and fertilizers in much the same way the oil man fills up the furnace tank. Customers rarely concern themselves with what chemicals they are getting, and if they do, they are apt to be disappointed because the various brews often are trade secrets. The lawn chemical delivery industry has been growing by about 25 to 30 percent per year. ChemLawn, the aptly named market leader (which has just bought out Techniturf), has grown from about $10 million in sales in 1973 to $113.5 million in 1980. At this writing, ChemLawn stock is worth $21.50 per share–not that impressive until you consider that, since the company incorporated in 1969, its shareholders have enjoyed several stock splits, with an accumulated ratio of 33.75-to-one. Today there are more than 150 ChemLawn branches in more than 100 cities across the United States and Canada.

It is widely reported in the "organic press" that America uses more chemical fertilizers to grow lawn grass than India uses to grow food. A major ingredient in most of these fertilizers is ammonia, made of nitrogen from the air and hydrogen from oil. Atmospheric nitrogen exists in tightly bound molecules of two nitrogen atoms, which must be broken apart before it can be utilized by plants. Fertilizer companies break this bond with heat—usually heat provided by natural gas. When the fertilizer has been distributed by oil- or gasoline-powered vehicles and applied by gasoline- or human-powered spreaders, the resultant grass is razed by mowing machines, about 50 million of which are powered by gasoline.

This energy binge is kept lively by the lawncare industry. Any lawngrower who reads his slick mailings knows that his crop is called "thatch" and that "thatch" is bad, something to be taken to the landfill in oil- and gasoline-powered vehicles. "Thatch" is said to do all sorts of awful things to one's lawn. But what it really does is to return more than 50 percent of the nitrogen to the grass. Of course the fertilizer salesmen and manufacturers recommend against "thatch." "If you think the 'thatch problem' is a bogus affliction, hatched by the marketing people in some fertilizer company," writes Jack Ruttle, managing editor of *Organic Gardening*, "you have been proven right."

Mort, and millions like him, have been conditioned by lawncare literature to poison off invading plants—white clover, for instance. But plants like white clover draw nitrogen from the air, break the double atom and release it into the soil so that other plants, like grass, can use it. White clover is a threat all right—not to lawns, but to the lawncare industry.

By keeping careful track of all the kilo calories (kcal) he expended in maintaining his property in lawn, Smithsonian's John Falk has provided lawngrowers with what is probably the most shocking illustration of their energy profligacy. Although he is thrifty and organically inclined, Falk's lawn costs him 1,865 kcal per square meter per year—mostly in gasoline and irrigation. Physical labor accounts for only 2.5 percent of the energy input. If Falk grew corn instead of "thatch," he would have to expend only 715 kcal per square meter per year.

The revenge of the lawn, of course, doesn't end with a drain on our shrinking energy reserves. Lawns drain our shrinking water reserves, too. They get us coming and going—first, by demanding extensive irrigation, then by polluting the water supplies into which they drain. One study found that urban (lawn-fed) streams contain two to four times more pesticides than rural streams, even though rural streams often drain heavily sprayed farm and forest land.

Lawns even pollute the air. In Oregon's Willamette Valley—literally the home turf of America's lawn-seed industry—the annual burning of grass stubble has befouled the atmosphere so grievously that a limit of 50,000 acres burned per year had to be specified in the state's implementation plan for compliance with the Clean Air Act. Although the City of Eugene—over which most of the smoke collects—filed suit to enforce this limit, the state legislature passed a bill in 1980 that establishes a new limit of 250,000 acres per year. On any given day up to 300,000 persons can be exposed to this pollution.

While Americans may now joke on the Sabbath with impunity, there is still a good chance they will be fined or thrown in jail if they don't get out there and mow their lawns. Most communities have "weed ordinances" that set legal limits on the height of one's grass and prohibit the cultivation of certain "noxious weeds." When Donald Hagar, a wildlife biologist with the US Forest Service in Wisconsin, failed to mow half of his 2.6 acres in New Berlin's Sun Shadows West subdivision, he incurred the wrath of town officials for violating the relatively liberal weed-ordinance height limit of 12 inches.

Hagar explained that he had been driven to crime by love for the wildlife that his unkempt property sheltered and fed. Still, the city hauled him into court, threatening fines that could have exceeded $4,000. The prosecution maintained that Hagar's property was a fire hazard and a rat haven. But a US Forest Service fire expert testified that fuel-loading tests in early spring when grasses and forbs were dry had revealed no difference between Hagar's land and the lot across the street tended by the city's weed commissioner. He explained that a fire on Hagar's land would not be a hazard to anything because grass fires can sustain heat for only 15 seconds—short by six minutes and 45 seconds of the time required of the same heat to ignite wood. He also explained that, during the growing season, Hagar's wild plants were too green to burn and that mowing them would create fuel for fire.

Next, a rat expert testified that "food [garbage and grain] is the key to rat abundance—not grass." After a thorough examination of Hagar's property he reported no trails, no burrows, no pellets, no rats.

The city darkly suspected that Hagar had been motivated by something more than concern for wildlife: concern for plants. "Are you or have you ever been a member of any of those groups interested in preserving all types of plants?" demanded the prosecuting attorney.

"Don't make it sound so un-American," said the judge. "Your wife or my wife might even belong to some of these groups."

But Hagar answered the question, confessing that he had indeed been a member of such groups and that he had been imbued with their alien ideologies. In particular, he disclosed, he wanted to save the various prairie plants that lawns (and livestock) had pushed to the brink of extinction. Among these, incidentally, are the wood lily and the bottle, cream and fringed gentians that may owe their existence to purposeful, Hagar-type violations.

On April 21, 1976, Donald Hagar was found guilty of growing "noxious" thistle and field bindweed. He was fined one dollar. But the grass-cutting section of the New Berlin weed ordinance was declared unconstitutional.

Kathleen Brown, of Midland, Michigan, has come up with an especially creative method for resisting forced lawnthink. In the fall of 1977, when weed authorities contacted her about the disheveled condition of her property, she wrote them as follows: "I've never received either written or oral notice that my yard is in violation of any law. I have been notified only of complaints. The last one, if I change but two words, would read: 'We have received a complaint about the [wart] on your [nose]. Will you please remove it? Thank you.' Is the city's role to be a conveyer of complaints, or to administer laws?" With that, she threatened to meet further complaints by setting out these *legal* lawn decorations: "yellow plastic sunflower-shaped windmills; pink plastic flamingo statues; large tractor-tire flower-planter; shrine with Madonna in cut-off, upended bathtub; toilet flower-planter."

The Borough of Emmaus, Pennsylvania, picked the wrong sparring partner when it took on Rodale Press in a weed ordinance bout in July 1979. Rodale had undertaken an experiment in which 65 percent of its property was to be maintained in traditionally manicured lawn, 25 percent in meadow and the remaining 10 percent in "natural area," where nothing except poison ivy was cut or killed. Rodale, publisher of *Organic Gardening*, was spoiling for such a fight and went jauntily to court. The defense cleverly proved that the Rodale property did not harbor the kind of weeds that "emit noxious odor" or "offer conceal-ment to filthy deposit." But the victory was incomplete. "It is unlikely," declared the court, "that the average suburban homeowner could muster the same justifications as Rodale for avoiding the require-ments of these ordinances."

"For Rodale to get a 'day in court' and limit the case to such a degree makes me furious!" exclaims naturalist and antilawn activist Lorrie Otto, of Milwaukee. When Otto first allowed her lawn to do its own thing, the weed inspector showed up when she wasn't home and gave it a crewcut. The weed ordinance prohibited only leafy spurge, field bindweed and Canada thistle, none of which she cultivated. She demanded that the weed inspector show her evidence of such weeds on her property, and when he failed to do so she collected enough in damages to buy her first original oil painting. Otto led the campaign to raise the $4,000 necessary for the defense of Don Hagar—her favorite folk hero who, as she puts it, "did not submit to the insidious peer pressure which forces suburbanites to mimic each other and preen their yards into lifeless, artificial landscapes."

Otto got started against the lawn out of concern for children, espe-cially her own. "What happens in a society when the young are not stimulated by a diversity of life?" she asks. "Since childhood we've been taught that one form of life depends on another. In adulthood we in turn preach it to the young. Yet in the areas where we could put our learning and teaching into practice—schoolyards, churches, hospitals, roadsides and, most obvious of all, our own yards—we neaten and bleaken, consistently and relentlessly destroying habitat for almost all life. It's as if we took off our heads, hung them up, and left them at the nature center."

Otto identifies plastic vegetation as the next logical step in America's quest for the perfect lawn. She has a point. A few years ago a couple in Renton, Washington, paid $3,500 for an artificial garden. The landscaper poured a large bed of cement, to which he glued artificial turf and 31 species of synthetic flowers. Los Angeles County even planted a $74,501 plastic forest, much of which was promptly clearcut by the public.

But Otto is a lot more than anti-lawn. She is *pro*-natural-yard. She teaches courses on the natural yard, lectures on it, writes on it. Wherever she goes, she senses a gathering groundswell of enthusiasm. Her neighbors, who at first had hotly demanded she tend her lawn like every other proper suburbanite, now are asking her to help them start natural yards of their own.

One indication that Otto has it right about the groundswell is the sudden shrill denunciation of natural yards by the lawncare industry. The Lawn Institute, one of the industry's mouthpieces, can't stop talking about how insignificant is the natural-yard movement. "It's been festering for years," says Institute director Robert Schery. "It's never been a big thing. It's usually found within the framework of the environmentalists who are talking mainly to themselves rather than the public."

In *Seed World*, after explaining that the natural-yard movement is really diffuse and unorganized, Schery writes: "It feeds upon a vague feeling of 'guilt' that America is unduly extravagant lavishing so much attention on what, offhand, seems to be 'nonproductive' lawn-growing while world conditions worsen. Well-meaning environmentalists encourage the reaction because of its conservationist overtones . . . . And, of course, anti-pesticide fervor reinforces whatever antipathy befalls lawns." Then, looking very hard for a resounding "yes" (and probably getting it from the readers of *Seed World*), Schery asks: "Aren't those capacious mowers, facile spreaders, diversified irrigation devices, the tailored fertilizers that feed lawngrasses gradually, the selective herbicides that weed lawns with surgical nicety, other pesticides if and as needed, really the pleasant, efficient way?"

Lorrie Otto and her crowd think not. She says she has a plan, or maybe a dream: "If suburbia were landscaped with meadows, prairies, thickets, or forests, or with combinations of these, then the water would sparkle, fish would be good to eat again, birds would sing, and human spirits would soar." She says her real goal is not to win legal acceptance of natural yards, but to live long enough to take people who have lawns to court.

When that happens, the ghost of Brautigan's friend Jack will be sitting next to her, gloating over *his* revenge. And if the Lawn Institute is still around then, maybe it can raise funds for the defense.

Planning a Natural Yard

1. In most of the area west of the Mississippi, your natural yard will be prairie, a climax condition. The site should be in full sunlight. A good way to maintain prairie, when and where legal, is to burn it occasionally. This gives the plants a quick boost of potash, phosphorus and calcium and kills alien weeds whose roots are not adapted to fire.

2. East of the Mississippi, in Western high country, and in the Pacific Northwest, a natural yard usually will progress from meadow to forest, unless you cut back invading trees and shrubs. In some areas it might be appropriate to plant or encourage evergreens on the north side of the house for wind protection in winter and shade in summer.

3. If you have hay fever, don't worry. Of the roughly 1,100 kinds of grass that grow wild in the United States, only a fistful are serious allergens. The only ones cited by the Asthma Allergy Foundation of America (AAFA) are: timothy, orchard, redtop, sweet vernal, Bermuda and "some blue grasses." All were introduced to North America from abroad (mainly for livestock forage), though evidence suggests that redtop and Kentucky bluegrass may already have been present in northern latitudes. Kentucky bluegrass, incidentally, is one of the most widely used American lawn grasses. And thanks to lawns, for which it is still popular, Bermuda grass has become a major pest plant in the South. Though trees produce more pollen than grass, they are less of a problem. Those cited by AAFA as most apt to make you sneeze are: elm, maple, birch, poplar, beech, ash, oak, walnut, sycamore, cypress, hickory and alder. The other potentially troublesome plants listed by AAFA are: sagebrush, pigweed, careless weed, plantain, spring amaranth, tumbleweed, Russian thistle, burning bush, lamb's quarters,

sorrel, cockleweed, marsh elder and, worst of all by far, ragweed. Goldenrod's association with hay fever is a bum rap.

4. Play politics. Obtain an audience with whoever enforces the weed ordinance and say, "Hey, I'm planning a natural yard with natural grasses and wildflowers. What are the weeds you want me to kill?" Then, when the complaints come in, the weedman can explain what your yard is all about and maybe feel like a bigshot. If he hears from someone else first, watch out.

5. You may decide just to stop mowing. "That's what we did," says Rodale's Jack Ruttle. "We're very near woods, so things start creeping in, and that makes it easier." But if you are surrounded by lawn or cement, you may not get much more than dandelions and crabgrass unless you bring in plants and/or seeds. Both may be collected in the wild where laws and landowners permit, or obtained through the mail. In the East, Herbst Brothers Seedsmen, 1000 North Main St., Brewster, NY 10509, offers natural seed mixes. Following are a few plant/seed sources in the Midwest, the epicenter of the natural-yard movement: Illini Gardens, Box 125, Oakford, IL 62673; Little Valley Farm, RR 1, Box 287, Richland Center, WI 53581; Natural Habitat Nursery, 4818 Terminal Rd., McFarland, WI 53558; Prairie Ridge Nursery, RR 2, 9738 Overland Rd., Mount Horeb, WI 53572. Ask for catalogs and further instructions.

UPDATE

Two years ago I decided to plant Meadow in a Can in our back field, which is surrounded by what we call the "Squirrel Woods"—a stand of oak, ash, butternut and maple entwined in Chinese bittersweet. In winter the starlings roost there by the hundreds. It would be smart, thought I, to plow the field so the seeds would take better.

The seeds took all right—the bittersweet seeds excreted like hail by the starling horde. Now the field looks and feels like Sleeping Beauty's castle was somewhere in the middle of it.

I don't like the lawn, but if we are going to have one (and Mace has ruled we are), by God it is going to be healthy. So I make Scott and Beth mow it and fill in the holes, dug by Wilton and the skunks, with edgings from Mace's flower gardens. They call me "The Turf Master."

Smallmouths at My Window

And pursuing them with a fly rod and a dry fly

Scientific Anglers' *Fly Rodding for Bass*, 1981

BEFORE ME, as I write, is a lake, a lake I have known intimately and loved well since I was first able to crawl into it. It is not the best smallmouth lake in New England, not even in the top 90 percent. Nor is it, in any sense, remote. On summer weekends one could surf on the motorboat wake. And this year there are whining, water-going snowmobiles, the purpose of which is to bear the operator around and around in ever-decreasing circles until he is sucked—temporarily, alas—into his own vortex.

Most of us have such lakes. One does not choose them any more than one chooses family. One is born into them. We love them, as Frost loved his waterless Hyla Brook, for what they are.

At least my lake has stayed clean these three decades, no doubt because of the constant aeration by jet skis and outboards. Her smallmouth bass are clean, too—hard and strong, with quick ruby eyes. There aren't very many of them, but I know where they are. (I should after all these years.) And I delight in exercising them with a fly rod.

In spring I could, if I wished, snatch them off their beds with popping bugs. But this, as someone (Nixon, I think) once observed, would be a cowardly act. And, besides, in the spring I am too busy with family responsibilities such as keeping wife and offspring supplied with wild brook trout.

I prefer to wait until the kingbird has taken his station at the point and the air is scented with sweet pepperbush, when paternal redbreast sunfish nip your toes, and copper dragonflies rise from their own reflections to flash through swirling clouds of midges. Now, on days when non-writers work, a hush falls over woods and water. I like it best on days like this one, when the air moves gently and the sun is muted through high, thin overcast, when redtails orbit our big, pine-clad island and my lake is still except for sailing boats under sailing gulls. Now the bass cruise the cool middle depths, two casts offshore, a long rod length below the surface. Now I am in my lake, waving a nine-foot graphite wand, wading on clean sand or mussel-strewn mud, swimming around the rocky points. I am buoyed by warm, soft, sweet-smelling water. There is no way of knowing a lake or her fish more intimately.

If you stare into the dancing sparks long enough, you may see a bit of a black fin or a dimple scarcely bigger than the splash of a hemlock cone. Sometimes it is illusion. Sometimes it is a sunfish. Sometimes it is a smallmouth that has drifted up to sip a squirming insect from the surface film.

If you think that you cast a good line under tough conditions, try presenting a greased grasshopper to a feeding smallmouth 40 feet farther out with the water lapping at your shoulders. If your line splashes and your leader collapses, don't be too hard on yourself. The nice thing about bass is that they seldom care. If you are in the general vicinity, mend your line and wait. Dance the fly a bit, and wait some more.

I love the way smallmouth bass take dry flies in summer. They are delicate and deliberate. They roll, and waggle their tails at you. There is no rush to set the hook. You lift the rod, always surprised by the weight of the fish. Your pulse races—not because you give a damn if you lose this fish, but because you need desperately to see him before you *might* lose him. In any kind of fishing the worst blow—after getting skunked—is losing an unseen fish. Unseen fish flap in the big, empty space inside an angler's head, waking him up at night. In that gulf between strike and first jump—when the smallmouth goes down for the same reason a pole vaulter goes back, and the water boils a full three seconds after the tail surge—you are more alive than you have ever been. And your mind stops to marvel at this thing called fishing. What an extraordinary pursuit, this obsession that makes graying men feel like little boys, that is called "a sport" by the rest of society, as if it were *bowling*.

When the line begins to angle up, you know that you will see him. The crisis is over. Your eye follows the line, and you lock in to his projected flight path.

Always, the smallmouth gives you the impression that he knows precisely what he is doing. His is not the frenzied fight of salmon. Everything he does is planned. He, not you, is in control. Finally he is there, exactly where he said he'd be, bulging the surface, breaking through the surface, rising, rising, trailing water, twisting, hanging, crashing back. It's OK to lose him now.

If I needed smallmouth bass in my refrigerator instead of in my lake, I think that I would still pursue them with a fly rod and a dry fly. In open water—which is the best smallmouth water—no method produces more fish per strike. They get the fly in the rubber edges of their jaws. They can't shake it out, as they can a lure, because it weighs nothing. They have no leverage. And the whippy rod provides a constant cushion against such ploys as head-shaking and tail-walking.

Sometimes you can hurt a bass with a popping bug, but you can never hurt a bass with a dry fly. No matter what, he is fighting only you, and 30 seconds later he has forgotten all about it. Nineteen years ago, when the state was foolish enough to stock my lake with scaleless, finless hatchery rainbows and I was foolish enough to fish for them, I saw a good smallmouth roll off Rhinoceros Rock. I eased the canoe over and dropped a big, buoyant Cahill on top of him. He slurped it in and I set hard, forgetting he wasn't a trout. The leader parted with an obscene crack, the fish jumped derisively, revealing his enormous bulk, and the line coiled around me like a corn snake on a rat. I shrieked an oath to the sky and continued fishing for hatchery trout.

A kingfisher rattled, dipped out of a big dead pine and sculled low along the Schneiders' cove. A bat appeared. The water went from pink to black. Mayflies danced. And off Rhinoceros Rock a smallmouth rolled.

I eased the canoe over and dropped another big Cahill in the middle of the newest, smallest ring. The bass rolled onto it and waggled his tail, and I set with restraint. I knew it was the same fish even before he jumped. He jumped only once, as is so often the way with really big smallmouth. I remember slugging it out with him in 50 feet of water in the dark with green frogs twanging and fireflies moving and flashing through the big island pines in the cadence of feeding trout. And I remember a big orange moon floating up over our point and the way a muskrat cut a silver V along the shore. Probably a barred owl was asking, "Who cooks for you?" (One usually does at that hour.) And I remember how the big bass felt in my hands and his pungent smallmouth smell. I held him for a long minute, not because he needed to be revived, but because I liked the thick, strong feel of him and the grand, powerful swishing of his tail. Before he glided off I slipped both my Cahills from his protruding lower lip.

Shortly thereafter, the fish and game department ceased its put-and-take trout stocking, not through any sudden shift in—or, rather, acquisition of—management philosophy, but merely because it had exhausted its funds in similar folly on other bass lakes. I became more diurnal in my fishing habits. While I still prowled the twilight by canoe whenever I could, which was often, there was something about these golden weekday afternoons that held me. Doubtless the fishing was not as good, but this way I could fish *in* rather than just *on* my lake, and there was something about seeing bass rising in full sunlight that intrigued me. I think it was that no one else saw. They said then and they say now that my lake is fished out, and maybe they are right. I guess it depends on how many decent smallmouth bass you need to keep you from getting grouchy. All I need is one per afternoon. Anything more comes as a pleasant surprise, brightening my mood still further. Bass from my lake are special, personal things, not to be compared with other bass from other lakes.

There was the day that I swam into the glare and out to the diving raft because a smallmouth, or something, had dimpled between me and it. Standing on the raft, with my back to the sun, I could see a fish working to my right and a fish working to my left, each a prayer and a grunt beyond my modest range. I turned left, with the wind, double-hauled, held my breath and shot. The grasshopper landed like a tin squid, and the fish gulped it. I felt the line go tight and wet against my curled index finger and, in my wrist, I felt the wonderful solid weight of a smallmouth. The line moved out and up in slow motion. I became aware of the shrill buzzing of cicadas, beginning in one tree-top and ending in another. Jays fluted. At last the bass was in the air, bright copper in the bright sunlight—a typical fish for my lake, 16 inches perhaps and very deep-bodied.

Those who know the smallmouth well—sober men who spurn superlatives—call him the strongest fish, for his size, that swims in fresh water. Perhaps those weird, hump-backed peacock bass that generate such flap in the big outdoor magazines are stronger, but I'll bet they aren't. As I write I can feel that immaculate little fish pounding for the bottom—through the rod, into my wrist and arm and shoulder.

Now dry and hot, I stood on the raft, stooping to rinse the bass slime from my soggy grasshopper. I turned to the right, and the wind—as if it were a divine wind—turned with me. The other bass was still rising. I whipped the fly dry, double-hauled, shot. He took, dipped and launched himself. Another 16-incher. A clean double on ruffed grouse could not have delighted me more.

All the while that I have been writing this I have been watching my lake like an osprey. From where I sit, 50 yards of seductive basswater is framed between a hemlock and an ancient white pine. It is now mid-afternoon, and I have seen two fish rise. I have been asking myself why I am in here writing down memories when I could be out there making them. The absurdity of it has been nagging on my conscience. Summer is as brief as the fragrance from sweet pepperbush. So goodbye; I'm going fishing.

UPDATE

Since I wrote the piece jet skis have been banned from New Hampshire lakes, largely as a result of lobbying by my parents (whose camp the jet skiers shot up one night in retaliation). Now I keep my Ruger Single Six in the liquor cabinet. If they shoot up my camp, they're going to get some return fire.

The smallmouths have been educated by catch-and-release bass tournaments. But fishing in deep water with worms, Kay and Jack Schneider catch smallmouths so enormous as to be obscene. When I wrote the piece there were no bluegills in the lake. Now they are everywhere; they're a pain, but the yellow perch are gorging on their fry. My friend Mike Hayden, Assistant Secretary for Fish, Wildlife and Parks under Bush, taught me how to make "shrimp" cocktail by boiling bluegill chunks in shrimpboil for one minute, then throwing them on ice.

In 1990 I caught the first crappie. Now they are almost as common as the bluegills and, as Kay likes to say, "we are learning to like them."

White perch, which had always been rare in our lake, are now less so, and I've been chasing them instead of smallmouths. One day last summer my childhood buddy Tricia Troup told me at 4:00 PM that all the Williamses and Reeds were invited for supper at six and please to go out and catch 30 white perch because Robbie, Judy and the kids were coming, too.

"*Patricia*," I said, "it's not that easy . . . ." She was busy and didn't care to discuss the matter.

"Just do it," she said.

In a panic I found brother-in-law Barry Reed and told him about my intimidating assignment. "Impossible," he said. "Does she think white perch are zucchinis? Doesn't she know that they make bass and trout seem *predictable*? Does she suppose that we'd be this obsessed with them if they behaved like bluegills?"

"My reputation is at stake," I said.

There were no whites at Trout Rock, none at Pickerel Rock, none at Rhinoceros, none at Escumbuet, none at Schneider's Cove. At 5:30 Barry caught the first at ML's weedbed—a 12-incher, with shoulders. From 5:31 to 5:55 we caught 32 more, all the same size.

"The bad news," I told Scott as I hauled the boat up on the beach and passed him the cooler, "is that you have to fillet these. The good news is that you get time-and-a-half."

We finished drinks on the Troup's porch at 7:15, just as Scott was walking in with the platter of fillets. Tricia didn't bat an eyelash, just took them into the kitchen and started rolling them in bread crumbs.

Fairy Diddling

Studying flying squirrels with a straight face—maybe

Audubon, November 1983

FROM THE MOUNTAINS of Oregon comes the story of this ancient log cabin that, along with a corporeal American family, was known to house the spirits of the early settlers who built it. In the attic was an old spinning wheel that had to go 'round, as the song says, despite the fact that no one was up there pumping. Night after night the family would hear the thing creaking away. Whenever anyone flung open the attic door the wheel would be in motion but decelerating—as if the spirit pumper had taken flight. At last, curiosity prevailed over fear, and an attic stakeout revealed that the operator of the spinning wheel was a fairy diddle.

"Fairy diddle" is one of several popular names—and in my opinion the only proper one—for any of the three closely related species of flying squirrels that inhabit North America and Eurasia. I can't verify the spinning-wheel tale, but I'm inclined to believe it—first, because tame rodents exercise in much the same fashion on and in smaller but similar wheels; second, because fairy diddles have a thing about attics; and third, because when it comes to haunting and puckish pranks there are no creatures more proficient than these merry wanderers of the night. Running nowhere on top of a spinning wheel is precisely like something a fairy diddle would "think of" and do.

Modern civilization has stripped nature of most of its magic and mystery, but what remains is largely preserved by fairy diddles. They are all about us, stirring in the twilight, abroad by dark, scuttering up bark and brick, spreading their flight capes, swooping over chimneys and rooftops, leering down and chirping as if in laughter at those who do not believe in things like fairy diddles simply because they cannot see them. Even where the earth grows buildings instead of trees and man has robbed night of everything up to and including its stars, fairy diddles thrive. In Washington, DC, for instance, there is an eight-story block of flats where unseen fairy diddles chase each other up the sheer cement walls and pop in and out of vacant rooms. Nationwide, they are probably more numerous than either red or gray squirrels. Sometimes there are five to the acre. Except in the Far North, they have two broods a year.

The spinning-wheel operator, if such existed, was doubtless a northern flying squirrel, *Glaucomys sabrinus*—from the Greek *glaukos*: "gray"; and *mys*: "mouse"; and the Latin *sabrina*: "river nymph." This is the larger and lesser known of the two North American species, dwelling in cool, dense coniferous and mixed forests from central Alaska through most of Canada to the Lower 48's high country and north country.

Our other fairy diddle is the southern flying squirrel, *Glaucomys volans*, *volans* translating from the Latin to "flying." It's America's smallest squirrel, averaging maybe nine-and-a-half inches in length, of which about four is tail, and weighing no more than two or three ounces. *Volans* inhabits almost all of the eastern United States, with a few isolated populations in Mexico.

Where the ranges of our two fairy diddles overlap it is exceedingly difficult to determine which species has revealed itself unless one has the specimen in hand. *Sabrinus* tends to be more brightly colored and is usually an inch or two longer and an ounce or two heavier. Often its dorsal pelage is browner and its belly hairs are lead colored at the base instead of white. Its head appears to be more rounded, its fur slightly longer, and its tail proportionally wider. Its "chirp" and "chuck" are softer and lower in pitch.

The fur of both species is thick and silky, the ears large, the whiskers long, the eyes black and prominent. There are no cheek pouches. When not in use the flight cape seems almost to disappear, shriveling into the belly, its sharp edge protruding a little from each flank, loose and folded like cloth on a collapsed umbrella. The flight cape doesn't hamper them much when they climb, but on the ground it renders them vaguely reminiscent of old men trying to walk with their trousers down around their ankles. In the water it renders them helpless, dragging them down within seconds. *Pteromys volans* is the Eurasian version of *Glaucomys*, which it closely resembles both in appearance and behavior. It occurs from Sweden to Japan. In Siberia it is hunted for its fur, which is dyed and sold under the name *moldena*: flying dog. There are 33 other species of flying squirrel (some say 34). Most, including the 36-inch giant flying squirrel, are native to Asia.

Once you start looking for fairy diddles, it never takes long to see one. Tap and scratch every woodpecker-ventilated snag you pass and sooner or later a beady-eyed, bewhiskered head will appear in one of the holes. A few more taps and the fairy diddle may scamper up and down the trunk. Or maybe you should settle in twilight or moonlight beside a hickory grove, or a feeding station baited with sunflower seeds and something smelly like bacon grease or peanut butter. Fairy diddles are remarkably trusting of humans, sometimes even allowing themselves to be scratched and stroked. Red-filtered light makes observation easier because it is virtually invisible to them, but they quickly become accustomed to the beam of an ordinary flashlight.

Perhaps you have encountered them before and never thought about what it was that you were seeing. They move across the violet sky like oak leaves on a gale, sometimes executing 90-degree turns, lateral loops or descending spirals (all by dropping a foreleg and thus creating drag on the opposite side of the flight cape) or just parachuting straight down from overhead branches.

It seems a shame that the first good look most of us get at fairy diddles is when they are pancaked on asphalt, regurgitated under sofas or floating high and bloated in the milk pail, maple-sap bucket and— maybe the most common observation site of all—the camp toilet. The beasts' perverse talent for drowning in liquid-containing vessels is the result of their prodigious thirst. They consume about two jiggers of water each night; were they of human size, that would translate to two gallons. Thus they rarely abide very far from streams or ponds (which might be how "river nymph" figures into the scientific name of the northern flying squirrel). And when they do, there is generally a year-round supply of standing stumpwater.

I was lucky. The first flying squirrel specimen I ever inspected up close was alive and well and busily engaged in gathering hickory nuts in front of "Countryside Apartments," where I once resided, briefly. I guess the nicest thing I can say about the place is that the developer had spared—or forgotten to cut—four large hickory trees from a stand that once covered the entire hillside. He had then seen fit to provide floodlights to illuminate the four trees, as if to extend to 24 hours the viewing of his good deed.

The flying squirrels—southern flying squirrels—didn't care a whit about the floodlights, which made the remnant grove as bright as any stage. Or about me and my new wife, who would sit among them while they "worked," if that word can be properly applied to the activities of fairy diddles. In virtually everything they undertook they had great difficulty maintaining a sober front. For instance, in the midst of nut gathering they would suddenly pause in order to bat the nuts around with their paws. Or they would pursue and snatch at each other through air and up shag bark, all the while emitting loud chirps, chucks and twitters.

For years after, I wondered why nature had bothered to provide them with owl-silent gliding ability if they were just going to squander the advantage by shouting at each other. Only last year did I learn—from flying squirrel researcher Nancy Wells-Gosling, of the University of Michigan—that the vocalization apparently has a Robin Goodfellow-like ventriloquial quality that may confuse predators.

The fact that a good deal of the vocalization is too high-pitched for human ears has led to speculation that flying squirrels navigate by echolocation, after the fashion of bats. It's a tempting hypothesis not easily wrested from those who fancy it. But Wells-Gosling cites an experiment in which a tame flying squirrel trained to come on command was released in a dark room equipped with vertical barriers. When its master called it, it launched, struck a barrier and crash landed, then ran in circles until it bumped into her leg, climbed it and received its nut reward.

It's said that fairy diddles can stay airborne for 100 yards, but the ones who lived at Countryside Apartments never made it past 30. Sometimes one would just materialize in front of us, hanging in the soft, still September air like a chamois on a clothesline. Or they would come fast, in twos and threes, barely descending, their stabilizer tails vibrating with tension. Just before impact they would decelerate with a sharp upward swoop, flip up their tails, balloon their flight capes and reach out with their thick-padded hind feet until their claws clicked on the bark. Usually, they let the excess momentum carry them up and around the trunk, a maneuver they probably evolved in order to frustrate pursuing owls.

I liked it best when they were getting ready to jump. On reaching a chosen launch site, a squirrel would gather itself up in a ball and chart its flight path with rapid side-to-side and up-and-down head movements—no doubt in compensation for its lack of binocular vision. Then it would spring forward. The flight cape would billow out, widened and supported by two crescent-shaped cartilage spurs that flipped from the "wrists," and the fairy diddle would be off into Massachusetts Electric's night. Or through the curtain sharply defined by the last beam and into the real night, where it belonged.

Before the boom in weird and ferocious pets there was much traffic in captive fairy diddles. They may make "good pets" compared with, say, monkeys—that is, they neither smell up the house nor rend your flesh—but when you're awake they're asleep, and to keep them breaks the spell. Stocks of "adorable flying squirrels" hawked in the outdoor magazines moved briskly. For one thing, the beasts are clean. While many rodents defecate and urinate in their nests, flying squirrels usually just urinate. They groom and clean themselves often, reaching almost every part of their bodies with claws and tongue. "He carried cleanliness to the extreme," wrote one owner of a tame flying squirrel in *Animal and Zoo* Magazine. In describing fairy diddle behavior, *Grzimek's Animal Life Encyclopedia* uses the words "fastidious" and "elegant."

And, of course, as the admen said, flying squirrels are "adorable." Grzimek briefly abandons his rigorous scientific decorum in order to convey the "adorableness" of two Southern flying squirrels owned by a friend: "As soon as the cage was opened, they ran to their human companions, did a few gymnastics on them, and investigated the insides of jackets, shirts, and trouser legs. They particularly enjoyed crawling into pockets where they liked to sleep . . . their owner could easily induce them to glide to him when he tapped his hand against his chest. Almost immediately they would land on his hand or whatever place he had tapped . . . . Sometimes they stood on his shoulder and delicately nibbled his ear, or they stuck their tiny noses in his ear and panted. They cleaned and looked through hair and clothes with their forepaws, teeth, and tongues. When they were still half asleep, they would allow [their owner] to pick them up and rub or scratch them. They would even hold out their heads in order to facilitate these caresses. Whenever any danger threatened—they were apt to be greatly afraid of rustling paper—they fled to as high a spot as they could find, or they sought refuge and security with people."

One can, however, write only so much about the engaging and gentle nature of flying squirrels before it becomes necessary to note behaviors that might be more readily attributed to, say, crows. Fairy diddles delight in stealing young birds from their nests. Not as changelings. As food. They are, in fact, rather voracious predators.

Deep in a Michigan forest one dark night, M.C. Nielsen, a noted authority on the state's Lepidoptera, reached for a moth that was feeding on some fermented bait he had applied to the trunk of a tree. But before his fingers closed around it, someone slapped him on the back. When he wheeled around he saw no one. The flying squirrel then climbed to his shoulder, leapt to the tree, snatched the moth and vanished into the night.

Fairy diddles are constantly getting caught in traps baited with such things as dead mice, and some trappers have it that cleaning out the local fairy diddle population is the first order of business necessary before you can get down to serious fur harvesting in a new area. So great is the fondness of fairy diddles for big caterpillars and pupae that they are thought to influence population cycles of the large silk moths.

One sultry August morning when the cardinal-flowers were in bloom and the night rain was steaming off the lush hardwood canopy of southern New Hampshire, I found a *volans* lolling in his doorway, trying to keep cool. His forelegs and part of his flight cape were draped over the edge of the woodpecker hole in a dead elm. He eyed me with distrust and disdain but declined to bestir himself. Not far from his tree I found several empty pignuts. He or one of his tribe had chiseled smooth, oval holes in them.

A week later I returned with my camera. My fairy diddle wasn't home, but every time I knocked with my tripod, a red squirrel in the next tree jumped two feet closer. I tapped him onto the fairy diddle's elm, down to the hole and, finally, into the hole. Evidently, he'd evicted the fairy diddle and was feeling possessive about the place. After that the holes in the pignuts around the dead elm were rough-edged and grated on my thumb. Gray squirrels and chipmunks, I discovered, don't bother to cut holes. They just chop.

I discovered also that the plainly audible tapping one hears on still autumn nights, which I had always dismissed as the work of elfin cobblers, is actually the work of fairy diddles. What you hear is their bared incisors hammering nuts into the forks in branches. They hammer with their snouts, too—when the cache site isn't a fork in a branch—but you can't hear that. If a *volans* mother (and doubtless a *sabrinus* mother, too, though they haven't been tested) has been storing nuts and is then presented with her offspring, she will sometimes store them, pounding each into place with sufficient force to elicit distress cries. And if provided with her offspring and then a nut, she will sometimes place it tenderly in the nest. (The researchers who dreamed up the experiment didn't say exactly what it was they'd proved. Maybe just that fairy diddles are absent-minded.)

Unlike other squirrels (one is tempted to write "normal squirrels") fairy diddles make no single store. Instead, in keeping with their characters, they simply pound their finds into whatever nook, cranny or hole happens to be handiest. When decreasing photoperiod triggers intensive fall hoarding they can store as many as 300 nuts a night. A nut is first scraped with the teeth to determine quality. If it passes this test, it is then turned over and notched on either side of the stem to make it easier to carry. Nuts are somehow scent-marked, though no one knows just how. If you present previously stored nuts along with "new" nuts to the fairy diddle who did the storing, it will generally drop the former in favor of the latter. And if you then wash the previously stored nuts in carbon tetrachloride and again present them along with new nuts, the fairy diddle will be unable to distinguish between previously stored and never stored.

Flying squirrels do not hibernate, although *volans* becomes torpid during excessively cold weather—even to the point that individuals may be plucked from the nest and held in your hand until your body heat awakens them. Not enough is known about *sabrinus* to say for sure that he does not become torpid in extreme cold, but it seems unlikely. Even at 20 degrees below he is abroad in the boreal night, burrowing straight down into the snow or excavating horizontal, weaselesque tunnels.

Both species conserve heat by packing nests (in or on trees) with whatever insulation is on hand—leaves, sphagnum moss, Spanish moss, feathers, grass, shredded bark, palmetto fibers—and by huddling together through the winter. The farther north, the more squirrels in a winter aggregation. One *volans* aggregation, packaged in a north country stump, contained 50 individuals. But of 29 *volans* nests surveyed in Florida, only two contained as many as three individuals.

Compared with most other small mammals, female fairy diddles kill and eat their young infrequently. Usually they are attentive mothers—imperative behavior owing to the excessively long development period of the young. It's a full six weeks between their appearance—as tiny, pink cocktail sausages with wispy whiskers, fused toes, flattened ears, bulging eyes sealed under tight, translucent skin—and the first tentative glides. Oddly, a *volans* mother (*sabrinus* wasn't tested) can't select her own young, usually numbering two to six, from a mixed group until they have lived outside her body for 40 days (exactly as long as they lived inside it). After that she will invariably select her own and attack others.

A mother doesn't teach her young to fly, she just pushes them into it. Before they learn, however, even when they weigh half what she does, she airlifts them—one at a time, holding them upside-down and, unless they are very young, with their legs wrapped around her head. A youngster's high-pitched distress cheeps draw swift response. In fact if you imitate these calls, you can sometimes fool a wild mother into searching through your clothing. Pick up a young fairy diddle and the mother may climb your leg and snatch it back. Dorcas MacClintock, in *The Squirrels of North America*, offers the following account: "A group of Michigan forestry students once felled a limb containing a flying squirrel nest. The students were curious and gathered around the nest, which one of them picked up and held in his hands. Undaunted, the mother squirrel fled to the top of a nearby tree, volplaned across a river to another tree, climbed up, and searched for a suitable hole [doubtless a previously selected emergency nest]. Then she glided back across the river, landed near the students, and climbed the trouser leg of the fellow holding the nest and her babies. With one baby firmly gripped in her mouth she descended the trouser leg, climbed high up a tree, glided across the river to the new nest-site, and poked her baby into the hole. She repeated the feat three times, only once making the mistake of ascending the wrong trouser leg."

And all that is pretty near as much as mortals ought to know about the doings of fairy diddles. The trouble with studying them is that no matter how clinical you try to be they set you laughing and even anthropomorphizing. Having worked with game managers and biologists at a state fish and wildlife agency, I know just how sinful this is— or at least I used to know. But for the past two years I have been called upon nightly to read aloud from Potter, Burgess, Lofting, White, Grahame . . . and still there have been no complaints about the roast grouse or woodcock stroganoff. Young naturalists ought to consult such sources, and if more of the old ones had, perhaps we wouldn't be so bereft of professionals who fight for wildlife instead of just studying it.

Now I'll admit that when, in *Bambi*, two autumn leaves strike up a conversation about their good looks, things have gotten thoroughly out of hand. But things have also gotten out of hand when someone watches fairy diddles up close, for prolonged periods, with a straight face and then reports that they are "rodents." We are talking here about an animal that stamps its feet when angry; lies on its back and kicks to discourage nest snoopers; embraces during mating, with the male throwing his flight cape over the female; greets members of the same denning group by literally kissing them. How, for example, does one seriously record the meeting of a group member and a stranger when the subjects are dancing and shouting and all the while attempting to sniff one another's genitalia but with scant success because each is constantly slapping the other in the face with the sole of its hind foot?

And what about the plight of fairy diddles? The fact is that they don't have one. Maybe there aren't quite as many around as there were before the forest-products industry decided that dead and dying trees were unclean appendages in need of surgical excision, but fairy diddles are still supremely abundant. They are one thing that we are definitely not running out of.

They are out there now, wherever the globe has whirled into its own shadow, haunting woods you thought were spiritless, flying between the cold moon and the Earth, jesting to Oberon—and accomplishing the important work of keeping night what it was meant to be.

UPDATE

Les Line is the best headline writer I've ever known. But I have to say I've never liked this one. It sounds downright depraved. If someone had walked into Big John's bar, in Waterville, Maine (where I spent most of my college days and nights) and accused me of fairy diddling, I'd have punched him in the head.

The fall after the piece came out, Beth and I had just returned from successful fairy diddling on Merriam District Road. She was going to bed, and I was pouring myself a drink when I heard her yell for me. I thought someone was in her room, and I was right. It was a fairy diddle. He was sitting on the curtain, watching us with obsidian eyes, fearless. I fed him peanut butter from my forefinger, and when he'd finished it he hauled the finger back and tried to eat that, too. He then swilled water from an eye dropper. Beth had two hamsters, both newly dead. (The female had eaten the male's face; apparently it had disagreed with her.) I took the exercise wheel from the deceased hamsters' cage and placed it beside Beth's bed. Beth set out a dish of peanuts and hung the hamsters' water bottle from the bed board. At about 3:00 AM I heard the wheel spinning.

The fairy diddle, whose name was Peanut, stayed all fall, coming and going, eating, drinking and spinning. I think he hibernated in the attic.

Peanut didn't show up the following year, and Grafton's fairy diddle population plummeted. (They tend to be very cyclical.) Now, however, they're back in force. Last fall they put on a spectacular show for Beth, Mace, me and our pal Bargo. Parked with the high beams on by Poler's Pond, we watched them swooping in twos and threes down Merriam District Road and chasing each other up the nut-laden hick-ory trees. Until we had dinner with them two months later Hank and Gail Poler thought they'd had deer jackers.

Resurrection of the Wild Turkey

Wildlife management gone right—but it didn't come easy

Audubon, January 1984

"EVERY NOW AND THEN we do something right, you know," announced my friend Carl Prescott, who supervises fish and wildlife management for the Commonwealth of Massachusetts and who sometimes gets a trifle annoyed with environmental writers. I scratched my head, chewed my pen, scowled as if in deep thought, then asked him if it was the new linoleum. But I knew what it was. It was wild turkey restoration.

In Massachusetts and dozens of other states this is some of the good news that game managers say gets skipped over. There are, of course, other successes—such as bald eagle recovery—but these are more dramatic, and a lot gets written about them. People need to pay attention to wild turkey restoration because it casts so much other game and fish department activity into proper perspective—the put-and-take stocking of cock pheasants, for instance. It shows what can be done. It's a prime example of wildlife management gone right.

There are only two species of turkey: *Meleagris gallopavo* of North America, domesticated by Indians about 2,000 years ago, and the smaller, more colorful *Meleagris ocellata* of southern Mexico and Central America. Other species, now extinct, lived on both New World continents, but apparently turkeys have never occurred naturally anywhere else.

By 1930 things looked mighty bleak for wild turkeys. All five subspecies of *gallopavo*—the Florida and Eastern and, in the West, the whiter, shorter-legged Merriam's, Rio Grande and Mexican—were at an all-time low. The total population, confined to 21 states, was probably somewhere in the neighborhood of 20,000. Habitat destruction—the razing of old forests—is commonly believed to be the cause of the wild turkey's demise. But this catchall theory for wildlife decline seems a bit too pat in this situation, and it has recently come under fire by some pretty knowledgeable authorities. Among them is veteran turkey biologist Lovett Williams, who makes the following observation in his new publication, *The Book of the Wild Turkey*:

"The blame for the turkey's decline during the 1800s has usually been placed on forest fires, deforestation, and agriculture. It is true that a large part of the turkey's habitat in the northeastern United States became unsuitable, but that happened after local turkey populations had already been eliminated. In early America, the gun came before the ax, and excessive exploitation depleted turkey populations well in advance of the more material signs of civilization, just as it did in the cases of the bison and the panther. The early activities of human settlement, including lumbering, family farming, pasture clearing, naval stores, and woods burning, practiced in the proportions to be expected in the 1800s, could only have improved much of the eastern hardwood forest as turkey habitat. It is now a moot point because overhunting was soon followed by the pressures of urban human occupation and the forest of change that went with it. I will always believe, however, that the wild turkey could have survived that in good shape if it had not been overhunted."

The habitat-destruction theory is also suspect in that the scrub resulting from forest removal turns out to be not-bad turkey habitat. Turkeys weren't supposed to be able to tolerate such conditions, but since restoration has been under way they have defied the experts. "The birds have been more adaptable than we thought," declares John Lewis, wildlife research supervisor of the Missouri Department of Conservation. Missouri is one of the states that has led the way in turkey restoration and (along with Florida) actually finished the job. "We moved birds up to the [sparsely forested] northern part of Missouri in the early 1960s, and they've done very well there. We felt that turkeys needed large blocks of fairly extensive timber, but this is not the case. They're doing much better in areas with less timber than we ever thought possible."

In addition to overhunting, alien diseases imported with European poultry may have had a lot to do with the wild turkey's decline. This has recently been suggested by blackhead-infected birds found dead in areas where farmers had been spreading poultry manure on the fields.

But if some of the reasons for the wild turkey's decline are a bit obscure, all the reasons for its return are immediately obvious. Granted, there has been some good luck, as when land-use patterns resulted in pole timber and abandoned farmland growing up into prime turkey woods. Mostly, though, there has been good management.

America's wild turkey population has increased 10,000 percent in the past half-century—from 20,000 to two million. And today the birds are found in every state except Alaska—including Hawaii, California, Nevada, Idaho, Oregon, Washington, the Dakotas and Minnesota, states where there is no record of their occurring previously. There are now an estimated 1.5 million turkey hunters in the United States, and turkey hunting is second in popularity only to deer hunting.

The good management didn't come easily. It had to be learned through years of trial and error, and it had to bubble up through a smothering scum of politics.

Rare is the article written about the wild turkey or bald eagle that fails to mention up front that Ben Franklin recommended the wild turkey for the national symbol. This is false. He recommended the *barnyard* turkey, and he did so not because it was a native American or because, as he wrote, the bald eagle was "a Bird of bad moral Character," "very lousy," and "a rank coward." He did so because barnyard turkeys were then, as now, ugly, dirty and stupid, and because he was a wag. But in addition to being ugly, dirty and stupid, barnyard turkeys also do not respond to confinement by bashing themselves to death against wire, and it was this attribute that endeared them to game managers and politicians.

It was obvious even to the politicians that a barnyard turkey could not tough it out in the real world long enough to be shot by a hunter. But the managers reasoned that if they could breed a little of its manageability into the wild turkey, they could mass-produce the birds in game farms and stock them as cannon fodder—much like they already did with ring-necked pheasants—or for restoration.

They tried it, and it didn't work. The trouble was that the birds needed all their wildness for survival in the wild, and even a trace of domestic blood usually doomed them. They survived just long enough to distribute their various diseases and infirm genes among the wild population, dragging it down, too.

In Pennsylvania, band returns on game-farm stock indicated an overall survival rate of 1.1 percent during the first six months following release. For winter releases, long-term band recoveries were nine times greater for wild stock than for game-farm stock. For summer releases, long-term returns for wild stock were 15 times greater.

Similar results were obtained in West Virginia. From 1957 through 1959 a private hunting club in the southeastern part of the state released more than 200 game-farm birds. Beginning in 1957 the area's annual hunting kill, which had averaged about 12, started to fall. By 1960 it was averaging about two.

A survey by the National Wild Turkey Federation revealed that of 354 restoration attempts by 23 states using 350,000 game-farm turkeys there have been 331 total failures, i.e., wipe-outs. This finding was published in 1978, but as early as 1944 wildlife biologist A. Starker Leopold had figured out that nature and game farms selected turkeys for precisely opposite reasons, and that survival in one precluded survival in the other. By 1959 this was so obvious that New York abandoned turkey farming in favor of trapping and transferring wild birds. In February that year, the turkey federation hosted its first National Wild Turkey Symposium, in Memphis. One of the speakers, Leonard Foote, of the Wildlife Management Institute, vented his spleen as follows: "Sickels . . . Hardy, Gilpin, and others presented crystal-clear evidence of the futility of playing with game-farm stock when restoration is the objective. Why some states continue, even for the sake of experimentation, is almost beyond my comprehension."

But continue they did. Though the biologists had long known it was worse than a waste of money, the politicians and the management bosses—who, together, called the shots—didn't want to risk offending the hunting-license buyers. Pennsylvania used to defend its put-and-take turkey stocking on the grounds that it was done only where *wild* turkeys weren't, and that the game-farm stock was 95-percent wild. But the game-farm turkeys wandered vast distances (preferring to travel by road and cleared right-of-way), and the 5-percent of barnyard blood—like the 5-percent of drowned rat marinating in a keg of 95-percent pure wine—rendered everything worthless.

The stocked turkeys were obscene pantomimes of the original items. One researcher determined that after two months in the wild some birds still allowed humans to approach to within six feet before showing alarm. At last, pressure from the great outside world of modern wildlife management became so intense that most state-sponsored stocking of game-farm turkeys ceased. In 1980 the revolution even spread to Pennsylvania, where the Game Commission, in a move that indicated it had absorbed at least some of the lesson, voted to convert its turkey factory to a pheasant factory.

Maryland, for the express purpose of humoring one well-connected individual, attempted in 1981 to establish a population of game-farm stock in the central part of the state, and achieved spectacular failure. Doubtless, some politician somewhere again will coerce or seduce a state into releasing game-farm turkeys, but for all intents and purposes it is finally over.

What is not over, however, is private release of game-farm turkeys. This is a problem in a lot of states, especially those that haven't officially outlawed it. Any turkey hunter or turkey fancier who wants to have "wild turkeys" in his back 40 can flip through any poultry magazine and order eggs, chicks or poults. But *real* wild turkeys are state property and can't be bought or sold, a fact that keeps the mail-order business booming. Instead of containing 5 percent barnyard blood— hopeless tainting, as aptly demonstrated by the states—the mail-order birds may contain 50 percent. Some are actually white. The written word cannot convey the absurdity of their behavior. They strut along the yellow stripes on highways, eat tomatoes from backyard gardens, defecate copiously on cartops and housetops, attack children and motorcycles. From my contact at the Minnesota Division of Fish and Wildlife word arrived that a flock of more than 100 privately stocked game-farm turkeys had just burned down a barn by shorting out the electric wires upon which they roosted each night. The public observes such behavior and, as one New Jersey biologist put it, asks questions such as, "How can you have a hunting season on such a stupid bird?" and "Why bother restoring such silly creatures to the wild?"

"If we really knew how many turkeys were being stocked around the country by so-called do-gooders, it'd probably scare both of us to death," the Wild Turkey Federation's research director, James Kennamer, told me. "These game breeders will raise these birds; and they're clean and in good shape when they hatch from the egg. And I have no doubt that they're doing a good job. But then John Doe out here buys the chicks and raises them in wire pens and he's got them in with all his chickens and guinea fowl and peafowl and the rest, and they pick all this stuff up. And then he turns them loose.

"I was doing some research over in the Mississippi Delta where they had a good turkey population, and this game warden living in the area had a domestic gobbler and a few [semi-wild] hens. The wild birds would come in and take the hens and whip the old gobbler. And

I remember one year he only had one tail feather left. But the bottom line was I kept telling the guy he was asking for problems. Not only was he polluting the gene pool by letting the hens go wild, but he had this domestic turkey that was immune to blackhead and other diseases transmitting them to the wild birds. The following year they had a die-off and found turkeys dead in the woods, which is very hard to do."

The states had learned a lot about what constitutes good turkey management well before they were able to practice it to any great extent. Part of the recipe called for seeding depleted turkey range with genuinely wild turkeys, but first they had to catch the wild turkeys. Killing one of these birds requires some luck, lots of time and prodigious hunting skill. Trapping a whole flock alive seemed impossible.

At first the states tried live traps, with scant success. Then they tried rigging drop nets over winter feeding stations, but the nets didn't work very well, and the turkeys would come to the bait only during severe winters. Finally, in the late 1950s, biologists in several states took to trapping turkeys with waterfowl "cannon nets" propelled by rockets or mortars.

I saw it done once. Jim Cardoza, a wildlife biologist with the Massachusetts Department of Fisheries, Wildlife, and Recreational Vehicles and one of the nation's top authorities on wild turkeys, had camouflaged the net with grass, scattered the corn, packed the plastic bag of explosive pellets into each of the two heavy metal rockets, rigged the ignition wires, screwed on the perforated, salt-shaker-lid backs, jammed the supporting steel rods in the dirt at the proper angle, then tucked me into the big, wild woods that shroud Boston's Quabbin Reservoir. Hours passed. I fell asleep to the hypnotic buzz of cicadas starting in one treetop and finishing in another.

And I awoke just in time to see Cardoza's hand easing toward the plunger and about a dozen wild turkeys, a beautiful bronze in the late afternoon sunlight, bending over the bait. There was a hideous explosion, and Cardoza and I were up and running toward the thrashing lumps under the net. I was appalled at the damage to the birds. Clumps of feathers with skin still attached were woven into the mesh. Later, when we released the birds at the transfer site, two limped badly. But we had done well. The damage had been inevitable and relatively minor. The big danger, Cardoza told me, is the turkeys' detecting you and coming up from the bait just as you fire. When this happens they literally lose their heads.

Another modern capture device is drugged bait, but occasionally the birds lurch drunkenly into the woods, where they become easy marks for dogs and wild predators. And sometimes they overeat and O.D. When this happens you've got to grab them fast, slice open their crops, squeeze out the bait, then stitch up their necks. Can cannon nets and chemicals really be efficient means of trapping wild turkeys? To this day they remain the most efficient. That's the difference between game-farm turkeys—which don't mind humans, provided they stay six feet away—and wild turkeys.

With the advent of the cannon net, states committed themselves to intensive trap-and-transfer programs. The same 1978 survey that recorded 331 failures out of 354 restoration attempts by 23 states using 350,000 game-farm birds also revealed 685 successes out of 841 restoration attempts by 32 states using just 26,500 wild birds. The game-farm birds had established themselves marginally on 635 square miles. The wild birds had established themselves strongly on 300,000 square miles.

The managers' learning process was not quite over, though. Many states tried to help their newly transferred wild turkeys by feeding them through the winter, thereby short-circuiting the natural selection process, facilitating the spread of disease and providing splendid opportunities for predators and poachers. Even in mild weather, feeders had to be kept full or the turkeys would forget where they were when conditions became severe. Gradually, the incredible toughness of wild turkeys became apparent. In one experiment—which would have sent the Humaniacs into orbit had they known about it—a wild turkey survived 24 winter days without food or water. Two other equally cruel experiments established that wild turkeys can recover near-normal fecundity after two weeks of starvation and 40-percent weight loss.

Once the harmful effects of winter feeding became known, the states quickly abandoned it. Massachusetts' Jim Cardoza was among the biologists who helped spread the word. "Weakened, poor-quality birds were surviving and subsequently breeding, thus lowering the vigor of the stock," he wrote in one of his many reports. "The wild turkeys were becoming dependent on artificially provided grains rather than adapting to the natural foods, and potential disease-transmission conditions were created by concentrating birds in a small area."

Weaned from its debilitating welfare diet, the wild turkey proliferated at an even faster clip, surging into vacant habitat, astonishing biologists with its vigor and survivability.

Vermont released 17 wild New York birds during the winter of 1968/69. The following winter it released 14 more. By 1973 the flock had expanded to 600, and in-state trap-and-transfer began. That same year, 579 Vermont turkey-hunting permits were issued. Now there are so many turkeys in Vermont that anyone who asks for a permit gets one. Vermont also has found the resolve to scrap its small but scandalously wasteful put-and-take pheasant program in order to channel the money to programs of real and lasting value. Like turkey restoration. Recently retired Vermont Fish and Game commissioner Ed Kehoe told me that there was "a lot of pressure" on his department to keep the pheasants coming. "But," he said, "the program was just too expensive." It cost the state about $25 for each bird shot by a hunter. At first there was much screaming and tearing of hair, but once wild turkeys started repopulating the state the sportsmen forgot all about pheasants.

In most states there has been great support for turkey restoration, from the non-hunting public as well as from sportsmen, and it is this support that has made and is making the programs so successful, particularly on private land. Missouri, for instance, elected not to advertise that it wished to release wild turkeys on privately owned turkey range. Instead, the Wildlife Division quietly seeded the information around the state. In this fashion the genuinely interested, genuinely committed land owners were selected. Once they approached the division, asking if they might be allowed to have wild turkeys on their land, John Lewis would survey the proposed transfer site. If he liked the looks of it, he would have the locals sign a petition to protect "their" turkeys from outsiders. "There was a little basic psychology involved here," he told me. "The people really got involved in the program. The birds became theirs, not the [state] government's." Last year, Missouri completed its twenty-fourth spring gobbler season, in which slightly more than 19,000 birds were taken.

In Massachusetts the wild turkey population has increased from 37 New York birds released in 1972 and 1973 to an estimated three or four thousand in 1983. There have been four spring gobbler seasons, and the annual hunting kill is approaching 200. In the southern national forests the wild turkey population has increased 500 percent in the past 20 years, and the annual hunting kill during this period has climbed from about 1,300 to 10,000. Real wild turkeys are booming just about everywhere.

Of course, there are still threats to wild turkeys—factory farming, urbanization and predatory logging being chief among them. But, for once, it looks as if things are going to get better before they get worse. The age of the wild turkey in America is at hand, again. The managers have done something right. Celebrate.

UPDATE

Picking the encyclopedic mind of wildlife biologist Jim Cardoza has become a reflex for me before starting any new wildlife writing project—straighten desktop, call Wilton the Brittany in to his desk-side dog nest, start new computer file, phone Cardoza. You won't find anyone on the planet who knows more about wild turkeys or black bears.

"We're almost done with our turkey restoration program—moving them around the state," he tells me. "We have about 10,000 birds in the fall population from Worcester County west, and several hundred to the east. They're doing very well; they've occupied about 95 percent of the available habitat."

Turkeys are now breeding in every state save Alaska—roughly 25 percent more area than before the first Thanksgiving. When I wrote the piece the Wild Turkey Federation estimated the national population at 1.5 million. Now it estimates it at 4.2 million.

Still, people are releasing game-farm "wild turkeys," usually in defiance of the law. Recently one of these birds chased and *bit* a lady bicyclist in my town. Outraged, she ran to the police. The police called Cardoza to ask what they should do. "I recommend CIFS," responded Cardoza, loftily. When they asked what this meant in layman's terms, he replied in his best professional voice: "Crush Its Fucking Skull."

Horses, Asses and Asininities

Destruction on the hoof

Audubon, September 1985

TIME WAS WHEN we Americans paid little attention to our feral horses and asses, permitting them to be sold to rodeos or ground into pet food. But then came "ecology," with ink and cathode images of streaming manes amid dust, and gentle, Biblical bundles of fur plodding around in the Grand Canyon. The crusade was won quickly and easily in 1971, with the Wild Horse and Burro Act (the Spanish "burro" being a more endearing, if less precise, appellation than "ass"). On property controlled by the Bureau of Land Management and the US Forest Service—i.e., most public land—it no longer was lawful to kill, capture, harass, sell or process these beloved symbols of the American West.

The humane activists who helped procure this legislation were and are offended by the word feral in reference to free-roaming horses and asses. Their reasoning goes like this: The family Equidae—which includes horses, asses and zebras—appears to have undergone its mainstream evolution in North America, eventually populating Europe and Asia via the Bering land bridge. Therefore, although equids became extinct on our continent approximately 10,000 years ago, they actually are proper Americans. By abandoning or accidentally liberating their riding and pack stock, Ponce de Leon and his successors were merely returning native fauna.

The argument—equally applicable to elephants, for instance—is technically correct. But neither horse nor ass reoccupied an old niche; both usurped new, post-Pleistocene ones. Whether they are considered wild or feral, native or alien, these beasts are sustained by habitat that never knew them and never developed a single defense against them. For 10 millennia, American deserts and grasslands were shaped by cloven hooves and lower front teeth that met toothless palates. Enter suddenly solid hooves and meshing incisors. Result: ecological havoc.

Consider the desert tree, palo verde, vital to countless wildlife species for food and cover. Birds nest in it and small mammals are nourished by its seeds. Desert bighorn sheep browse on the new growth at the tips of the twigs. Reptiles are sustained through summer by its shade. Asses eliminate it. Because palo verde never had to cope with equid incisors it is extremely brittle. Foraging asses break off large branches—five, 10, 15 years' worth of growth—eat a little and leave the rest to die. This done, they bite the green bark from the trunk. They also destroy other important desert trees and shrubs—mesquite, acacia, ocotillo, to mention a few—leaving in their place monocultures of such unpalatable fare as creosote bush, which is almost worthless to wildlife.

Even under the best conditions, life on the American desert is fragile and stressed. What it absolutely does not need is a plague of heavy-footed, 500-pound ungulates from northeast Africa, each consuming 10 pounds of greenery per day. The increasingly rare desert tortoise, for example, is apt to be pancaked by ass hooves. If it escapes this fate, it may suddenly find itself without the shrubs that provide it shade and without sites to dig the dens and tunnels that get it through extreme heat and cold. Digging in the open may be impossible because asses have compacted the soil. As with other creatures that share its arid habitat, the tortoise gets much of its water from a wildflower, the leafy-stemmed coreopsis. But asses have acquired a taste for it and rip it permanently from the scene. Thus do species like the desert tortoise pass into extinction.

"They [asses] affect everything you can think of, from burrowing animals to songbirds to quail to chukar," declares Dick Weaver, a biologist with the California Department of Fish and Game. "They just denude the landscape . . . . They so deplete the annual growth of weeds and forbs that rodents are eliminated, and this reflects on up the food chain to raptors and other predators. They are devastating." In one study, vegetation within an ass-free enclosure in Death Valley National Monument recovered to 73.8 plants per square meter, compared with 26.7 outside. The ratio of dead shrubs outside to dead shrubs inside was 27:1.

Research ecologist Steven Carothers has noticed an interesting feature of ass grazing: The steeper the slope, the closer the trails. This, says he, "allows the burros to get every last shred of available forage that is on the slope. They can reach their heads out from one trail almost all the way to the next. These soils are so fragile and so thin that it may take several decades before you could see a natural vegetative cover again."

Asses are gentle only in mangers. In the wild they have been seen to seek out and trample small animals. They are particularly aggressive around water holes. Native species—bighorn sheep, for instance—will move in, drink their fill and leave. Asses will move in, drink their fill and stay, driving off native species, bathing, wallowing, urinating, defecating, razing the ring of lush vegetation and smashing such man-made water enhancement devices as cement troughs and plastic pipe. In the Panamint Mountains, on the west side of Death Valley, more than 170 springs (virtually all the springs in the park) have been grossly fouled by asses. Because summer hikers can't carry sufficient drinking water into the Panamints, asses have displaced people, too.

Principally out of concern for bighorns, California wildlife managers tried adding more water to various desert habitats by setting up contraptions to catch and hold rain. But they found that in so doing they also were adding more asses. Now they are directed by official department policy to "achieve complete removal" of feral asses from all bighorn habitat. But it's not that easy. The asses have virtually no predators and few diseases. And herds expand by roughly 20 percent annually, with the average jenny bearing young before she is two years old and every 14 to 16 months thereafter until she is 12. All over the American desert, wherever asses have existed for any period, populations of bighorns keep flickering out. What remains are little units ravaged by inbreeding, separated by ruined springs and broken range.

As destroyers of wildlife, feral horses are more subtle than asses. Generally, they do not take over water holes, and because they did not evolve in a desert situation—as did asses—they are obliged to inhabit more resilient range where water is less of a limiting factor. They may compete with elk, damage winter deer range and stress other species by stripping choice vegetation. But they don't lay waste to the earth. On the other hand, feral horses are far more numerous and far more widely distributed than feral asses.

In 1976, five years after Congress passed the Wild Horse and Burro

Act, the Bureau of Land Management acted to check expanding populations of feral equids with its "Adopt-a-Horse [or Burro]" program. It has been pursuing this with enormous energy and expense ever since. BLM and various humane groups go on and on about how good it is, but the following statistics say everything that needs to be said about how well it works. In 1971 there were an estimated 17,000 feral horses and feral asses on Forest Service and BLM land. Today the figures are, respectively, 51,880 and 12,090.

Feral horses are big and very dangerous. The "adoption fee," which doesn't begin to defray BLM's investment, is $125—down in desperation from $200 two years ago—but you also need a trailer, a shelter and a corral. Just to keep a horse in hay, grain and medicine can cost more than $1,200 a year, and horses commonly live for a quarter-century. One woman I spoke with said she heard of a man who could break feral horses in three days, although she allowed it took her a year. Another adopter told me that it took him six months "to get comfortable" with his feral horse. You can never get comfortable with, or near, some of them.

Feral asses are different. They are about half the size of horses, about half as expensive to keep and much easier to tame. The adoption fee is but $75. The problem is that today there are scarcely any uses for an ass. Therefore, our national ass-adoption effort draws forth weird-pet fanciers of the sort who drag ocelots around New York City. Robert Ohmart, a zoology professor at Arizona State University who has vast experience with feral asses, puts it this way: "What kind of a nut would want one?" It is a question I am tempted to relay to my parents, who kept an ass loose on the premises for the single purpose of calming their horse, which mission it accomplished admirably enough. I recall that it and its sign seemed to be everywhere at once, that it never ceased eating and that it brayed loudly in the middle of the night.

The Bureau of Land Management is very good at rounding up its feral equids, but not so good at giving them away. "That's the big bottleneck," acknowledges BLM's rangelands person, John Boyles, a little sadly. Having unloaded 51,000 over the past decade, the bureau has noticed that the demand is down. "I think they've saturated the market," declares National Park Service biologist Chuck Douglas at the University of Nevada. As evidence he cites the fact that adopted asses are mysteriously reappearing in the wild. They do get boring, and if you sign up for one you may get two. I checked into 14 ass adoptions and discovered seven pregnant asses.

Legally, the Bureau of Land Management can kill unwanted horses and asses, but the humane lobby has made it promise not to. According to the American Horse Protection Association, the rejects ought to be placed back on public land. Hal Baerg, of the Animal Lovers Volunteer Association, says this: "There's nothing out there on the desert anyhow . . . . Maybe if a guy is interested in goddamned bighorn sheep only, to the exclusion of everything else, then he wants to get rid of a burro, a fox, or whatever the hell else might compete."

The US Navy, which is not constrained by the Wild Horse and Burro Act, viewed with alarm the irruption of feral asses at its weapons center at China Lake, California. The beasts were threading through jet traffic, causing major highway accidents, ambling along rocket-sled runs and realigning MIDAS missile tracking pads by using them for scratching posts. Abruptly, the Navy shot 649. Abruptly, the humane groups sued. Now BLM rounds up the Navy's asses.

Neither is the National Park Service constrained by the Wild Horse and Burro Act, but under intense pressure from humane groups it too has promised not to kill its feral equids. So unadopted feral equids are backing up in Bureau of Land Management holding pens. Each is maintained at an annual cost of roughly $730, and there were 3,500 at the end of 1984. Last year BLM managed to find homes for only about 6,000 animals. This year, with an appropriation of $16.7 million (up from $5.8 million for fiscal 1984), it plans to capture 17,000 more. It can't unload them all on the public; it dares not kill them; and it cannot sell them for slaughter. Legislation to allow the agency to sell them is again before Congress, having failed last session. Again, it appears headed for defeat. The humane lobby says it's a bald ruse by cattlemen to free up public range for more overgrazing.

That pitch does have a certain appeal in that public range is scandalously overgrazed. But a reduction in feral equids doesn't mean an increase in livestock. The equation isn't that simple. For one thing, the industry is limited by countless factors other than forage. For another, the habitat appropriated by asses is too dry for livestock; and horses, because of their different grazing behavior, don't compete much.

But one gets nowhere with mere reason. Confronted with indisputable documentation of ass and horse damage to wildlife, the humane groups simply say it's all made up by hunters and cattlemen. Or they cite a National Academy of Sciences report that they claim, wrongly, establishes that feral equids don't hurt anything. One high-ranking Audubon official who asked me not to use his name made this comment: "A lot of these groups have one position—that absolutely no horse or burro should be harmed in any way, shape, or form. The only death they will accept is death by old age. And they can really break out a formidable group of opponents. I kind of backed out on the issue to be truthful; it's the worst hate mail I've ever gotten."

Actually, the process of wrenching equids from the wild and shipping them around the country isn't all that humane itself. Frantz Dantzler, who directs the north-central office of the Humane Society of the United States and has observed scores of BLM roundups, reports that major injuries, including broken legs, are routine. "The animals," he says, "are severely stressed and traumatized by the whole experience." One researcher determined that a high percentage of mares—approaching half—are sufficiently stressed to abort their fetuses. Other mares are separated from foals.

Phyllis Wright, also of the Humane Society, reports "a great deal of misuse" by adopters. She has discovered that adopted equids have been sold at auctions, transported to foreign slaughterhouses under inhumane conditions and "have ended up in various bad situations where they weren't receiving proper care."

The brutal truth is that no matter how hard we strive and how much money we spend, life is not going to be any less tough for feral horses and asses than for other animals, wild or domestic. However ghoulish the pet-food entrepreneurs, at least they kept feral equids under control and used them. It wasn't their basic idea that was unsavory, just their execution.

So what ought to be done about feral equids? "I suppose," says Wright, "we are in the same position with surplus horses and burros as we are with surplus dogs and cats. And humane euthanasia has to be done at this point because of man's stupidity in allowing them to breed." Processing plants in Canada, Mexico and even the United States butcher unwanted domestic equids and ship the meat to Europe and Japan where, sensibly, it is relished. "I myself have eaten a lot of burro meat, and it's quite good," says Ohmart. He'd like to see BLM sell permits to buyers. It would then be their responsibility to remove surplus animals however best they could, including by rifle.

Will it happen? Not a chance. Only in America could it be a misdemeanor to poach a desert bighorn and a felony to annoy a feral ass. Ours is a society willing to spend $16.7 million to place on permanent welfare two destructive exotics that we find "magnificent" and "cute," and an average of only $84,000 to keep on Earth each of more than 300 endangered native species that we won't hike in to see and couldn't identify anyway. As stewards of our land and wildlife there's not a lot of hope for us.

UPDATE

BLM is still having major ass problems. In Arizona, for example, it may have to completely de-assify its Tassi-Gold Butte unit as part of the desert tortoise recovery plan. Ass manager L.D. Walker reports that rounding up the 100 asses—to a large extent with helicopters—will likely cost more than $100,000. Think what could be done for native species with that kind of bread.

You can still adopt a "wild" horse for $125 and an ass for $75. Lo, some genius has devised a purpose for feral asses—predator control—and now demand outstrips supply. "They take to mothering them sheep, and they just kick the tar out of a coyote that tries to get in, hollering and screaming as they're doing it," one range manager told me.

The Park Service—which has much more freedom in wildlife management than BLM—has shot a few feral asses here and there, very quietly. Grand Canyon National Park is now almost ass free, manager John Ray proudly reports. "We think we've got five or six left," he says. "And if anyone wants to adopt them, they're welcome to go down there and catch them."

On Lake Mead National Recreational Area, the Park Service still rounds up feral horses and asses with helicopters and net guns. Manager Nancy Hendricks told me that she and her colleagues had worked with BLM to rid the land of asses, but that "it didn't seem like we were getting enough; we kept suffering impacts." So they spent three years developing a management plan and EIS. Even in drought feral asses increase at about 18 percent a year. "If you get behind on your captures, you're in trouble," she says.

The Politics and Pleasures of Releasing Salmon

Gently bucking the system in Newfoundland

Gray's Sporting Journal, Winter 1986

THE TORRENT is one of the more spectacular rivers that drain the tip of Newfoundland's Great Northern Peninsula. It rushes down to Hawkes Bay through a dark, rocky gorge lined along the top with stunted spruce and fir that lean out from both sides and almost meet in the middle. From the south bank you can fish most of the lower gorge to where you can see the upper section, but then you have to backtrack along the limestone and granite outcroppings and cut through the woods. Above, you can fish up to the fast water, where you run out of footing. Here the gorge curls north so that you can't see the big falls. But you can hear them and see the high, swirling mist. In late July the sun rises behind the mist at about 8:45 AM, making rainbows and lighting up the canyon walls.

As dawn broke on July 21, 1986, the Torrent looked as if it had been named by some effete wag from Idaho's Salmon River country. It was more a Trickle, eminently fordable in any of a dozen spots. When I go fishing I expect to be told that I have landed in an "off year" or that I should have come "last week" or "next week." This I can handle. I cannot handle what the guides and Bill Maynard of Viking Trail Salmon Outfitters were telling me; if distilled and amalgamated, it came approximately to this: "There is no water. The fishing isn't just bad; it's vile. Morbid. Wretched. Accursed. Ghastly. The worst in memory, doubtless history."

All this, however, did not mean that there were no salmon. The river was alive with them. I could see 10 in Shady Pool, holding in two's and three's just back from the dropoff. One had a red-and-white fly—almost a Parmachene Belle—stuck in its upper jaw. I tied on a Green Butt and cast to them for an hour. They never even looked. On the opposite shore three locals who had been there when I arrived cast to the same fish. Presently, they lost interest and went away, and I waded deeper. I reached out with my rod tip and touched a salmon, feeling it shudder through the graphite. I touched another. Briefly, I considered stoning the pool, but instead I waded right into the middle of it, nearly shipping water into my high-fitting chest waders, but then gaining a flat rock that gave me a foot or so of freeboard.

"Hey Skipper, you're standing in the middle of the pool," someone called from the bottom of the gorge.

"I knows," I hollered, having had Newfy talk lessons the previous season from a number of able instructors.

I bit the leader and re-tied the fly, this time adding a Portland hitch—two half-hitches around the head (each affected by making a loop in the line and twisting it back upon itself) so that the shank angles away from you when you face downcurrent. The ruse evolved by accident at Portland Creek, a few miles south on the Viking Trail, during the age of gut and eyeless, snelled hooks. When the gut rotted off the fly one could fish with it only by re-tying directly to the shank. Sometimes a hitched fly worked better than a new one because it cut a seductive, arcing V-wake over glassy glides. Sometimes, because salmon are such capricious beasts, it worked not at all.

From my new position I could just reach the smooth lip where the pool spilled away into fast water. It took all my line, but the brave little Green Butt sliced down across the lip and hung there, flirting with the edge and looking delicious. On the far bank one of the Newfies had silently returned and was sitting on a rock, hugging his knees, sucking a cigarette and watching me with a quizzical expression. Surely, thought I, he knew enough to realize that my sloppy backcasts resulted mostly from the height I had lost by wading so deeply.

On about the tenth cast I saw a flash in back of the fly. Two casts later, a little bulge. I rested the fish, feigning application of insect repellent and inspection of my fly so that the Newfy wouldn't get any ideas about flogging the pool again. On the next cast I got another flash, and on the next a bulge and a solid take.

I hauled back and instantly the fish burst into the air, catching the sun on her slender flank and turning a somersault. She looked reasonably fresh and bore only minor net wounds. I judged her weight to be about four pounds—fair to good for Newfoundland fish, virtually all of which are grilse. She felt splendid on the wispy trout rod.

Rod aloft, I backstepped to the bank, getting out of a bad position. Now I used reverse psychology on my fish, leading her toward the fast water and feeling smug when she surged up into the pool. There she leapt again, even higher than before, spinning through the air like a throwing knife. But, with that, she shot back toward the rapids and disappeared down the chute, thereby becoming the first Newfoundland fish to show me my backing. The Newfy smiled and turned up his palms in sympathy, and I galloped over the rocks.

Twenty yards down, the leader caught around a boulder and I slacked off quickly so that the casting line would slide down and take the beating instead. The fish hung in the rush of water, mouth agape, thrashing, planing to one side and then the other. With the low water, I thought I might have a chance of wading close enough to the boulder to get my rod tip out behind it and lift the line away. Except for one tense moment when a standing wave slammed me in the gut, it proved easier than it had looked. Now the fish was tired, and with modest luck I'd slide her, tail first, into the next pool.

I got my index finger on her back just above the still water. Once I touch them, they count, and now it was just a matter of getting her close enough to twist out the hook or letting her get off by herself, even break off if she insisted. So I tucked my rod under my armpit, waded deeper and hauled her toward me by the leader. It was, I must now confess, titillating to see the reaction this created among the dozen or so anglers on both sides of the river. They were jumping and gesturing. "No, no, no," they screamed. "Get 'im ashore. Get 'im ashore." Someone brandished a net.

In this harsh, impoverished land there is scarcely any understanding of pure recreation, none whatever of voluntary surrender of victuals. One might better busy himself entreating the heavens to release rain than Newfoundlanders to release salmon. So, rising to my audience, I stumbled and splashed and hauled on the leader. A gaunt fisherman in a white sweatshirt clasped the top of his head with both hands, sank to his knees and said "Arrrrrgh."

A foot under the surface, I slid out the hook, having to touch nothing save her lower jaw, and she wrenched free and swam quickly away without waiting to be revived. Then I stumbled and splashed some more, and when I came up empty handed and turned toward shore there was much rolling of eyes and raising of arms. *Stunning incompe-*

tence. Leave it to an American with a fancy rod who stands in the middle of salmon pools. It was to be the major topic of conversation at all the bars that night.

Now, if the American had been a bit perverse, at least he preferred the company of honest perverts to that of holier-than-thou no-kill types who prate and simper and misquote Shelley and turn in disgust from the sight of that same American hunched like a fish hawk by some stream bank, mantling and eviscerating brook trout.

It is not that I am against releasing trout, etc. In fact, when not hungry, I do it a good deal myself. But the thing to remember is that Atlantic salmon aren't comparable to other fish. They are endangered—in fact, if not by official decree—and all the altruistic reasons for releasing them are therefore the more compelling. Also, they are better than other fish.

And there are pragmatic reasons for releasing Atlantic salmon. To begin with, in Newfoundland at least, it allows you to keep fishing after you have taken two fish in the same day—a feat which, on any normal day in any normal year, is downright likely before lunchtime. Also, there is no scaling, gutting, lugging, tagging, wrapping, paper shuffling, extended sessions with customs officials or waiting around airports while your fish soften up. If you can afford to fish for Atlantic salmon, you can afford to buy Pacific salmon (just as good) or sea-farmed "Norway salmon" when you return home. It will be better tasting because it will not have to be frozen in preparation of transport and, if your time is worth more than, say, $8 an hour, it probably will be cheaper.

What is black and blue and floats?" the lithe and beautiful Sheila Maynard had inquired of me at 4:30 AM as I munched corn flakes at Maynard's Motor Inn, the main base of Viking Trail Salmon Outfitters. It is, she explained, a Yankee who tells Newfy jokes in Hawkes Bay. But it wasn't a joke, I insisted, opening and reading aloud from a pamphlet provincial biologists had gotten out on how to release salmon (since anything over 24.8 inches may not be killed). Actually, I thought it was superb advice, and I said as much to Sheila. "Do not," the biologists instructed, "use gaff to handle fish."

Other than that, however, most advice one reads on how to release fish is just plain common sense. While much has been written, some of it by me, regarding the techniques, virtually nothing has been written regarding the politics. I mean what do you do when your guide chases you and your fish around a pool, stabbing wildly with a gaff even as you shout, "No! No! No!"? If you release the fish in his presence, you deliver to him a monumental insult. You tell him that the welfare of this cold-blooded vertebrate in your hand is, to you, worth more than his welfare and that of his kin.

If a Newfoundland guide happens to be around when you return a salmon—which, according to my experience, is more the exception than the rule—you will have to do some careful explaining. I will say that the guides I had accepted it with grace, but several others were plainly offended. One told me that if I didn't like salmon I could give them to him. My tip for releasing in front of guides is this: Tell them that your faith forbids you to kill fish, that you perceive them as sacred beings. People the world over can relate to religion.

My favorite Newfoundland guides—they're also commonly held to be the best raconteurs on the peninsula—are Earl Pilgrim of Roddickton, a huge game warden who runs down moose/caribou poachers with no less enjoyment than beagles run down varying hares, and Uncle Kad of Main Brook, a lean old waterman with the gaze of an osprey. Both know and love this big, wild country and both find humor where lesser men find pique—like in the releasing of salmon. Uncle Kad, for example, told me I could "kiss 'em and he'd club 'em," and, when I was into fish, he'd discreetly position himself downstream with a landing net because "once the salmon was back in the drink it was fair game." Uncle Kad allowed that the Lord had been good to let him live near these woods. Work had been tough to find but he'd gotten by. He used to cut pulp for Bowater Company. Everyone in these parts did at one time or another. One day he'd been cutting at the very spot where we were fishing and a bull moose had chased him into the woods and up a spruce, keeping him there all day. Finally, the moose had trotted down to the river, found a beaver and brought it back to fell the tree. The beaver was three-quarters of the way through and Uncle Kad was preparing to meet his maker when the Bowater whistle blew and the beaver quit. It was, explained Uncle Kad, a union beaver.

Many anglers one encounters along Newfoundland streams are accompanied by young children—not because they wish to "take a kid fishing," as it used to say on the back of my old split-shot boxes, but because they wish to double their kill. The kid gets to reel in the second and third fish that the adult hooks. On the morning of July 22 I rose before the ravens, determined to be the first to lay line on the lower gorge. Arriving at Shady Pool in semi-darkness, I flushed fishermen from both sides of the river. With kids in tow, they sprinted to claim their spots, but not to fish, because legal hours had yet to commence.

Such streamside receptions, I guess, are foremost among the reasons blue-bloods I meet at Boston salmon dinners don't fish Newfoundland. There is no private water, therefore no privacy (except when you hoof it way in or travel by boat or plane); anyone can go fishing anywhere. Another putoff is that virtually every salmon is net cut, often grotesquely. Poaching with nets is a way of life in Newfoundland. One sees "cod traps" at the mouths of major rivers during the peak of the salmon run—illegal but permanent fixtures. When one flies in to remote spots poachers look up from their nets and wave. Guides readily admit poaching to those who disrupt it by hiring them. Further, the provincial government has pretty much determined, for everyone's convenience, to keep the arm of the law feeble. It has assigned its thoroughly inadequate warden force either to hunting or fishing and has forbidden each group—idle during half the year—to dabble in the regulatory affairs of the other.

But you will note that I *returned* to Newfoundland. If you must compete with locals, at least you may do it when the urge seizes you; there is no waiting in line during prime fishing hours for some slow loris of a bureaucrat to assign you a beat you didn't want anyway, as in the settled regions of Quebec.

If the fish are little, at least they are aggressive to the fly—the theory being that because grilse return a year early the imprint of insectivorous parrhood remains sharper. If the fish are beat up, at least they are prolific. With the orgy of poaching one wonders how this can be so, but it is so. In 1985, during a week of what was said to be poor fishing, I hooked 28 grilse. And the locals did as well or better. In 1986, during four days of perhaps the worst fishing of this century, I hooked six.

What astonishes about Newfoundland streams is the abundance of parr. Wherever you step they dash around like brook trout in a mountain rill. Everywhere they dimple glides, and on every drift they peck your fly. One can only fantasize about the kind of salmon fishing Newfoundland could have if ever it resolved to restrain its poachers. Finally, of all Atlantic salmon fishing in which you can pretty well count on catching fish, Newfoundland's is probably the cheapest. A week at Maynard's Motor Inn costs $1,500 Canadian, guides included. Rex Boyd, the peninsula's other outfitter—on the wilder east side— charges more because he flies you around, but not much more. In 15 minutes he can put you on salmon that haven't seen a fly all season, and in under an hour he can set you down on the best part of Labrador and show you caribou, whales and icebergs on the way.

I declined to engage the sprinters but instead walked purposefully up to the bottom of the gorge where the channel narrows and where I'd seen fish holding the day before. There I found a rock of my own and sat down to set up my rod. Across from me, a leader length away, a boy of about eight clasped a thick rod with both hands, skidding a buoyant dry fly hither and yon. It was his first try with a fly rod, he announced superfluously.

Another thing I like about Atlantic salmon is that they have a wonderful way of pricking bubbles. I could think of half a dozen lavishly equipped popinjays who needed to be at my side when I saw the salmon drift up, turn and follow the fly downstream, waggling its dorsal a little. "Here he comes," I hissed. The fish broke the surface, sucked down the fly and was on when the kid snatched away the line for another cast. There were three frantic jumps on a very tight line before it was off. "Dern," said the fisherman, but there was no major anguish.

When the sun rose above the conifers I dug my polaroids from my vest, wiped away the crusted salt and sunscreen from the last bluefish trip and studied the river from a new perspective. Half a dozen shifting white blurs six feet down became wounds on salmon backs. I found nine fish holding over clean gravel, one about 20 pounds. A few big salmon still ply the Torrent, but they blast through fast and early. As in other Newfoundland streams gillnets—legal and otherwise—have selected for grilse, which occasionally can squeeze through the mesh. Hence the enlightened new regulation proscribing killing of the larger fish.

I worked the lower-gorge lies for the next two hours, shaking parr from the Green Butt at about 15-minute intervals. Then, when I had all but given up and was casting on automatic pilot, there came a lusty swirl at the bottom of a drift, about where the kid had hooked his fish. A dozen or so heartbeats later, on the opposite side of the river—eight feet away—a raw-backed grilse took solidly and beat the black glide white. I landed and released it, this time dispensing with the theatrics but eliciting no less distress from onlookers. "Fer shame," admonished the kid.

My main mission that day was to release a salmon in front of Knowles. I have to get my licks in some way; and, besides, he really deserved it, carrying on about salmon steaks to the extent that it seemed he might even offend the locals. So I made my way back to

Shady Pool and hiked to the upper gorge. Knowles (who with the guides had done the bars till five that morning, eliciting only a belly laugh from a 250-pound cod fisherman when he had informed him that he danced as if he had his "left knocker caught in his zipper") had long since put up his rod and now was reclining on a throne-shaped boulder, telling stories and jokes, looking and sounding like Toad of Toad Hall. Spence and Tom listened. Up by the fast water, where he couldn't hear, Paul flicked a dry fly. Lynn, who had had a fish up 10 minutes earlier, listened and rested her arm.

"Look at that Ted Williams now," cried Knowles. "He's going to elbow his way right into the pool. Shove, shove, shove, shove. Push, push, push, push. Here he comes."

I tied on a white Samson Special.

"Now watch him catch her fish," he shouted.

I looked at Lynn. She shrugged. A pod of five grilse held tight against the bank. On the first cast with the short line one came up and looked. He came perhaps 10 more times, never closing to within less than a foot from the fly. After awhile I moved up the pool to get a better drift, positioning myself directly in front of Knowles and eliciting raucous splutter.

Now I couldn't see any of the salmon. After a few dozen casts I switched back to the Green Butt, and the fish came to it like a pickerel to a pork rind. So magnificent was the first series of leaps against the sunlit cliff that Knowles—for once—was speechless. But he recovered quickly, launching into a rambling harangue about how I owed him this fish and about how he planned to cook it.

No fish ever hooked was played with more care. How desperately I needed to land it, to cradle it inches from Knowles' enormous, clutching hands and then to slip it back into the run and say, "Oh, did you want that one?" And how my stomach twisted when the fish started eel-spinning on the bottom. I could see that it was going to break off; and, alas, it did.

But all fish come to him who waits. And the following morning, at the same spot and in the same company, I landed a fine grilse, returning it in front of Knowles, getting him to scream and dance and call me a "low-life bastard."

Our last morning I found myself alone on the Torrent. Paul and Lynn had gone trout fishing, and Spence, Tom and Knowles were sleeping in, having exhausted themselves in celebration of Knowles' first salmon. It had rained the night before, and I was hoping for a fresh run of fish. Right away I caught a miniature grilse no bigger than the hatchery landlocks one encounters in Grand Lake Stream. But as the day progressed and the sun dried the mossy, rich-smelling woods, hope faded, and I wandered down below the gorge to all the lovely but marginal water I hadn't explored.

Dragonflies buzzed and clattered in the brush. Kingfishers rattled. The locals picked up their landing nets, cranked their leaders down onto their reels and walked out to the road. I perused my flies, finally selecting a Green Highlander because it was the most beautiful.

I walked quickly along shallow pools where the water seemed to turn to air and along gentle riffles where it went silver in the sun. I probed the little pockets between shale slabs, as if for trout, and I forgot that I was fishing. I could safely afford another 20 minutes. Then I'd have to go find my guide, gather up my jacket and rod case and get back to Maynard's or I'd hold up the ride to Deer Lake.

There was no disturbance in the water, no motion or warning of any kind; the salmon was just on—a heavy cock fish up on the morning tide, fluorescent silver and barely touched by the nets. He hung in the pocket a long while, then jumped and moved out into the main flow. He never jumped again, partly because I babied him.

Every time I worked him into slack water he surged back out again.

I knew I'd never land him. A real fishing trip doesn't end this way. But finally he slipped into water less deep than he was, and I ran over and touched him, and it did.

UPDATE

After this piece was published a bigshot in Hawkes Bay said I'd insulted Newfies. Maybe he didn't read carefully. In any case, he didn't understand why I went back or how much I delight in the humor and honesty of his countrymen or how I savor the music of their language or how refreshing I find it to get away from the pomposity and snobbery that pervade American fly-fishing. I like Newfies almost as much as their salmon.

If you want to *really* learn about their humor and honesty and really hear the music of their language, read *The Shipping News*—a weird, funny, happy, Pulitzer-winning novel by Annie Proulx, who lived in Newfoundland for a year before she started writing, just to watch and listen. She was the best wordsmith I ever worked with at *Gray's Sporting Journal*, and I'd always tell her she was going to be famous. Back then she used the by-line E.A. Proulx because, well, what red-blooded, red-flanneled sportsperson would read stories about brook trout and ruffed grouse told by a *girl?*

Something really wonderful has happened in Newfoundland. In 1992, at a cost of $40 million, Canada bought out commercial salmon netters who had virtually wiped out local stocks and were intercepting about 70 percent of New-England-bound fish. I never would have believed it, but on March 14 of that year—at the annual dinner of the Theodore Gordon Flyfishers, in Rye, New York—I heard someone refer to "those courageous Canadian fisheries ministers." It was Joan Wulff, rising and calling for a round of applause for the Newfoundland net ban. Somewhere her late husband, Lee, gasped, laid down his rod and clapped with us.

Up to Our Necks in Canadas

Can we control them? Should we try?

Connecticut Audubon, Fall 1987

THEY COME ON A RUSH of arctic air that shakes the golden aspen leaves, or with a warm front rolling up from the Carolinas that sets the wood frogs croaking in starwashed forest pools. Wispy V's penciled on azure, wafting toward Polaris or the Southern Cross, so high you have to strain to make them out. And yet the wild, discordant symphony is all around you, loud and close, lifting your spirit and whisking it over dark taiga, blossoming tundra, bright bays, rippling marsh grass and clean, crashing surf. So fine and rare are wild geese that, by moonlight, they even are among Julie Andrews' favorite things. Breathes there a Yankee who does not thrill at their arrival? Yes.

Sometimes they never go away or go only a few miles to the coast, where they squat, burning ample fat, till the brief Eastern winter releases inland reservoirs, park ponds, golf courses, highway median strips and lawns. They are astonishingly efficient at converting grass to guano, the size and odor of which make the suburbanite nostalgic for the time bird droppings meant dainty chalk marks on the windshield. Along the Atlantic seaboard from Maryland to Massachusetts, geese are rapidly losing popularity, sometimes taxing the minds of animal behaviorists, wildlife managers and would-be pest controllers.

Of all victims of pest geese, golfers are most ardent in their hatred. "Golf," wrote Aldo Leopold half a century ago in his essay "Goose Music," "is a sophisticated exercise, but the love of hunting is almost a physiological characteristic." Yet when a golfer recently combined the two, dispatching a goose with one of his clubs, he landed in court.

This week, as I write, another golfer—on the Tashua-Knolls course, in Trumbull, Connecticut—has birdied before reaching the green, folding a goose with a perfect chip shot to the white cheek patch. "He didn't want it," reports greenskeeper Ed Zenisky. "We had to bury that one in the woods."

Bernard Martin, treasurer of the Connecticut Audubon Society, has been golfing in the state for 40 years, the last 10 of which he has slipped and slid between holes. "They are beautiful animals," he declares, "but . . . the stuff covers your shoes. You get into an area where there are thousands of them and they don't move very far. When the ball lands in it, you have to be careful when you swing."

Such is the proliferation of geese in Connecticut and other Atlantic states that parks and public swimming areas have been deemed unhealthy for humans and temporarily closed. About half Connecticut's water companies have reported goose problems. There is good evidence that some of the algae blooms that increased the cost of water treatment were caused by geese.

In the 1950s, Connecticut's coastal winter goose count averaged 138; in the 1960s, 358; in the 1970s, 2,543. Now it's about 7,000 and, statewide, the Connecticut Audubon Society tallies 35,000. Of these, 25,000 are just passing through, while 10,000, mostly in southwestern Connecticut, are residents.

There are those who say humanity should welcome the wild goose, especially the suburban subspecies, the giant Canada—*Branta canadensis maxima*, a semi-legendary creature discovered in the 1930s by examination of museum skins and classified extinct until 1962, when it turned up alive and begging bread in downtown Rochester, Minnesota. This was a discovery acutely embarrassing to the experts, among them nature writer John Madson, who had pooh-poohed the old-time wildfowlers' tales of 18-pound honkers with six-foot wing spans, declaring that such birds had not existed since "the days of hoop snakes and wampus cats."

It's likely that the birds evolved in the Midwest and southern Canada. Because they were relatively bold and calm, more or less non-migratory and nested far to the south of other geese, they prospered in captivity. So, early in the nation's history, giant Canadas became the live decoys of hunters and, when live decoys were outlawed in 1935, they were liberated in the East where they waxed fruitful, especially as urban sprawl proscribed gunning and the land, with all the new grass and ornamental ponds, took on the aspect of their old prairie habitat. The state of Connecticut also released a couple of hundred geese in the 1950s, and possibly a few hundred more were released by sportsmen. The genetic background of those geese, however, is unclear. "Because the giant evolved on the prairie and is presumably less suited to New England than the native Atlantic Canada goose, it is doubtful that the giant will ever become common in this region," I and a biologist wisely reported in the May/June 1972 issue of *Massachusetts Wildlife* magazine. And then, to make it worse: "Few things are valued so much as those that have been taken away from us, seemingly forever, then suddenly, inexplicably returned."

Now we have devised all manner of "controls" for the reborn beast. Last year Connecticut tacked five days onto its goose-hunting season. If this significantly reduced giant Canadas, which is debatable, it merely created a vacuum into which others will rush. The season might be extended further, except that you run the risk of intercepting the spring migration of Atlantic geese.

Another trouble with hunting giant Canadas is that, usually, it doesn't work. They're too smart. The same bird that in a city park will reach into your pocket to get the rest of your sandwich will detour two miles to avoid a marsh full of waterfowlers. One goose hunter says he is considering a new kind of decoy—an inflatable human mother clutching a loaf of Wonder Bread.

Then there are automatic firing, gas-powered noisemakers that farmers use to scare away grain-eating birds. "They scare the heck out of the geese," one greenskeeper told me. But they scare the heck out of the golfers, too. Another greenskeeper says he is partial to hand-launched rocket bombs. Basically, these teach the geese to feed before 8 AM (when the golf-course staff arrives) and after 5 PM (when it departs).

Geese are said to dislike balloons bobbing around on ponds. If this is so, they quickly master their aversion. However, balloons remain popular because there is always the possibility, however remote, that without them one might have even *more* geese.

Occasionally, during nesting, mute swans attack geese. So people with goose trouble commonly erect swan decoys. They repel geese about as efficiently as herb necklaces repel disease. This is because the geese see that the swans are fakes.

Dogs can successfully goose-proof small areas, but their enthusiasm for goose chasing wanes as they discover that they never catch one. Sometimes dogs get beaten up by geese, and dogs defecate on grass, too.

In Connecticut and elsewhere giant Canadas have been captured during molt and deported to places like Maine. But when their feathers grow in, they fly back.

The Connecticut Agricultural Experiment Station has established that the chemical Methiocarb, when sprayed on grass, can keep geese away for several months. It washes off after about two weeks, but it gives the geese stomachaches and they remember. Methiocarb, however, is an insecticide, and mild and short-lived though it apparently is, environmental groups (the Connecticut Audubon Society among them) don't like the notion of spraying it all over suburbia.

The Experiment Station also has established that geese prefer tender grasses, such as Kentucky bluegrass (with which the banks of many reservoirs are seeded) over coarser varieties such as tall fescue. Goose haters can plant tall fescue but, if nothing else is handy, geese eat it, too.

Habitat alteration offers relief. "But," says waterfowl biologist Greg Chasko, of the Connecticut Wildlife Bureau, "in many cases the alterations are even less desirable than the geese. [As an example he offers killing your grass and planting something geese won't eat, like pachysandra.] If you build an estate and put a pond in and want to have expansive grass around it, you're going to have goose problems."

What about serious goose control: poisoning, lethal injections, traps—the big-league stuff they do to coyotes out West, for instance? First, most state resource agencies, with maybe a few exceptions, have progressed to the point where they wouldn't do this. Second, the feds wouldn't let them if they tried. "Geese," Chasko tells me, "are considered a migratory species even though most of the nuisance problems we have are from birds that are year-round residents. The ultimate authority for managing these birds is the US Fish and Wildlife Service." What about more moderate reduction/management plans? "None," says Chasko.

The message I get from all sources is that there is no solution to our problem. The geese will continue to do as they please, no matter what we say or think or do.

Somehow it cheers me, and not just because I am antisocial and dislike golf. Here is a symbol of wildness that humanity has not been able to crush and that, instead of going gentle into that good night when we convert the world to asphalt and green monoculture, takes over and doesn't get out of our way. "People just can't stand stepping on goose [droppings]," declares Priscilla Feral, national president of Friends of Animals. "They get real emotional about it. I don't. It doesn't bother me. Maybe golfers have to be a little more tolerant of goose droppings . . . . Where do robins defecate?"

I think the central message in all this goose flap is that, basically, we are hypocrites. We profess delight in the rediscovery of the ivory-billed woodpecker, for instance. We want the species to prosper, but on our terms. If 10,000 ivory-bills descended on each Atlantic state and took to prying off shingles, we would try to chase them back to Cuba.

"Babes," continued Aldo Leopold in "Goose Music," "do not tremble [with excitement] when they are shown a golf ball." This I have noted myself. But what worries me is that we appear to be breeding people who will.

UPDATE

Non-migratory Canada geese continue to humiliate humans who fancy they have some sort of control over nature. Minnesota birds have proliferated to the point that managers are conducting roundups and slaughters. Now the US Fish and Wildlife Service is talking about turning jurisdiction of Canada geese over to the states between the first of April and the end of August.

In 1989, two years after my article appeared, a survey of the Atlantic flyway from Maine through Virginia reported 70,613 *pairs* of resident geese. In 1995 the figure was 230,000. Some of these birds can be vulnerable to hunting when they fly over areas where it is permitted. (You set the season in early fall, before the wild birds fly.) But other flocks learn to stay downtown.

Recently, I toured the Department of Agriculture's Denver Wildlife Research Center—the only facility in the world dedicated exclusively to shielding humanity from the living inconveniences of nature. When I inquired why Building Number Three smelled like grape I was told that it was full of the artificial additive used in soda pop. The center has discovered that geese hate the stuff, that it affects their olfactory nerves the way ammonia affects ours. Now, say the Animal Damage Control agents, suburban grass will be as repulsive to them as it will be delicious to kids. Sure.

With populations of wild, migratory Canadas faltering, goose-hunting seasons along the Atlantic flyway have been closed. So resident town birds are expanding faster than ever. "How do you deal with them?" I asked waterfowl biologist H.W. Heusmann, my former colleague at the Massachusetts Division of Fisheries and Wildlife. Of the several suggestions he gave me, my favorite was: "You learn to live with them."

Jiggermen

For them, spring always comes too fast

Gray's Sporting Journal, Winter 1987

WHEN ALDERS along wild rivertops are burnt with frost and the brook trout pair off and hover under scarlet maple leaves, when the Great Bear walks through pine spires and New England slouches from the sun, lesser anglers sip bourbon by black-cherry fires, wax mellow about the season past, and clean and store their tackle. Jiggermen sip bourbon by black-cherry fires, wax mellow about the season past and set up their tackle. For them fishing never ceases and northern winters never are long.

Of course, I am not so pretentious as to claim that I am a jiggerman. At 40 I am far too young, and I haven't quite mastered the lingo or attained the proper stance or gut. But I am striving, making fair progress. I have been told that I have potential. At 50 and with new false teeth, Adamona is closer to it than I. He talks like Fess Parker, which helps but, at six-foot-three, he looks like him as well; and he doesn't even have gray hair. He has far to travel. Knowles, beefy, grizzled, fluent in clipped Cape-Codese, 78 and a master curmudgeon, has everything he needs to be a jiggerman except a proper chisel. He chops with some bent, spoon-billed Kmart contraption that I cover with a slicker when it must repose in the back of my truck. It saddens me to see such potential squandered.

Anyone can jigger, but few can become jiggermen. It takes monumental dedication, and there are rigid qualifications. First, one must be a Yankee. (A friend of my brother once said his barber knew a jiggerman from New York, but I never believed it.) For those who would delete the "er," referring to the art as "jigging," there is no hope whatever. He who catches pickerel on purpose by any means will never amount to anything more than an ice fisherman—the sort who builds fires on shore, sits on bait buckets, skims his holes and drills instead of chops. Jiggermen pursue yellow perch and only yellow perch. They have it right when they observe that tilts are cowardly devices more accurately called "traps," and that fishing with them is to winter angling what cut-rate prostitution is to holy matrimony.

In my state of Massachusetts there are perhaps 100 jiggermen, if one counts apprentices. Most know each other. They meet only on ice, and their conversations consist mainly of grunts and nods. None can quite match The Russian. Paunchy and ancient, he fishes 365 days a year, never more ardently than when the ponds are walkable. Ten or 20 years ago he realized that somewhere in some season his wife had stalked permanently from the house, maybe, he idly hypothesizes, because he had turned the cellar into a personal bait concession and didn't pay enough attention to all the dead stuff. When lunch time arrives The Russian does not go to the sandwiches; the sandwiches go to The Russian. While eating, he places his jiggerstick between his knees and maintains jigger action with pelvic thrusts.

Food is apt to fly from our forks, so twitchy are our wrists by mid-December. Then one night the wind drops and the unlit moon shows plain around its bright rim—too big, it seems, to fit. The geese leave Glen Charlie before midnight. We know that by dawn there will be shuffling ice, so-called because we shuffle over it and reach way out with our chisels so the jagged silver fractures don't quite radiate to our feet. One chop and we are through.

At times such as these, people summon the police to rescue us from our folly. I suspect that these are the same souls who, when I worked for the Massachusetts Division of Fisheries and Wildlife, would try to muster me to the aid of ducks who hadn't moved in such a long while that their feet "obviously" had frozen fast to the ice. When the cops arrive, they ask if they can talk to us. If Knowles is present, he'll holler, "Sure, come on out." And the cops, who know nothing of ice or jiggermen and have tried to order us off ponds that were not just walkable but driveable, will splutter and tell us that they prefer to remain on shore, that they have received reports that the Three Stooges were stumbling around the skimmed-over pond, and that they just want us to know that they are there to fish us out, animate or otherwise. So far, only Adamona has required fishing out—half a dozen times, perhaps—and always he has attended to it himself. He drives to a laundromat, runs his clothes through the drier twice—while robed in a tarpaulin—and is back fishing inside an hour. Knowles and I have been through a few times but only to our waists.

Until the ice frosts over or the snow falls, our normal, shallow beats are off limits. There the perch can see our every motion. Sometimes we glimpse them as they flash away or see the green weeds shudder. So now we fish deep water. Even 12 feet down we can spy our jiggers dancing. When the jigger is motionless the bead wiggles to a stop, and it is then that the perch eases in, moving only its pectorals, and takes: Twitch, twitch, flutter, flutter, stop . . . bump. I snap my wrist; the three-foot fiberglass jiggerstick dips and the drag on the taped-on spinning reel slips half a turn. I crank the fish up, watching it dash around under my feet, turning its lovely black-and-golden bars toward the sun. Then it is on the ice, twisting and glistening. A good perch, maybe nine inches, its pelvic fins redder than any brook trout's.

A week later the real cold settles from an azure sky. Now the blue woodsmoke rises straight from the cottages along the stark shoreline, and in the low, bright sun the ice chips fly like welding sparks to Adamona's chin. Jiggermen by nature cannot effervesce about how the *thunk, thunk, thunk-keyoo* of good steel on hard ice so stirs their blood or why they find clean, precise, efficient chopping almost an end in itself. You do not hit the ice in the same spot each time but, rather, you work gradually toward your foot so that the cut—preferably in the ice—is chisel width and four or five inches long. One chop for each inch of ice—unless, of course, you are equipped in the fashion of, say, Knowles, in which case you may count on at least 10. Sludge is not skimmed; it is shunted to the sides by holding the shaft still for three seconds, then extracting it in slow motion like a screwdriver used to mix paint. Usually the perch fit through OK; you don't care about the pickerel or bass. A jiggerman may be tracked by his hole trail.

Today the kids are skating and passing pucks. One, a 10-year-old who says his name is Bryan Herman, advises us to chop over air pockets because he has heard that fish frequent them to obtain additional air. Also, he says that we should note the way the perch were swimming when we haul them up so that we can determine the direction of the school. I tell him that if he is not careful he will grow up to be an outdoor writer. Bryan doesn't like the cracks that start at one end of the pond and howl and groan along its length like summer loonsong. But we explain that it is the sound of safe and thickening ice, the music of the jiggerman.

Why, Bryan wonders, are we wasting our time with little fish when we could be catching great big ones like his uncle down the lake? Adamona sighs an indulgent sigh and smiles a patient smile, a smile born of nearly half a century of plodding the frozen surface water of this tired old planet. He knows, as I do, that it's no good explaining. Bryan—as with the society to which he still is affixed—places a premium on sheer bigness. With luck, he one day will spring from that society like the free-swimming medusae of pond anemones, but for now he is anchored in the muck.

I am trying to raise Scott and Beth to be jiggerpeople, but I know that I will never live to see the fruition of my work. For them, too, the words "bigness" and "quality" are nearly interchangeable. Both, for instance, lust after oversize burgers from undernourished cows. Like Bryan, they have this perverse fascination with pickerel and "loud-mouth bass," as Beth calls them. Long ago I told them that I would take them jiggering only if they asked politely. But they never ask, so I have to force them to come, and always they require constant herding and fetching. Once, though, I dealt with them in a harsh and fitting manner.

It was one of those days in mid-February when the springtails hop in corn snow and little pods of crane flies dip and bob and hang around at head level. We were at the "Big Lake," the haunted island/forest where all three of us learned most of what we know that is worth knowing.

"How about we go jiggering?" I inquired, picking up my chisel.

"Nah," said Scott and Beth.

"I'm gonna walk around the island, though."

"Nah," said Scott and Beth.

"All right then. This is your last chance. I'm going right now. I'll leave you here. I really will. Do you want me to go without you?"

"OK," said Scott and Beth.

So I struck out "all alonely," as Beth says. It is five miles around the island. When I reached Rhinoceros Rock a tiltman accosted me. "Do you like pickerel?" he asked.

"No," I announced, firmly.

"Weeell," he declared, kicking at the wet ice. "You might as well take these heah."

"Why?"

"'Cause I ain't goin' ter."

"You mean you don't like pickerel either?" I asked in disbelief.

The tiltman shook his head and dropped his jaw so that he looked like a dental patient posing for inspection.

"Then why do you kill them?" I asked. "Why are you out here? Why are you going to all this trouble?"

The tiltman looked surprised and hurt, dropped his jaw farther and said he didn't rightly know. So I took off my Bean's belt and strung up his pickerel. There were five—bright, fat fish, all more than two pounds. The fangs left long, white trails down the linseed-darkened leather.

Now and then I'd catch a perch. I breathed deeply of the fresh, warm air fragrant with pine needles and pondwater. I shucked off my shirt and let the vitamin D soak into my winter itch. I didn't even have to chop because there were plenty of old tilt holes, all connected with bootprints and ringed with cigarette butts, shiner parts and muddy wisps of kabomba weed. It was a fine morning to be alive and jiggering in.

Between the bridge and Muskrat Island snowmobiles shrieked and tore back and forth across the ice. How colorfully, how thoroughly Knowles would have cursed them and their operators had he been at my side. "Don't it frost your ass," he would have said. Presently, a snowmobiler paused and, leering at me from the saddle, asked if I would watch his tilts for him while he raced. Lacking Knowles' quick, acerbic tongue, I could think of no more appropriate comment than, "No."

I regarded the snowmobiles as they flickered through the heat waves, fantasizing that the Big Lake opened like a pickerel maw and sucked them in. And, lo, as I stood there, it did. At least it sucked in one. It happened beneath the bridge where the current flows even in the dead of winter. First the hat bobbed to the surface, then the snow-mobiler. With that, the racing ceased.

At the head of First Perch Cove a tiltman hollered at me. I couldn't comprehend him across the wide expanse of ice, but I thought I knew what he wanted. When I came abreast of him he asked if I liked pick-erel.

"No," I said, sternly.

He had 11, all big fish. I better take them, he explained, because otherwise he was going to feed them to his neighbor's hogs. *Not even his own hogs.* He had a long piece of clothesline, so I shook the pick-erel I was carrying off my belt and threaded the line through 16 sets of gills. Now there was no carrying the pickerel; I had to drag them the way Knowles used to make me drag stripers off dawn-washed Nantucket beaches, leaning far forward with the cord cutting into my shoulder. I struggled toward camp, cogitating all the while: If I was going to go to all the trouble of making pickerel chowder and if tiltmen gave away their pickerel, I might as well do it up big.

So I went around to all the tiltmen in view, soliciting pickerel. I collected two more and two pot-bellied loudmouth bass. And when I gained our beach and moved up the path like a Clydesdale hitched to a stoneboat, Scott and Beth dropped their plastic sleds and goggled at my load. I left it by the turn-around circle, wiped the sweat from my forehead and proceeded nonchalantly onto the porch. Still, they did not speak.

I opened a beer, stretched out on the davenport and flexed my little jiggerstick.

"Fair jiggering," I intoned. "You should have come."

More than anything, jiggering is a philosophical state of being, but to reach it one first must master the simple mechanics. Therefore, brief tackle instruction is necessary. If Knowles, for example, only would pay attention to it, he could be a journeyman jiggerman in a week.

The jigger: A willow-leaf spinner blade filled with solder that embraces, at the hole end, the eye and a quarter-inch of shank from a clipped perch hook and, at the other, the rest of the hook. It takes a good man to keep it all straight with a nail and a pair of needle-nose pliers while blowing on the hot solder. Adamona insists on building his jiggers backward, so that the solder is on the outside. You do not want to do this because, among all sorts of other things, the hook hinders polishing of the brass. The trouble with Adamona and Knowles is that they carry their Yankeeness to preposterous extremes. They are too stubborn, too set in their ways and too opinionated. They have these notions about jiggering, of which virtually all are wrong.

But, to get back to tackle talk. At least Adamona is correct when he observes that a proper jigger is like a piece of fine jewelry, and he is offended when one is treated otherwise. A former friend of his, whom he had presented with a brace of jiggers, actually took sandpaper to them; a decade later Adamona still tells the story.

Let me hasten to explain that we are not snobbish. We feel that, on occasion, it is perfectly acceptable to bait a jigger with a worm or perch eye. But "the bead" is far more sporting and, usually, equally effective. By "the bead" we mean red, pea-size glass beads with holes through the center. Once I spent a whole day trying to find beads. "You get them from women's necklaces," Adamona had instructed. But, as usual, he was wrong. All the women I phoned said they didn't have any (although I will say that they sounded a little brusque, giving me the impression that they hadn't hunted very hard). At length, I unearthed a batch from the chaotic bowels of Paul's Tackle Shop, in Worcester, Massachusetts, where supposedly they were to be strung onto spinners. One threads the bead onto a common pin, clips the point and, with a combination of fingers and pliers, wraps it twice around the jigger hook so that the bead is tight up to the metal and so that it wiggles seductively but does not slip off the barb. Believe me, it takes a good man; even The Russian doesn't do it on his first try.

The chisel: Again, one does not acquire it at a store. Nothing that is sold commercially is remotely usable by real jiggermen. One makes one's chisel or has it made. The head is hardened steel, no wider than the shaft and steak-knife-sharp. Off ice this is protected by a cowhide sheath (best made by a cobbler) so that sharpening is never necessary. The shaft, to which the head is welded by a professional versed in attaching hard steel to soft, must be solid stock with a milled aluminum cap three-and-a-half inches in diameter and machine-pressed onto the top (to catch in the ice if, God forbid, you drop your chisel). A quarter-inch hole is drilled in the shaft just under the cap, and through this is inserted a length of quarter-inch nylon cord tied off in a loop so that, should the chisel slip to the bottom despite the cap, it may be retrieved with a treble hook wired to a bamboo rug pole. You can stick your hand through the loop, too, although jiggermen rarely do this. A jiggerman must chop with one hand, so take care that the shaft is not too long.

Boots: felt lined.

Clothing: Wool pants and parka. Stripeless snowmobile suits also are acceptable if sufficiently grimy.

"High pressure," grunts Adamona, meaning that it is cold and clear and the perch "won't eat," as he puts it.

"They could of et Thursday in the rain," I remark.

"Could of," allows Adamona.

But then my jiggerstick bends sharply and my hand is taken to the hole. The drag clatters. Stalemate. I fear a pickerel. Slowly, carefully I argue the fish to the ice. It sticks in the hole. I increase the pressure.

"Want my gaff?" inquires Adamona, referring to a length of curtain rod, one end of which he has smashed with a hammer around the eye of a barbless striper hook.

The jigger rips out and orbits my head.

With my knees I pull the slime-darkened glove from my right hand

and gingerly probe the hole. Joyfully, I feel toothless perch lips. I pinch one between thumb and forefinger and pull. Nothing. I pull and wiggle, feeling tissue rip. I get my index finger under a gill plate, and out she slides—a bright, foot-long cow.

"Gawd, ain't that beautiful," cries Adamona.

I insert my hand in my armpit, feeling the blood sear back into my fingers. Then I put the glove back on and swing my arm around. The big perch arches and lies still; within seconds her rigid fins turn white with frost.

By two o'clock I am toting 17 perch, better than I had expected with the bad jiggering weather. About a dozen—all Adamona's—are scattered over the ice. I never can get Adamona or Knowles to promptly put their perch in their jiggering bags (over-the-shoulder canvas affairs made by wives). Instead, they leave them where they fall like kids leave gum wrappers on living-room rugs, and they pay for it because when they finally get around to picking up after themselves they find that the gulls have assisted them. Knowles, who has much in common with gulls and long has identified with gulls, always yells at them to "get the hell off [his] fish," but they obey only when he shakes his jiggerstick and lumbers after them like a baited bear.

I would as soon leave woodcock around a birch run as yellow perch around ice. Nothing in freshwater rivals them as table fare, certainly not their larger, coarser cousins—the saugers and walleyes about which so much fuss is made—and certainly not the much-flapped-about and mushy salmonids. To clean perch properly one must: Slice off head, angling toward pelvic fins so that these, head and guts rip away in one unit. Slice off front dorsal. Slit hide to tail. Flip. Slice belly to vent. Slit hide from vent to tail. Peel hide off left flank. Peel hide off right flank. Pull—never cut—back dorsal and anal fin. Scissor out rib cage. I've been cleaning perch this way for 35 years and am now down to 20 seconds per fish. Adamona, on the other hand, insists on filleting perch, wasting time and meat. Like I said, he is a stubborn Yankee set in his ways. "Thank God I'm different," I always tell him.

Because I tend to forget important details I keep a fishing journal, and if the following details seem important to you too, then you have potential as a jiggerman. Thus far, I have related them only to Knowles, Adamona and the League of Women Voters, which I frequently find meeting in my living room when I return from jiggering. The members listen politely but seem unimpressed, and I frankly doubt if any has much potential. Anyway, my entry for the next outing reads as follows:

"Jan. 29—Sunny, 10 degrees but warming fast. To Caragrimseg at 8:15. Got in with only two-wheel drive. Saw red grouse in road. Guy waiting for his son and setting up tilts. He had loud beagle. I found partly cooked chicken with feathers still on, frozen into ice among burnt logs. Mist from waterfall had made hoarfrost on tree. Beautiful in sun, but melted fast. Ice getting thicker, but still good chopping. After 40 minutes got perch on bead. When I broke his neck and took eye he threw up live mummichaug. Didn't know they were in here. I put it in hole but it was hurting. Ruggles pissed on tiltman's sled and got yelled at."

I remember telling Ruggles that I too looked down on tiltmen but that this time he had gone too far. At this point, I suppose, I ought to explain that Ruggles is not my butler. He is my jiggering dog. When the popples are yellow and the milkweed blows he doubles as a Brittany spaniel, pointing woodcock and bringing the dead ones halfway back to me. When I pick up my chisel and ask him if he wants to go jiggering he responds by spinning and yelping and biting at my pant cuffs. While jiggering dogs help a lot, they are not absolutely essential to the sport. They are used mainly for barking at fish, investigating cottages, retrieving discarded ice chunks, participating in hockey games, sniffing the crotches of fellow jiggermen, running around and, especially, saluting all matter that breaks the gray monotony of a winter pond: logs, sleds, tilts, bait buckets, radios, thermos bottles, jackets. Everything. Ruggles, for example, has accomplished the Herculean task of teaching Knowles and Adamona actually to adapt an aspect of their jiggering routine; he has conditioned them always to wear their jiggering bags.

On this day, because no other jiggermen are abroad, I do something that otherwise would betray the cub in me. I chop a big hole, rake out the chips with my fingers, get down on my belly and study what is happening beneath me. The chill water feels wonderful around my nose and upper lip; it rides up with the surface tension, smelling of swamp and summer. It is clear but even now flecked with suspended bits of protoplasm that drift like stars in some grand and imperceptible pattern. The universe beneath the ice comes into focus when I cup my hands. Browning coontail undulates over lush, green bottom moss. The white spot becomes a wound on a pickerel's beak. I wiggle the line with my fingers, and he regards the jigger with wicked, reptilian eyes, then flattens his head, flares his gills and snatches. But I do not set. I get him to strike four times before he loses interest. Three perch, one a good one, materialize and hang around the jigger as if from a mobile. Tails motionless, they fan their pectoral fins and arch their needle-ridged dorsals. Suspiciously, coyly, they drift toward their comrade's ghastly, wrinkled, fluid-drained eye, peck it and drift back. Twitch, twitch, flutter, flutter . . . bump. I yank the line and, incredibly, the perch is on. Not the big one, though. I slide him onto the ice and break his neck. Soon there are eight perch surrounding the eye like wagon spokes. They move in and out and will not take. I watch them, hypnotized.

"Hey! Hey!" Someone is yelling at the north end of the pond. It is the tiltman, who has been joined by his son. He is wondering if I am dead. I wave, and he sits down again. The shadow of a red-tailed hawk sweeps across the ice, and the timeless fluting of jays drifts from the woods. I roll back onto my stomach and return to my voyeurism. Ruggles whines and prods me in the neck with his cold nose. Jiggering dogs won't let you die without noticing them first.

I do not want another season to slip by without finding Sandy—the semi-mythical pond, discovered by The Russian, that Adamona fished in the distant past. All he remembers is that it was somewhere north of Caragrimseg, deep in the woods, and that a troupe of hippies had set up a commune there, getting the place posted. Unaware that there haven't been any hippies anywhere for a good long while, he never went back.

So on this misty March morning we find ourselves trudging a tote road through the pine barrens of southeast Massachusetts and the feral, forgotten cranberry country they embrace. Pitch pine. Scrub oak. Wintergreen. Bull briar. Old burns. Cranberry bogs. Sand. The sun cuts through. Water beads sparkle on teaberries and pine needles and unshed oak leaves. The air is heady with the scent of pine and wet earth.

"This ain't right," says Adamona, backtracking and striking off on another tote road. "It oughta be over this next ridge." I recall how colossal is the quantity of next ridges in my life that were supposed to have worthwhile things in back of them and didn't. Here is yet another.

Finally, though, the right ridge gets in our way, and Adamona is wild with excitement, which, for a jiggerman, means grinning and saying, "Theah, b'Gawd." The pond even looks mythical. The woods around it and the sky over it are clear and bright while it remains shrouded in mist with the tops of drowned cedars poking through. A 40-foot band of open water obliges us to harpoon an ice raft and ferry ourselves to main ice, poling with our chisels, watching the bow and stern slip under the surface and the water rise almost to our boot tops.

"This is worse than when you drug me onto Turnpike," I observe, referring to the time I'd been fishing alone at Turnpike Pond with a spinning rod and bobber in April. Adamona had shown up and, with great disgust, asked why I wasn't jiggering. I'd laughed. But then he had fashioned a bridge out of planks and picnic tables, and we had drifted around the pond all afternoon on a tiny ice floe. Such is the attitude that keeps his business with laundromats so brisk.

There is no need to chop. Rain has swirled out holes everywhere. The ice is punky and honeycombed. We move over it, probing with our chisels as through a mine field. Sometimes, in the darker sections, we can push our chisels through. The perch come slowly, but they are lovely cows. There are just enough to give us unquiet dreams through summer nights.

"Next week this'll all be prayer ice," declares Adamona, as if that which we are standing upon were something else.

With a sound like French police cars, two mute swans beat through the mist and scull off toward Caragrimseg, now open. Redwings, perched on blushing swamp maples, are shouting "oklaree," and in the pitch pines a chickadee chants "feebee." We can hear the ice sputtering and popping in the sun. It is going. At noon we are driven off.

Adamona sighs. "Spring," says he, "always comes so fast."

UPDATE

I'm progressing splendidly in my apprenticeship. The paunch still eludes me, but I've mastered the stance and diction. Wilton is the first jiggering dog I've had that will actually retrieve perch; and, like the great Ruggles, he pees on everything that breaks the monotony of the winter icescape. When teaching jiggering to Peter Bogle and Howard Humphreys I call each of them "Grasshopper."

Knowles died with his fishing boots on.

Adamona is now a genuine jiggerman. To push his button, I mailed him an ad I saw for the "Electric Ice Fish Jigger"—a battery-powered, vibrating jiggerstick you're supposed to leave by the hole while you sit by the fire and drink coffee like a *tiltman.* Mozart would have been less appalled if I had asked him play "The Wabash Cannonball" on the crow call.

Whoever invented the Electric Ice Fish Jigger must also have invented the bulbous, green-and-black plastic eyeballs. I was fascinated with the concept—an artificial imitation of a bait procured by jiggermen because, in the dead of winter, they can't get anything natural. Anyway, I bought a package (they're about three times normal size) and kept them in my pocket until I'd iced a cow perch on a new pond Adamona was showing me. When he had gone to get his sandwich I replaced the fish's real eyeballs with the counterfeits—a difficult operation. They made the perch look like Rodney Dangerfield. "What the *hell* is wrong with the fish you got in this gawdammed pond," I demanded when Adamona trudged back out. For once he was speechless.

More recently I ran into a bunch of jiggermen on a Cape Cod pond. From their chisels I could tell they were from Worcester, Massachusetts, which is to jiggering what Vienna is to opera. In an emotional outburst, one looked at my Worcester-style chisel and grunted approvingly, then showed me an eyeball remover he had invented. Finally, he spoke: "We take this serious."

Well, of course.

The Blues

Question: What does the bluefish have in common with the

wolf, the passenger pigeon and the bison?

Fly Rod & Reel, May/June 1988

THEY ATTACK with primitive, savage frenzy. Up against the beach and along the leading edges of offshore rips, in quiet slicks and wild surf, wherever bait mills or tumbles, they cut, rip and slash, killing even when sated. Not the bluefish—the bluefish fishermen.

I watched such mayhem this past September where the Merrimack River merges with the North Atlantic off Newburyport, Massachusetts. The morning was warm and misty, the sea glassy and sliced everywhere by dorsal fins of enormous bluefish—choppers down from the Gulf of Maine on the first cool currents of autumn. I'd waited all year for this. Anglers effusing about the plentitude of bluefish have selective memories, forgetting all the days the fish were somewhere else. It's a big ocean.

Now I stood on the deck of my Mako and fired a long, yellow streamer on a floating 10-weight shooting-taper. I let it sweep along the south jetty, holding the big rod between my knees and stripping fast with both hands. Marking the course of the fly were flashes and violent upwellings. Blues are a wonderful flyrod species, provided they are present in large numbers. If you have someone with you, they can cast a hookless plug, getting the fish closer and madder.

I love to eat fresh blues, so I was clubbing mine. The people in the next boat—a cabin cruiser—were releasing theirs. First, however, a fellow I took to be the mate was gaffing them. Gaff-and-release angling. It's a new trend among coastal sportfishermen from Maine to Florida. "What the hell are you doing that for?" I asked, as the mate skewered another 12-pounder through the gut cavity. He looked at me as if I had immigrated from Ganymede.

Among the bluefish I have caught in the past five years two have been dead. The first of these was taken along the Galls en route to Nantucket's Great Point. Knowles, the scale-stuck, beslimed curmudgeon with whom I prowl the Yankee coast, had spotted the slick, and we had the fish to ourselves for a minute or two. Presently, however, beach buggies descended on us like herring gulls, eliciting shocking profanity from Knowles (despite the fact that he responds to bent rods in precisely the same fashion). Knowles kills bluefish in considerable (but not piggish) quantity and consumes everything; he even condemns me for filleting my fish and thereby "wasting the flank." He used to quit when the box was full, but on this day I had introduced him to single, barbless hooks and we let our surplus fish shake off in the wash without touching them. It was a whole new concept for Knowles, and he was bubbling about it.

But now a steady line of dead bluefish floated by us on the tide. All along the beach fishermen were stepping on fish, grinding them in the sand, ripping them, punting them back into the sea or just letting them flap at the wave line. Finally, 50 yards out, I snagged one by a protruding gill raker, and we moved.

The behavior I have observed while bluefishing does not seem aberrant to Stuart Wilk of the National Marine Fisheries Service, for he routinely observes behavior even more grotesque. Wilk has devoted his whole career—more than 20 years—to studying bluefish. He fishes them constantly, rarely killing one. Marine biologists call him "Mr. Bluefish."

"I've seen people walk off a party boat and leave bags full of bluefish hung on the rail," he told me. "I've seen dumpsters full of bluefish. I've seen people bring them into the dock where I keep my boat, hold them up and take pictures and just throw them over the side. You can see it all the time. Somebody catches a fish on the beach and they throw it up on the sand. And then they walk down the beach for maybe half a mile, catching fish as they go along and throwing them up on the beach. And they never go back to pick them up. Why?"

Why indeed? It's an interesting question, a question not so easily answered. Whatever the answer, the behavior is not just a symptom of our age. In his newly revised book, *Bluefishing*, Henry Lyman cites an item from the January 6, 1883, edition of *The American Angler*. Sailing from New York City to Fire Island, the author, who signed himself

"Old Issak," noted that "the water was perfectly alive with fish" and that he "repeatedly killed bluefish on the surface with [his] revolver," regretting only that he didn't have a shotgun.

Bluefish appear in vast schools, so humans, driven by a kind of coon-in-the-chicken-coop mentality, kill more than they can ever use. But there is more to it than this. "There's a real anger about bluefish," observes Bob Pond, creator of Atom lures and crusader for steward-ship of the seas. "There are an awful lot of people who actually hate the fish because it so often interferes with other kinds of fishing. If you want a striped bass and catch a bluefish, you're angry at the blue-fish. If you want a cod and get a sand shark, you physically carve it up. It's an amazing reaction, and I don't really understand it because the guy thought he had a good fish and was enjoying the fight."

And humans fear bluefish. Out of water, blues are the only fish I know that will attack and wound people on purpose. They follow you with quick, unrelenting eyes, biding their time. Underwater, they attack and wound people by mistake. (Once I heard Knowles howling in the dark because he had gotten a good lip-hold on what he thought was a striper but was really a bluefish.) Fearing the awful teeth of bluefish, fishermen often let them die before dislodging the lure, though with a single hook—barbless or otherwise—there's nothing to it. I also think that humans envy bluefish, as perhaps they envied the bison, begrudging them their speed, power, freedom and fecundity.

Finally, and seriously, I've noticed that fishermen take on some of the characteristics of the fish they pursue. The way trout, for example, pursue insects is not unlike the way some humans pursue trout. (I'll leave the big-mouthed bass and walleyed pike to Ed Zern.) The selectivity of bluefish, on the other hand, usually doesn't extend much beyond motion, i.e., if something moves, they seize it. As for delicacy, blues don't have any. They appear suddenly in droves, staining the water red in killing orgies that can last the better part of a tide. I have seen their prey beach itself in mile-long windrows rather than face the terrible jaws. Apt indeed is the blue's scientific name: *Pomatomus saltatrix*, translated loosely as "a sheathed, leaping, cutting edge."

I am just a fisherman without much biological training, so I had long wondered if the wanton waste I was seeing along the Atlantic coast was really a threat to bluefish stocks or just moral/aesthetic squalor. Actually, I suspected it was the latter, and I had to admit I believed the case, made by some biologists, that the slaughter was preventing the population from reaching that maximum biomass that triggers self-destruction.

Now I know better. The bubble principle works with creatures such as white-tailed deer, whose habitat is sharply defined and food supply limited by permanent boundaries. If Friends of Animals, for example, prevails in deer management (as happens from time to time on various reservations and islands), the deer cease to be killed by hunters and instead starve to death. It is as simple as that. But species like bluefish keep the bubble from breaking by expanding their range. Wilk puts it this way: "Fifteen years ago there were few if any blues in Maine or the Canadian maritimes. Even in Massachusetts Bay, as opposed to Cape Cod. Now they're all over. They've spread out. Their ability to survive throughout continental shelf waters is well documented. They can live almost anywhere. If they're pushed because of crowding, they just go east and west or north and south. Their criteria for being happy may change, but they're still within a range of conditions they can tolerate."

But if the killing is not preserving the bubble, is it really threatening the population? After all, seasoned anglers don't need any fancy data to see that there are more and bigger bluefish now than there have been for decades. Never have catches been higher—some 33 million blues a year. A third, by weight, of all fishes caught along the Atlantic coast are blues. In 1960 anglers killed 51 million pounds of bluefish, making the species the sixth most important, by weight, of all American fish. By 1970 the overall rod-and-reel catch had risen to 120 million pounds (it has remained in that vicinity) and bluefish ranked first. In the face of all this, they've expanded their range.

So why worry? This was the attitude of Reagan's Department of Commerce, which rejected a management plan proposed by the Mid-Atlantic Fishery Management Council in part because "there was no immediate urgency for management at the time."

Of course, there was "no immediate urgency" for striped bass management in 1970. Or Atlantic salmon management in 1790. We only begin managing things after we run out of them; it's a tradition. Just once, suggested the Mid-Atlantic Fishery Management Council, it would be nice to manage something *before* the crash. This way we could determine the beast's potential, chart its range, study its true behavior, avoid tedious and expensive restoration.

Now the council, assisted by the Atlantic States Marine Fisheries Commission, is trying again. A stock assessment has been completed, a draft management plan printed. At this writing the process seems to have bogged down, but participants expect fruition in a year or so.

Bluefish, it turns out, are a lot more vulnerable than we had supposed. They are short-lived. Maximum age is thought to be about 12 years (half that of striped bass), so strong year-classes don't last and populations are extremely volatile. My friend Knowles, for instance, remembers when there were virtually no bluefish off New England—circa 1941. Slightly before his time—in 1764—bluefish suddenly disappeared, not showing up again until 1810. The population boomed from 1880 to 1905, then dropped off. So it goes with *Pomatomus saltatrix*.

The point, however, is that with management, fluctuations need not be so wild. Abysses can be alpine valleys, peaks wide plateaus. "Recreational fisheries are predicated on overabundance," notes Randy Fairbanks of the Massachusetts Division of Marine Fisheries. "Recreational fishers are very inefficient. That's why we have a tackle industry, because people lose what they throw. Blues are great. They hit lures, they cut lines, they strip reels. They're there for everybody. It's that overabundance that we're enjoying right now. If we want to have this consistently good fishing, we have to preserve it."

Currently, commercial landings amount to only 10 percent of the kill. This is because bluefish spoil quickly and don't freeze well. But things could change fast with new technology. In the late 1970s, markets in Africa and South America stimulated test purse seinings of bluefish by tuna fishermen. In 1982 Florida fishermen used runaround gillnets to make enormous hauls in Chesapeake Bay. Blues, like any schooling, pelagic species, are easily netted, and they are dangerously concentrated at certain points along their migration route. Accordingly, the pioneers of bluefish management propose to restrict commercial fishermen if, based on average landings of three previous years, they account for more than 20 percent of the total catch.

As the management plan takes shape it is becoming apparent that blues are being killed at about the maximum sustainable yield. On top of this, estimated spawning stock has dropped 66 percent—from 549,567 metric tons in 1979 to 185,587 metric tons in 1986. After three dominant year-classes in 1977, 1981 and 1984, reproductive success has been mediocre or poor. But recruitment is a function of natural events on the continental shelf. Managers worry much more about protecting fish already hatched. "We are very concerned about the rising fishing rate," declares Vic Crecco of the Connecticut Department of Environmental Protection and author of the stock assessment. "We'd like to cap it."

Toward this end the would-be managers have suggested a 10-fish daily limit. Knowles would approve. I certainly would. Maybe 10 bluefish is too generous. Say they average six pounds. That's 20 pounds of meat, 35 pounds if you save the flank and cheeks! But the charter/party skippers, who coastwide account for the largest portion of the kill, are screaming like the Sabine virgins. "Why worry about a migratory species," exclaimed one captain at a recent meeting of the Maryland Charter Boat Association, at which a motion to support the limit was soundly defeated. "If we don't catch them here, they'll get them in New Jersey or the Carolinas." Imagine the quality of water-fowling we'd have today had Joe Knapp, sire of Ducks Unlimited, talked that way in 1937.

The story of how I caught my other dead bluefish is significant in that it provides further revelations about charter operations and because the experience shocked me into the realization that it is time for decent people to agitate for bluefish appreciation and bluefish man-agement. An artist friend of mine books this Cape Cod charter boat several times a season, more often than not killing 100 or 200 bluefish, keeping three or four and letting the crew sell the rest (this after they've collected $250). Learning that the skipper was one of the few who permit anglers to use light tackle, Knowles and I went out with him. He proved to be a nice guy—not greedy, arrogant, bossy or abu-sive. But his mate made up for him, getting his back up when we asked to keep our fish instead of letting him sell them for lobster bait. (It was August and the fish stores were glutted.)

Off the Old Man Rip the skipper announced that he'd spotted on the screen a big school of blues 40 feet down. This meant marlin rods and wire line. Knowles, who didn't believe depth finders could record anything but the bottom, told the skipper that he was "as full of crap as a Christmas goose." But soon Knowles was winching in 15-pound bluefish, all of which the sullen mate threw back after hacking out the fillets. And, as each fillet came off, he would fling it against the side of the boat because he was still mad.

I just watched, but there were two rods out. The mate would grab one, set the hook and thrust it into my hands; and, not wishing to anger him any further and having nothing else to do anyway, I would crank the reel. Presently, I felt something really big. "Bass," announced the mate. Knowles fumbled for his camera. I strained at the rod, gaining and losing wire. The fish was amazingly strong but didn't swim around much. At last, I worked it to the surface.

"Oh," said the mate, putting down the gaff. I'd hooked a bluefish by the tail and had been dragging it, gills spread, against the current. It was one of the filleted ones.

UPDATE

The bad news is that the blues have fallen way off. The good news is the big bluefish-netting operation off the Carolinas has been banned and that there are now more stripers than when I chased them with Knowles in the 1970s. My theory is that there can only be so many cows in one pasture.

This past summer Wilton's vet, Dr. Neil MacKenzie, took a 20-pound blue in Ipswich Bay while casting a pencil popper from my vessel, the venerable *Gin Lo III* (a 17-foot Mako I bought secondhand in the early 1980s, never having learned who Gin and Lo were or are). When Neil's wife, Barbara, hung an even bigger blue from the same school, I got so excited I put a bass-style thumb-hold on the lower lip of Neil's fish.

"Look at all the blood," chirped the lovely, enthusiastic, ever-innocent Barbara after I'd gaffed her 23-pounder.

Steelhead Factories

Haig-Brown had it right; why can't we listen?

Fly Rod & Reel, July/October 1988

ON A STEELHEAD fishing/fact-finding expedition to Vancouver Island five years ago I made a pilgrimage to Campbell River to read Roderick Haig-Brown's unpublished papers and talk with Ann, his friendly, energetic widow. We walked along the dry bed of the once and future Kingfisher Creek, then imprisoned in downtown storm sewers but today, in the most fitting of all possible tributes, full of coho parr and restored by Haig-Brown's admirers to roughly its original course through the 19-acre property.

Ann and I talked about her husband's writing and his enormous influence on steelhead management in British Columbia. And after dinner she ushered me into his office/library. His glasses were on the desk, exactly as he had set them down when he'd gone out to tend the lawn on the last morning of his life. I could even smell his pipe tobacco. Then Ann closed the door from the outside and, alone in the late-December twilight in front of the high, gray Campbell River, I visited with Roderick Haig-Brown's ghost.

As I read, I became increasingly envious—not of Haig-Brown nor his fishing nor even his writing, but of *Canada*. God knows, we Americans need him more than they ever did. Basically, he made British Columbia understand the difference between steelhead management and steelhead production. He coaxed and badgered the province into 1) stocking only a handful of degraded streams incapable of sustaining natural runs; and 2) forbidding anglers to kill wild steelhead. There was some real culture shock. But, as BC biologist R.S.

Hooton put it, "The choice is simple—some fishing or no fishing." Angling effort fell off by about 75 percent. Then, as catch-and-release caught on, it returned to normal.

In America's Pacific Northwest, however, the line between steel-head management and steelhead production is blurred. And fish and game departments, the federal government, Indians, fillet-and-release anglers, foresters, farmers, courts and water districts have the steel-head resource by the gills and are pulling from all directions.

The recent trouble started in 1970, when the federal government mounted a lavishly funded lawsuit against the State of Washington on behalf of commercial Indian gillnetters. Chosen to preside was Federal Judge George H. Boldt, a well-known champion of "Indian rights," as they were perceived at the time. When the case came to trial in the fall of 1974 there was no doubt about the outcome. With creative interpretation of ancient treaties—not one of which used the words "50 percent" or "half" in relation to fish—Boldt determined that 1,500 Indians had the right to 50 percent of the state's har-vestable steelhead and salmon resource. One problem was that no one had the slightest idea what the harvestable resource might consist of.

Swiftly, the Indians dealt steelhead runs a blow from which they have yet to recover. For instance, on the Skagit River—at that time probably Washington's most prolific steelhead producer—they virtu-ally wiped out a whole year-class, and the "50-50 split" translated to 5,000 for the Indians, 800 for sportsmen. If one can accept Boldt's Old Testament notion that wrongs to dead people can be righted by paying off their descendants, there is still the problem of natural recruitment. The Boldt decision might have made sense in a world where anadro-mous fish behave like Treasury notes. But on this earth, even in man-made setups, anadromous fish can be generated only by themselves; and when the brood stock is gone, that's it.

Four years ago, when I talked to Bob Gibbons of the Washington Game Department (which, through the vagaries of bureaucracy, has charge of steelhead), he told me he felt "encouraged" even though the Skagit's escapement goal wasn't being met. In 1988 he's still encouraged and the Skagit's escapement goal still isn't being met.

"We're having a hard time," he acknowledged. "We don't seem to be getting the wild returns from the protected escapements that we thought we'd get. The sport catch this year is quite good for wild fish, so we're hopeful that maybe we have a good run." But maybe they don't. And, even if they do, how many will the commercial Indian gill-netters kill next year?

The terrible pressure on steelhead has caused the State of Washington to grow impatient. Impatience breeds hatcheries; and hatcheries breed carelessness with land and water. After all, by current values, rivers don't need to produce steelhead anymore; fish factories will take care of it.

But hatcheries cannot produce steelhead. What issues from them is something else, something less. Fish best adapted to hatchery life are least adapted to the real world simply because conditions within a concrete trough are in every respect the antithesis of those within a river. Moreover, wild steelhead are genetically adapted to their natal water so that instead of one subspecies native to the Pacific Northwest, we have—or had—hundreds. Of known Columbia River stocks, for example, 57 are presumed extinct, including one that traversed 1,400 miles to a tributary on the upper Snake.

By nature a young steelhead spends two years in fresh water, but by selecting for earlier eggs, hatchery technicians can send it to sea in one, thereby slashing costs. Hatchery technicians also tend to select earlier-spawning fish for brood stock because they fear the run will peter out and they might not get enough eggs later. Dick May, president of California Trout, puts it this way, "They take these early fish and spawn them and fill up their trays. And then all these other steelhead come knocking at the door in dead winter or maybe early spring and there's no room at the inn. And they're blocked off by the dam that this hatchery was supposed to mitigate. So they've got no place to go." This is why so many American steelhead streams that used to have three runs—in fall, winter and spring—now have just one.

Because of this tendency of hatchery steelhead to ascend rivers earlier, interbreeding with wild fish occurs less frequently than one might suppose. But in every case where natural runs have been "supplemented" by the hatchery product wild steelhead have declined. "Once you get hatchery fish into a system they become the primary focus of management and the wild stocks are set up for extinction," declares Bill Bakke, the executive director of Oregon Trout.

Bakke, who has done extensive research on this subject, reports that wild steelhead are: Six times more effective than hatchery fish in producing the next generation; 144 percent more likely to survive from fry to smolt; and 74 percent more likely to survive from smolt to adult. "Salmonids are renewable resources," he writes, "but gene resources are not easily renewable and decisions to reduce genetic resources should be made carefully, with good information . . . . The goal of the hatchery program . . . should be to maintain the genetic characteristics that allow the fish to perform well in the natural stream environment. For example, a four-week advance in spawning may reduce the survival of offspring by as much as 50 percent."

Yet Haig-Brown-style steelhead management still eludes Americans. Perhaps we are too rich or in too much of a rush. Whatever the reason, we tend to get caught on fake-fish treadmills: The faster we lose our wild fish, the more we depend on hatcheries. And the more we depend on hatcheries, the faster we lose their wild fish. A steelhead hatchery has just been reopened on the net-blighted Skagit. The Northwest Power Planning Council plans two major steelhead/salmon hatcheries. Congress has appropriated funds for new steelhead hatcheries for the Snake River. Oregon and Washington still play Johnny Appleseed with hatchery stock, most of it dangerously inbred. In Oregon 53 percent of the fish division's budget for 1987/89 has been earmarked for hatchery production; and 78 percent of the rivers are being polluted with hatchery genes. It's just as bad in Washington.

"Fish agencies continue to claim more hatcheries are needed, not more wild fish or habitat protection," laments Bakke. "Hatcheries have become a form of orthodoxy, and anyone questioning them is criticized as unrealistic . . . . With hatchery dominance in place, we then are free to develop our watersheds."

Washington Indians, who operate some two dozen hatcheries with federal money, are pushing for more and have proposed to saturate all available steelhead water. At least the states minimize interbreeding by taking the earliest eggs, but some of the Indians don't make even this token effort.

"Although the Indian tribes give lip-service to wild-fish preservation, the biologists and lawyers employed by the tribes repeatedly have demonstrated a disregard for native stocks," charges an irate manager from Idaho, the one state that does emphasize wild-fish management. "The pushing of widespread hatchery programs is a transparent attempt to cover up systematic overfishing."

The Indians like to sell hatchery steelhead well enough, but wild fish are bigger and yield more dollars per carcass, so the less cooperative tribes want these, too. This spring the Quileutes hadn't taken their 50-percent quota, at least according to their figures, from the Quillayute system on Washington's Olympic Peninsula and were still netting when the wild runs started. "It irritates the hell out of us," one veteran steelheader told me.

The states are making some effort to protect wild stocks by clipping the adipose fins off hatchery smolts and requiring that adults with full adiposes be released. But they presume that the highest and best use of a wild steelhead is to pass through the gastrointestinal tract of a human being, and as soon as a run seems healthy again, and just as anglers have adapted to catch-and-release, no-kill regs get dropped.

These days, all summer-run steelhead planted in the Columbia River Basin are being clipped, and no-kill is on for wild fish. But here and elsewhere such distinction is rarely made with winter runs. With some wild Columbia River stocks candidates for endangered status, mixing in unmarked hatchery fish is an especially irresponsible practice as well as an especially effective means of ducking the requirements of the Endangered Species Act.

Not all the news is bad, as they always say. But this, alas, is a piece about bad news, i.e., American-style steelhead "production." If there is any good news to report here, it is that there are groups like California Trout, Oregon Trout and S/SPAWN (Steelhead and Salmon Protective Action for Washington Now) working hard to bring us to our senses.

Perhaps if we pay more attention to Haig-Brown's writing, we will acquire better taste in things natural and learn to appreciate wildness in fish. Once, to compensate him for speaking at a forestry convention, the Government of Saskatchewan flew him north, away from his steelhead, to fish for Arctic grayling. "What did I want of them?" he asked in *Fisherman's Summer.* "Not to kill them certainly, nor to eat them, though I would probably do both these things. Not even to match my skill against their instincts, because I cheerfully assumed they would be rising freely, as Arctic grayling so frequently are, and present no problems. Nor for the excitement of setting light tackle against their strength and watermanship, for I had long ago learned to handle faster and stronger fish on lighter gear than they would make me use. Really, it was only to see them and through them somehow to become more intimate with the land about the streams their presence graced."

In the Pacific Northwest, just to start with, that passage ought to be printed on all fishing licenses and tribal membership cards. And it ought to be set backward in brass—onto the business end of a one-foot-square wood-burning iron—for inscribing, just to start with, the desktops of all fish managers.

UPDATE

In some ways the Pacific Northwest is getting smarter about taking care of its wild steelhead. Washington has been a leader in no-kill regulations. Oregon is following suit. But the population decline continues. Bill Bakke, who now runs an outfit called the Native Fish Society, believes much has been learned about wild steelhead since 1988 but that "what we've learned and how we manage are two different things." Basically, American steelhead are still being "managed for meat," says Bakke, and the current situation throughout the Pacific Northwest is "an ecological crisis." For example, Idaho reports that its wild steelhead have declined to where they're now at the level of the Snake River chinook salmon when they were listed under the Endangered Species Act.

A study in Washington reveals that "while hatchery winter steelhead had the potential to produce 55 percent of the winter-run offspring [both hatchery and wild], natural production by these hatchery fish appears to be zero, based on the 1990-brood adults returning to Kalama River during the 1993-94 winter-run cycle." So while hatchery fish are producing lots of juveniles, they're not surviving. The preliminary data collected in the study indicate "that the reproductive success differentials between hatchery and wild winter-runs in the Kalama River are similar to that previously estimated for Kalama summer runs. Hatchery winter-runs have the potential to breed with wild winter steelhead. Therefore findings of low hatchery winter-run success have serious implications regarding the potential genetic effects . . . on wild populations."

Budget cuts forcing closure of hatcheries are good news for wild steelhead. Domestic stock can't cope with the kind of habitat variability facing steelhead since I wrote the piece—poor ocean environment and poor freshwater environment due to draught. Wild stock can.

The National Marine Fisheries Service has been petitioned to list steelhead under the Endangered Species Act. They may well do it; they should.

"The states are in denial," remarks Geoff Pampush, the new director of Oregon Trout. "These agencies are directly dependent on the revenue stream associated with license sales and fish landings. Even a short-term blip makes them scramble. That translates to an extreme reluctance to shift to a wild-fish management policy."

Kurt Beardslee, director of Washington Trout, says too many wild fish are still being killed. "We need to err in favor of fish. We've been erring in favor of making sure we have a harvest, quite obviously to the detriment of fish we don't have enough information on."

In 1995 the Skagit's escapement goal still wasn't being met.

Driving Out the Dread Serpent

A day at a rattlesnake rodeo

Audubon, September 1990

WERE IT NOT for the Opp Jaycees' Rattlesnake Rodeo, which attracts some 50,000 visitors a year, few Americans would have heard of Opp, Alabama—"The City of OPP-ortunity," population 7,000, deposited, as if by a passing buzzard, on the dry, sandy pinewoods of southern Alabama. "This is what put us on the map," declares Mike Carnley, president of the Opp Jaycees.

Publicity on Opp and its snake show reached me in far-off Yankeeland last winter. But it came from *Audubon* readers Nela and Jim Godwin, two young wildlife biologists from Snook, Texas, and it wasn't the kind of stuff the Jaycees were handing out. The Godwins have some pretty aberrant notions about snakes—they love them, even (or especially) rattlesnakes. They seriously urge people who live near rattlesnakes not only to be nice to the serpents they catch—feed and water them, for instance—but to desist from cutting off their heads when they finish using them to raise money for charity. The Godwins are *environmentalists*, a word much used these days in rattlesnake rodeo country and pronounced *enn-vie-meddlists*, with the accent on the *enn*. So there I was on March 3, 1990, at Opp Jaycees headquarters, inspecting all the polyurethaned rattlesnake gew-gaws and reading material hanging on the walls. There was the Jaycee Creed: "We believe . . . that Earth's great treasure lies in human personality." (The enn-vie-meddlists, of course, would argue that biodiversity is worth more.) And the glass-framed *Opp News* editorial about a four-year-old boy who had been killed by a rattlesnake and, therefore, had received the posthumous honor of having one entire Opp

Rattlesnake Rodeo dedicated to him: "During the past few years the hunting of rattlesnakes in south Alabama has come under attack by a number of self-styled ecologists who cry long and loud that the poor rattlesnake is being persecuted . . . . Frankly, these people make us a little sick to our stomachs . . . .

"So strong has their movement become that they have even been successful in introducing legislation in Alabama that would prohibit the hunting of rattlesnakes. Thanks to the clear thinking of our legislators, however, it was defeated—this time.

"The truth is that a rattlesnake is a very deadly, and often a very vicious reptile who will strike and kill anything that happens to irritate him at the moment. He knows nothing about peaceful coexistence, nor is he capable of learning." The piece was dated May 23, 1974.

Presently, Mike Carnley appeared for a quick, pre-rodeo interview. "We get so much flak from these enn-vie-meddlists," he lamented. "Most of the people who criticize us have no concept of what it's like to live in an area where rattlesnakes live. They have no concept of what it's like to get out of your car and walk to your front door and know you might get bit by a rattlesnake."

I never have been frightened by the rattlesnakes I live with, which cause significantly fewer injuries to humans throughout their range than do house cats. But my snakes are timber rattlers. Carnley's are Eastern diamondbacks, just as shy and docile but much larger. What, I asked him, was the human death toll from snakebite in Alabama. "There was a little boy that got killed in 1974," he told me. "I've got a little four-year-old myself, and that's how old that boy was. People don't know what it's like to live in an area where your kid could walk up on a snake."

After the interview I wandered back outside and watched the Eastern diamondbacks in the trailer. Their slanting, bony "eyebrows" made them look very deadly and vicious. Some were stacked on top of each other, and their feces were piling up on the green Astroturf. But there were lights for warmth and plenty of water. They seemed happy enough, if that's the right word for what rattlesnakes feel when they have more or less what they need. Even an environmentalist couldn't claim they were being treated inhumanely.

The six cages were encased in thick glass with a layer of heavy wire beyond that. But still the Jaycees weren't taking any chances. DANGER LIVE RATTLESNAKES warned the sign. That's the thing about the Opp Jaycees. They stress safety. "We tell what to do if you encounter a rattlesnake," says Carnley. "And we do education—where he stays, what he eats, such as that. You won't see no freak show or daredevil stuff. No one ever got bit [unless you count one nip on the finger, which Carnley did not], and we're the only rodeo that can claim that."

My conversations with the snake handlers of Western rodeos (or "roundups," as they are more commonly called) seemed to confirm what Carnley was saying. Cotton Dillard, of Brownwood, Texas, for example, has received 25 venomous bites from Western diamondbacks while on the roundup circuit and he "doesn't keep up" with the scores of nicks and dry bites. Only three of the venomous bites—on the nose, lip and foot—were acquired in the "snake pit," where participants (though not Dillard) have been seen to engage in such activities as: "Goin' for a Sixpack" (in which they hold up, between their fingers, three snakes in each hand); "Stackin' Cow Pies" (in which snakes—prodded into the defensive, non-strike position with their heads tucked behind their bodies—are stacked on one's head, shoulders, knees, arms and crotch); "The Kung Fu Walk of Death" (in which contestants sashay barefoot through defensively coiled serpents, kicking them soccer-style against the plywood walls); and "Stomping" (in which contestants compete to see who can crush to death the most snakes with their cowboy boots).

Dillard, however, specializes in "Sacking," in which he got his other bites and for which he claims to hold the world record. Amateur and professional sackers (he counts himself among the latter) compete to see how many live rattlers they can stuff into a burlap bag in the shortest time. A trick of the trade is to stay sober: "A lot of these guys get tanked up. That's why they get in there. Seems like the last few years it's got a little worse." Once Dillard sacked five snakes in under three seconds. He also claims to hold the world record for "Lifting"—25 live rattlers in each hand.

Sometimes Cotton Dillard will have as many as 10 rattlers on his shirt, in his pockets and around his neck. "I handle them real liberal," he confides.

One of Dillard's fellow sackers and a Brownwood neighbor died after being bitten in a contest. Another sacker was bitten in the hand (for which points were taken off), continued sacking, was bitten in the other hand (for which more points were taken off), continued sacking, observed with chagrin that he had lost the contest and then was rushed to the hospital. When Dillard is bitten, though, he doesn't even get sick (except once when he "was compromising for a friend and the good Lord didn't go along with it"). It was the Lord, in fact, who sent him on the roundup circuit. As Dillard explains it, every time he survives a bite in public, it demonstrates just what the Lord can do. "I do this as a way of witnessing for the Lord," he told me.

Snakebite is (or at least used to be) such a non-problem in America that the Red Cross saw fit to drop it from its multimedia first-aid course. But as rattlesnake roundups proliferate, more and more contestants are getting bitten. And, with all the new cases of snakebite, there are more calls for roundups as a means of snake control.

Virtually all the roundups are sponsored by civic groups, mainly the Jaycees. There are 25 or 30 events in Texas, five in Oklahoma, one in New Mexico, one in Alabama, four in Georgia and usually about a dozen in Pennsylvania (although here native snake parts can't be sold and timber rattlers have to be released at point of capture within 48 hours).

"God cursed the serpent," says Dillard. "There's no doubt about that, but I disapprove of being cruel to anything." That's why he doesn't go for "the kicking and stomping." In this, at least, he has the support of the enn-vie-meddlists. They don't like the kicking and stomping either. Nor do they like the public "Butcher Shop" shows where, for a nominal fee, Moms, Dads and kiddies get to watch or participate in decapitations, where headless bodies writhe from metal hooks and where severed heads exhibit brain activity—erecting fangs, snapping at heat sources and dilating pupils in response to light—for more than an hour.

The enn-vie-meddlists even object to the practice of sewing shut the mouths of live snakes so you and your kiddies can safely get your pictures taken with them wrapped around your shoulders. And they fret about the slow starvation and desiccation of snakes when they are stockpiled months before the roundups in cramped cages. "What they don't sell for skins or meat they send off to the next roundup," declares Joe Branham, a herpetologist with the Oklahoma City Zoo. "At the end of the year they're in terrible shape. You see a lot of them with mouth rot, big, swollen, infected heads. They're jammed into tight corners and agitated, and they bite each other."

Python breeder David Barker, of Stevenson, Maryland, claims to have seen roundups in which people: 1) disemboweled live snakes, throwing the mortally wounded animals into their own gut piles; and 2) sliced off the tails of live snakes. However, he suspects that these particular activities probably aren't happening anymore now that the Jaycees and other civic groups are worried about maintaining their image, such as it is.

Enn-vie-meddlist Jim Seippel, of the Greater San Antonio Herpetological Society, goes so far as to worry about snake back pain. "Snakes can't cry out," he says. He has it that diamondbacks are so heavy-bodied their vertebrae separate and their ribs break when they are held aloft or tossed around.

Always, the complainers get stuffed along with the snakes. "Have you hugged a rattlesnake today?" jeered the *Daily Oklahoman* after protesters tried to stop the 51-year-old Jaycee-sponsored roundup at Okeene, Oklahoma.

Rattlesnakes hibernate underground, a problem for roundups until recently. But now when a snake hunter happens on a likely looking hole or crevice he applies gasoline, and the fumes either kill the snake (in which case it is lost) or send it topside. Eastern diamondbacks winter in the frequently occupied holes of "gophers," which, on the Southeast coastal plain, have shells rather than fur. Actually, they are tortoises—gopher tortoises, to be precise, a species in steep decline throughout its range and listed by the US Fish and Wildlife Service as threatened.

Since gopher tortoises can excavate tunnels that are nine feet deep and 30 feet long, you need a garden hose to apply the gasoline. Be sure to shove it all the way to the end of the burrow or you'll just drive the snake deeper into the earth. First, you hold the hose to your ear, and if you just hear the gopher blowing at you—*pooof, pooof, pooof*—move on to the next hole. But if you hear pooof, pooof . . . *buzza-buzza-brrrraaap*, fill her up with the regular. As the Jaycee announcer put it at the Opp Rattlesnake Rodeo, "that ole gopher, he don't mind that snake being down there any at all." But he does mind the gasoline.

In the West, where there are no gopher tortoises, snake hunters apply gasoline to holes and crevices by means of hand-powered pesticide sprayers and compressed-air fire extinguishers.

Naturally, the enn-vie-meddlists complain about gassing, too. In with the snakes are whole communities of mammals, reptiles, amphibians and arthropods, some of which are rare and endangered, some of which are found nowhere else, and most of which die after inhaling gasoline fumes. Studies in Texas, where gassing is permitted, reveal hideous, irreversible lung damage in a host of burrowing creatures. Another study, in Alabama—where gassing also is permitted—shows high mortality among non-poisonous snakes, including the Eastern indigo, the longest snake in North America, a natural enemy of the Eastern diamondback and an endangered species. Unfortunately for the indigo, it's an "obligate inquiline"—the kind of label biologists dream up to make you ask them what it means. It means an animal that has no choice but to live in another animal's home, in this case the gopher tortoise's.

"Wherever there's gassing in the sand hills, we've done research that shows it kills all the indigo snakes that come in contact with it," reports indigo recovery plan author Dan Speake, of the Alabama Cooperative Wildlife Research Station. "I'm worried that if the roundups stay popular and the kids think it's glamorous to go and dump gas in all the gopher holes, trying to run rattlesnakes out and win prizes, it could be the end of the indigos." Frankly, I suspected that Speake himself was an enn-vie-meddlist, and as we talked it became clear that I was right. He said rattlesnake roundup people made him so "mad" and he found their shows so "irritating" and "disgusting" that, despite the data to be had, he no longer attended, making his graduate students go in his place. "I hope you're gonna give 'em hell for gassin' gopher holes," he told me.

Apparently, gasoline fumes don't kill the dusky gopher frog, another vanishing obligate inquiline of gopher tortoise burrows and a candidate for protection under the federal Endangered Species Act. Instead, they force it above ground, where it dries out and dies if it isn't first eaten by a predator. Gassing is also permitted in Georgia, Oklahoma and New Mexico.

There even are enn-vie-meddlists who cry about roundups causing localized, and possibly national, rattlesnake extinctions. Rattlesnake parts are used to make belts, hatbands, vests, pants, wallets, paperweights, key rings, key cases, knife sheaths, earrings, handbags, suspenders, guitar straps, rifle slings, barrettes, wristbands, neckties. And, in a fitting memorial of their perceived place in the universe, whole animals are now being molded into clear plastic toilet seats. A two-pound diamondback fetches at least $45—$12 for the meat, $12 for the skin, $15 for the head, $5 for the rattles and $1 for the gallbladder, which, when soaked in liquor, is relished by Asians as a health tonic. Therefore, the 11,709 pounds of rattlers weighed in at the Jaycee-sponsored Sweetwater (Texas) Roundup in 1988 had a commercial value of $263,452.50. In Texas alone, roundups kill half a million Western diamondbacks a year. There is no bag limit in any of the Eastern or Western diamondback roundup states and no season, save in Oklahoma, where it runs from March 1 through June 30—the time of year when rattlers can be most efficiently caught.

The Oklahoma Department of Wildlife Conservation, which recently attempted to legitimize rattlesnake roundups in its magazine, maintains there's no evidence of stress in Western diamondback populations. But, say the enn-vie-meddlists, this is because no one, including the state wildlife departments, has seriously bothered to collect evidence.

And they claim that the status of the much rarer Eastern diamondback is being staunchly ignored as well. One of the foremost authorities on the species, Bruce Means, of the Coastal Plains Institute, predicts (albeit with no good data) that within 25 years we will have succeeded in driving this serpent from our nation except, perhaps, where habitat has been protected on public land.

I am not a rattlesnake hugger; but I do have an aversion to reptile viscera, at least in large quantities. So I was just as glad to have avoided the Western roundup scene. The Opp Rodeo, say the Opp Jaycees, is a lot better, and I believe them. Freak show and daredevil stuff, indeed, was not to be seen. In the double-walled pen, the diamondbacks buzzed almost contentedly, like grasshoppers in a summer hayfield. Waves of spectators broke against the wire, aiming kids and cameras at the Jaycee handlers who pinned snakes to the ground with modified golf putters, draped snakes around their necks, made snakes strike their boots and pressed thumbs into snake skulls for open-mouthed mug shots. I witnessed no gross snake abuse. As far as I could tell, all the animals were treated more or less humanely before being privately and discreetly butchered.

There were 275 Eastern diamondbacks turned in this year, but Mike Carnley claims the number isn't important: "We have arts and crafts, greased-pole climbing, buck dancing, live bands, a beauty pageant, car show, road run, stock-car race, and horse show. We could put on the rodeo with two snakes."

And while only two snakes might seriously reduce the suspense in the race to determine "the world's fastest rattler" (various "heats" of which take place during both days), there might be a mechanical solution, which I offer herewith to the Opp Jaycees. When Florida banned gopher tortoise races, the organizers went to radio-controlled, "bionic" gophers. Because they are a lot faster and "pop wheelies," fans enjoy them more than the older models. The best thing about them is that when you run out you just order new ones.

All the money brought in by the Opp Jaycees goes to very worthy charities. And this year the Jaycees collected venom "for research," sending it to Ventoxin Laboratories, in Frederick, Maryland. "Researchers aren't looking at much of the venom from Eastern diamondbacks," says Ventoxin director Glen Womble. "But, at the same time, it's worth taking advantage of." In the past, Womble had avoided venom from roundups because of the poor quality. A lot of the snakes have infected venom glands and bloody mouths from being gassed and slung around. The roundup staffers will be collecting venom, and all of a sudden a snake will "unload a whole fang's worth of bloody infection into the jar." The pus and blood ruins the whole batch, but they just swirl it around until it blends in. Then they let it all fester in the hot sun for a few hours. And sometimes, says Womble, if there doesn't seem to be enough venom, they top off a jar by urinating into it. (This he has from one of his colleagues—a federal researcher with a PhD.) The venom provided by the Opp Jaycees, however, was in splendid condition and contained no urine at all.

At the 1989 rodeo (which I saw only on videotape), the Opp Jaycee announcer had said: "We are as enn-vie-meddly minded as anyone, probably more so. And we have not been forced to release snakes back into the wild. We do this [a few, outside Opp] on a voluntary basis, hopefully to avoid any confrontations with the enn-vie-meddlists." Snakes would be released this year, too, Carnley assured me. I asked him if any communities had requested them. "Noooo," he said. And the 1989 announcer had explained that the Opp Rodeo would no longer be cooking up 800 pounds of Western diamondback meat because "we had a lady from *National Geographic* down here last year, and she said we had a very well-organized event. The only thing she didn't like was that we sold snake meat. So rather than have to deal with a potential problem, we decided to head it off at the pass."

The Opp Rodeo is also unique in its policy of not accepting snakes that have been driven out of gopher holes by gasoline "the way the old-timers used to do it . . . a long time ago." The Jaycees can always tell a gassed snake because it's "groggy."

When it came time to pay out the "bounties" on the snakes, Carnley, wearing a rattlesnake-skin vest, thanked the hunters for their charitable work. "These men that go out and hunt snakes, they put their lives on the line every time," he announced. Live rattlers more than three feet long fetch $17, smaller ones, $10. There is $200 for the most, $150 for the second most and $100 for the heaviest. There even is a bounty on "other type snakes," provided the Jaycees can find someone to buy them.

After the bounty payments, it was time for me to put my life on the line for *Audubon* magazine. I was going snake hunting with the legendary J.P. Jones, the St. Patrick of Alabama, the man who founded the Opp Rattlesnake Rodeo and who now serves as its official "Grandaddy." As the Jaycees explain in their promo: "Mr. Jones said that he worked for years trying to find an organization that would work with him to rid Covington County of the dreaded menace, the rattlesnake. He couldn't have found a more supportive group."

"Them old snakes is tough as can be," J.P. told me sympathetically as I gnawed on a hunk of deep-fried Western diamondback I had purchased for a dollar. (The *National Geographic* lady apparently hadn't shown up this year.) It tasted pretty terrible, about like a freezer-burned chicken neck. The trash cans were full of it.

We hauled up into J.P.'s old pickup truck and headed out of town toward the 90,000-acre private tract looked after by his son, Jody. It was good to get away from all the sweaty gogglers and spilled food and out into the bright, clean, bluebird-filled Alabama countryside. To extract the snakes from gopher holes, J.P. uses a garden hose with a treble fishhook attached to one end. "It's just like fishin'," he said. "When I hook a rattler I hope he's the biggest one I ever caught."

I gave up on the snake meat and stuffed it into my shirt pocket. "That there's a mockin' bird," pronounced J.P. "He can mock any bird they are." I thanked him for the information and asked if he'd heard of anyone being killed by rattlesnakes in Alabama. He had indeed. "They was a little boy got bit 16 years ago, about four or five miles from here. He was playing with a lil' ol' ball. And he was about four year old."

Would we be releasing any snakes today, I inquired? "They don't turn many loose," said J.P. "That's a bunch of shit. That's just for the enn-vie-meddlists." This year they had planned to release four, but Jody had nixed the idea, declaring that he "had to walk in them woods." The snake covert was dry and sandy and lined with planted slash pine about five inches in diameter. Crickets chirped, black swallowtails fluttered, and the cobalt sky was full of wobbling turkey vultures. I dismounted and inspected J.P.'s snakin' hose in the back of the truck. He'd drilled two small holes on opposite sides about an inch up from one end, and through these he'd inserted a length of wire, which ran through the eye of the hook and held it in place. J.P.'s snakin' hose reeked of gasoline.

"Everybody uses gas," he admitted when I asked him about it. "We make like we don't, but we do." In fact, he was worried that the 11-

pound trophy diamondback he had planted in the gopher hole earlier that morning was dead from all the gas. Before inserting the snake, he and Jody had jammed a burlap bag two feet down the hole so the quarry could be quickly caught during the filming of the TV program *The Sportsman's Showcase*. As Jody put it: "We didn't have time to go out on an actual hunt. You know, you might go out all day and not find one sometime. But the snake outfoxed us. He got around the bag and went to the bottom of the hole, and we couldn't git him out. Hawh! Hawh! Hawh!"

"We have to drive 100 miles from here [on real snake hunts]," lamented J.P. "They a lot scarcer now. When I started we just hunted in the woods around here. We used to get 15 a day. You won't get none today."

Over at the gopher hole, Ken Tucker, host of *The Sportsman's Showcase*, was cramming chewing gum into his mouth. "You and I are gonna have to go to town and get us some Redman," he said to his video man. "I just have one bag, and they gonna make me start chewing . . . . Hey J.P., you want some Redman?" Tucker guffawed when J.P. allowed that he never touched the stuff. "That ain't what you sup-posed to say, J.P."

Jody inserted the hose into the hole, rammed it to the end and churned it around like a plumber unclogging a toilet. Presently, he hooked the snake and hauled back on the hose. But the rattler, who had had enough of humans for one day, wedged its thick, muscular body against the sides of the burrow. I could hear its skin ripping.

Jody kept hooking and pulling, and the snake's skin kept ripping. After about 20 minutes Tucker said: "He's a pretty good-sized snake isn't he? Whatjathink J.P.?"

"I think he's a good snake," said J.P.

Turning toward the camera, Tucker said: "I'm ready to dig, if that's what it takes. If folks think snake hunting's not work, they just don't realize. Three hours of fooling with him."

Jody fetched a shovel from J.P.'s truck and began excavating the gopher hole. After about 10 minutes Tucker said: "I think he's a pretty good snake. Four hours! He better be a good one."

At last we could see the rattles. They were not moving. Gingerly, Jody reached down and grabbed them. Then he held up the trophy for the camera. The deadly, vicious serpent hung motionless, muddy and wet with gasoline and body fluids. Jody laid it in the back of the pickup. After J.P. doused it with water it managed to move its head.

UPDATE

The Opp Rattlesnake Rodeo, still sponsored by the Opp Jaycees, is bigger than ever. "More snakes, more people," says spokesperson Liz Lindsey. Snakes are still fried and "some" are still released, though the Jaycees aren't saying what percent. "There are mixed feelings about releasing them," says Lindsey, "because in this town there was a young boy named Wyatt who was bit. We improve it some each year. We've still got our arts and crafts, snake races now with audience participation, snake shows. They milk the venom. We're trying to have some of the Olympic teams in." Now, according to the brochure, 25 to 100 beautiful Rattlesnake Rodeo Beauty Pageant contestants "come seeking the title and honor bestowed upon our Queen."

Somehow one of my similes offended Ms. Evelyn Smith of Opp, whose letter to the editor appeared in the following issue of *Audubon*: "Williams' article was in poor taste, inaccurate, and degrading to the people of Opp. Opp DOES NOT look like it was deposited by a passing buzzard."

He's Going to
Have an Accident

Idaho cattle barons lose to a tough forest ranger

Audubon, March 1991

WINSLOW BECK (W.B.) WHITELEY, of Oakley, Idaho—the man who has done more than anyone to save Don Oman's job—tipped back his white cowboy hat, placed his hands on his desk and glowered at me through gold-rimmed glasses.

I was infinitely happier about the interview than he was because I knew it would be the last he'd grant on the subject, save to government prosecutors. Further, I'd arrived with only minutes to spare; the morning papers were shouting reports of W.B.'s citation for threatening a federal officer in performance of his duty.

The officer was Don Oman, the US Forest Service ranger who presides over the 500-square-mile Twin Falls District of Idaho's Sawtooth National Forest, where W.B. grazes cattle. W.B. didn't mean to save Don Oman's job. On the contrary, he's been crusading to do away with it and says he'd like to know "how such an individual with rampant hatred toward livestock grazing [could] be placed in a position of authority to administer multiple-use public land, of which livestock grazing is a use." And he accuses Oman of "making war against a group of tax-paying citizens whose property rights on these rangelands have been violated."

W.B. has complained about Oman to just about everyone who will listen, including *People* Magazine, which had quoted him as saying: "I want Don Oman out of here. I hope it can be done peacefully. I haven't talked with the Secretary of Agriculture yet, but I might have a session with him if Oman isn't moved. I know my way around

Washington. I don't need all this s - - - and I don't need him."

W. B. got more specific with *The New York Times*, which on August 19, 1990, filed this report: " 'Either Oman is gone or he's going to have an accident,' said Winslow Whiteley, who has one of the biggest herds in the district. 'Myself and every other one of the permit holders would cut his throat if we could get him alone.' Asked if he was making a specific threat on the life of the district ranger, Mr. Whiteley said, 'Yes, it's intentional. If they don't move him out of this district, we will.' "

W.B. was born in 1910 on the 4,000 acres he still ranches, and he's been running cows out of Oakley Valley since 1930. Like other wealthy stockmen who fatten their herds on the public's 307 million acres of designated range (about 70 percent of public land in the West), W.B. is used to doing things his way. And doing things one's way had been a tradition on what is now the Twin Falls District from 1872, when A.J. Harrell first drove cattle into the lush riparian meadows of the Goose Creek Mountains—then teeming with trout, bear, deer, elk, moose, bighorn sheep and mountain goats—until Don Oman arrived on the scene in 1986 and first attempted to reverse the process of cow-induced desertification. Oman's unpardonable sin was to violate the Forest Service's Prime Directive—"Cooperation, Coordination and Communication." "The Three C's," as it is called within the agency.

I had been granted my audience with W.B. only after delicate negotiations with his lawyer, in which I'd agreed to the vetting of all direct quotes. But, as it turned out, W.B.'s blond, heavy-set son Robert did most of the talking. Robert pulled up a chair next to his father, scratched his thick mustache and glowered at me. "You ever write for *High Country News?*" he demanded. Until that very instant I'd regretted that I had not, but now I sensed that even a freelance relationship with this environmental conscience of the Rocky Mountain West would have earned me instant passage back through W.B.'s door. "Frankly," continued Robert, "I was disappointed when Dad made the agreement to talk to you. I don't have any faith in the press whatsoever. I think the whole industry is devoid of integrity and honesty." I told him I'd do my very best to get the facts exactly right.

According to Robert Whiteley, Oman is "abrasive," "arrogant" and unwilling to *Cooperate* with ranchers. And Robert charges that Oman deeply offended the very people he was supposed to Cooperate with by "coming into this country in 1986 and saying he'd been on eight different forests and that this was the worst he'd ever seen."

Oman said this because it was true. I met him in his office in Twin Falls the day before I met the Whiteleys. He is powerfully built, with intense brown eyes and thinning, salt-and-pepper hair. If he's the Hitler the ranchers say he is, he's learned to mask it well, coming across instead as honest, intelligent, soft-spoken and well-spoken. He's been married to the same woman for 24 years, has helped her raise their three sons, serves on the board of his church, teaches Sunday school and renders outdoor scenes in oils and watercolors—an avocation he says helped teach him to appreciate nature. For 26 of his 47 years Oman has worked for the Forest Service—always with ratings that qualify him as an agency superstar. At age 13, when growing up on a ranch in Montana, he read a book about forest rangers. He's wanted to be one ever since.

The first thing Oman did when he arrived in the Twin Falls District—even before he made his offensive pronouncement—was tour the Goose Creek Allotment where W.B. and the four other ranchers of the Wild Rose Grazing Association run their cattle. "We saw this heavily used area down by Trout Creek," he recalls. "I'm being told this is one the Fish and Game Department is really worried about. It's got native cutthroat trout in it. And it was just beat to pieces, banks all caved in. And then we came down on the north side of the district. And, my gosh, I was just appalled. It was bare dirt. This was in November, and Ralph Jenkins [the range conservationist] and I looked at each other and said, 'Gosh, it's awful late in the year; what are all these cows doing out here?' So we got back and we looked at the permit, and even with all the abuse, those guys had been given a two-week extension, *and that extension had ended two weeks earlier.*"

When Jenkins contacted the permittees, they said they'd always done it this way—just opened the gates and let the weather drive the cows down out of the national forest and back to the ranches. And if the cows tore up public land for a few weeks after the permits had expired, well, so what? Oman told the Wild Rose Association that this sort of thing "was going to change," and with those words he started a range war.

During his first year on the job Oman collected 45 documents detailing violations by the association. In one case he reported that the Goose Creek range boss had told him cattle had been moved onto the fall range when, actually, they'd secretly been moved into remote, sensitive stretches of Trout and Jay Creeks. This in itself should have resulted in cancellation of the entire permit and possibly federal court proceedings. But when Oman presented the documents to the forest supervisor for enforcement action, he was scolded for not following The Three C's.

Over the next three grazing seasons Oman documented violation after violation, and not just on the Goose Creek Allotment: failure to maintain pipelines, failure to maintain water troughs, placing salt licks near water (all of which send cattle into riparian areas), failure to get cattle out of riparian areas, failure to maintain fences, failure to move cattle, disruption of archaeological sites, construction of unauthorized facilities . . . .

"Remember The Three C's," Don Oman's superiors would chant whenever he complained. But Oman kept forgetting. In April 1989, during a session at a Forest Service National Range Workshop in Albuquerque in which participants were asked to vent their spleens, he again violated The Three C's. This time he was deficient in the area of Communication—not that he *failed* to Communicate, just that he Communicated the wrong sort of information. Specifically, he referred to his forest's "ingenious ways of being able to avoid taking any actions against permittee violations." When this got back to Sawtooth headquarters, Oman reports that Range Staff Officer Bert Webster ordered him to shut up about such things and said: "I can ruin you." Webster claims he doesn't recall using those precise words but allows that he did come down on Oman for "talking about his problems everywhere, openly and outwardly."

About this time district rangers throughout the Forest Service, at the discretion of the individual regions, were extended authority to take enforcement action instead of just recommend it. That's when Oman moved, doing something truly outrageous. He actually *disciplined* a group of permittees—the 10-ranch Pleasant Valley C&H Allotment, which habitually had flouted grazing rules and ignored Forest Service orders. What he did was reduce by 10 percent the number of cows that could be grazed on the allotment for 1990. Hardly Draconian, but the first enforcement action against cattlemen in the history of the Sawtooth National Forest. Oman was hoping to send a message to ranchers who graze their livestock on public land that it is important for them to live by the terms of their permits.

Actually, the terms of the permits are pretty generous. Although cattle grazing in the West has polluted more water, eroded more topsoil, killed more fish, displaced more wildlife, destroyed more native vegetation than any other use, the American public pays ranchers to do it. A permit for one Animal Unit Month (AUM)—the forage base required to sustain a cow and her calf for a month—sells for $1.97, less than one-quarter fair market value. The public buys ranchers fences along highways with its gasoline taxes. It buys them fences on range-land with its income taxes. It pays federal agencies to erect the fences, to tear up native vegetation, to plant alien grasses hurtful to wildlife, to trap, poison and shoot native predators. It buys ranchers water pipe, water troughs and cattle guards. For every $1.97 it collects for an AUM, it spends $6 for "range improvements," resulting in a net loss to the US Treasury of $50 million a year. And, after all this, grazers of public land produce but 2-percent of America's beef. The system amounts to cowboy welfare, evoking the image of John Wayne grov-eling for cigar butts and cheeseburgers in dumpsters.

The cowboys, though, have come to expect it. W.B. Whiteley says he feels the grass and water on public rangeland belong to the ranchers. In a letter to one of Oman's bosses, he accuses Oman of sneaking onto the Goose Creek Allotment without permission of the Wild Rose Association. At one point the Wild Rose Association took it upon itself to enlarge a cattle holding area by about 10 acres, incorporating a del-icate riparian zone and an inventoried archaeological site in the process. When Sawtooth Range Conservationist Ray Neiwart sug-gested that next time the ranchers ask permission, Wild Rose President Ray Bedke responded that it was "the American way" just to forge ahead and "un-American to ask." When the association took it upon itself to dig up another protected archaeological site to lay a water pipe, Neiwart got testier.

"There will be repercussions," he told Goose Creek permittee Kyle Adams, "but I guess you expected that when you decided to put in the pipe." To which Adams reportedly replied: "I guess I don't know what I expected, but I've put in a lot of pipe and never had to put up with all this archaeological crap."

When I phoned Adams to confirm the quote he told me to take it up with the Idaho Cattle Association (ICA) and hung up.

As Oman continued to tell ranchers what to do on rangeland they fancied belonged to them, they continued to threaten him. When he informed permittee Mike Poulton that the spring range wasn't ready for his cows, Poulton reportedly announced he was turning them out anyway. "No you're not, Mike," said Oman. To which Poulton report-edly responded: "It's a good thing I am 40 miles away from you right now. I am crazy mad. Crazy mad!" (Oman had an idea of what "crazy mad" might mean because when other Sawtooth personnel had sug-gested a reduction in the Goose Creek Allotment, Poulton reportedly had declared he "wouldn't be above shooting a man out of the saddle, if things got too rough.") When Oman took Poulton on a range tour and contradicted some of his copious pontification, Poulton reportedly began dancing around with his fists up in the air, yelling: "Come on. Let's get it on, right now!"

When I phoned Poulton to see if he'd really said these things he told me to take it up with the ICA. When I explained that the ICA appeared bereft of useful insights into unseemly rancher behavior, he said: "Everything that we have said has turned agin' us so I refuse to make any comments."

"Have you ever threatened Don Oman?" I persisted.

"I don't know," cried Poulton. "I refuse to talk. Goodbye."

Bud Bedke, a fourth-generation Oakley rancher and Ray Bedke's second cousin, was reported to have told the attorney who represents the Twin Falls District permittees that she had one month to get rid of Oman, "or he would do it his way." According to Oman, Bud Bedke "has a reputation for violent behavior" and is considered "the most dangerous of the people associated with the Goose Creek Allotment permittees." When I asked Bud Bedke about Oman's charges he told me this: "He's a lying son of a bitch. I never spoke to the woman, wouldn't know her if I seen her . . . . He's heard me tell him I might bend him over my knee and spank him before. That was nose-to-nose. That was not hearsay. But as far as me gonna kill him, I never said that. I have told him I might just spank the shit out of him. I meant what I said at the time, probably don't now. In the heat of things, things can be said that maybe's not proper."

In light of all the threats, Oman thought it prudent to bring along two Forest Service law enforcement officers when he ventured onto the Goose Creek Allotment to conduct a "cattle count," a fairly routine Forest Service tool for encouraging ranchers not to cheat on their permits. It had become apparent to him that the Wild Rose Association was running more cattle than it had permits for, and when he shared the evidence with one of his superiors, Regional Range Staff Officer Ray Hall, he was told to do a roundup. Instead, Oman opted for a less disruptive count.

On the morning of October 13, 1989, he arrived at Piney Cabin (the Wild Rose shipping facility in the Sawtooth National Forest) with two state brand inspectors, a BLM official, Ralph Jenkins, and the two officers, one of whom displayed his police-style duty belt complete with holstered pistol. The day went so smoothly that Oman and his team finished their work before nightfall and didn't have to sleep in the Ryder van they'd rented for that purpose. And, save for a nose-to-nose encounter between Oman and an hysterical Mike Poulton, the atmosphere was friendly, even warm. They were served cookies by the children, and the wives asked them in for breakfast and lunch (invitations they declined because in both cases they'd eaten). Ray Bedke told them to come back anytime.

The count revealed astonishing fecundity among cattle belonging to Mike Poulton and Bruce Bedke (Ray's cousin)—better than one calf per cow. This struck Oman and his staff as compelling evidence of permit violation because, after a full season on the open range, a ratio of three calves to four cows is considered excellent. But Oman explains that many animals had apparently wandered out of the allotment toward home so that, even with the unnatural abundance of calves, the total count was within legal limits. He took no action.

Still, the count incensed the ranching community. The *South Idaho Press* ran reports of government "sentries" on the surrounding hills and "federal marshals armed to the teeth." Idaho Cattle Association president Tom Shaw characterized the incident as "heavy-handed intimidation of unarmed men and their families by armed Forest Service bullies" and asked US Agriculture Secretary Clayton Yeutter to investigate. *Western Livestock Journal* editor Fred Wortham complained about Oman's "Gestapo tactics" and his "caravan swooping down on the cow camp." In a letter to the *South Idaho Press*, Bud Bedke charged that the Forest Service had "paraded around with their guns, sticks, radios, guards on gates." In other reports the Ryder van became "a paddy wagon" and Forest Service trucks—of which there were but six—were said to have "encircled the area" so that ranchers (who came and went in their vehicles all day) couldn't escape. Livestock operators, congressional aides and county commissioners convened in Twin Falls to explore ways of getting rid of Don Oman.

Forest Service officials publicly deplored Oman's "tactics" and spoke of the need for agency personnel to Cooperate, Coordinate and Communicate. Two of Oman's bosses—Ray Hall and Bert Webster—attended the November 1989 meeting of the Idaho Cattle Association where they pow-wowed with outgoing ICA president Tom Shaw, incoming president Bert Brackett, several congressional aides (including John Hatch from the office of US Senator Steve D. Symms, of Idaho), Idaho Public Lands Council president Randal Brewer, Scott Bedke (Ray's son) and other Twin Falls District permittees.

The cattlemen proposed a secret deal: They'd withdraw their complaint to the Secretary of Agriculture if the Forest Service would dump Oman. *No problem.* He'd be gone within the year, promised Hall. After all, when special interests complain that an officer charged with regulating them has "lost the ability to Cooperate, Coordinate and Communicate," why, then, "it is in everyone's best interests" that he be disappeared. It's a long-standing tradition in federal resource agencies.

The trouble was that, two months and several lateral-transfer offers later, Oman figured everything out. Once again he violated The Three C's, this time by refusing to Cooperate. Instead, he filed a "whistle-blower's complaint" with the Inspector General, a recourse by which federal employees may protect themselves from being fired or transferred while their cases are being examined. Findings of the seven-month investigation filled 330 pages. And when the report was delivered last August 24 it established that Ranger Don Oman had done nothing wrong or even inappropriate, that he had only carried out his duty and earned his keep, and that not once had he asked ranchers to do anything they hadn't agreed to do when they signed their grazing permits.

When I asked range conservationist Ray Neiwart if the Sawtooth was just an agency backwater or if cowardice and malfeasance similar to that chronicled by Oman and the Inspector General was the norm on other National Forests, he didn't get three words out of his mouth before violating The Three C's.

"My first trespass [this word is *verboten* in the Forest Service] case was in Austin, Nevada. The son-in-law was running the ranch for his wife's dad. I saw all these wrong brands on the allotment, and I figured out that they belonged to Dick, the son-in-law. So I said, 'Dick, you can't run your cattle on this allotment. You either have to get your father-in-law's brand on your cattle or get your father-in-law's name on your brand.' I notified him seven times. Finally, we took up trespass [that word again] action, which would involve a reduction in his father-in-law's program. The end result was my ranger, the forest supervisor, a state senator from Nevada and someone from the regional office all took an overnight pack trip down to the Toiyabe Range and drank a gallon of wine. And when the ranger came back he had a $100 silver belt buckle as a gift from the state senator. And they said, 'Well, the case is not gonna be.' We drove out to the ranch to tell the rancher that; and, as we passed through Forest Service land, we had to honk the cattle off the road. That's the way we've trained these ranchers as long as I've been in the Forest Service."

But in 1991 Oman—the harbinger of change in federal resource agencies and the hero of the Earth Day generation moving into positions of authority—is sitting pretty. While his superiors are frightened of the ranchers, they are even more frightened of the press, which has been infatuated with Oman's case ever since W.B. Whiteley was quoted in *The New York Times*. And they are more frightened of President George Bush, who was outraged by the quotes and ordered a full Justice Department investigation. And more frightened of environmentalists. And more frightened of the newly formed Association of Forest Service Employees for Environmental Ethics, which Oman has just joined. And maybe even more frightened of the Inspector General. Now Hall is telling the ICA that the secret deal to dump Oman is definitely off, and he has ordered up an official letter reconfirming Oman's authority. The ranchers, of course, are apoplectic. "We as Twin Falls permittees still feel we have an agreement with Mr. Ray Hall," declares Robert Whiteley.

On my last day in Idaho I went on patrol with Ranger Don Oman— up into the South Hills that he is restoring to health after a century-long savaging by bovine hooves and teeth. That very morning one of his superiors had cluck-clucked at him for not following The Three C's. Specifically, he needed "to improve his Communications both externally and internally." Rancher Bill Brockman, herd boss of the Rock Creek permittees, had accused him (falsely) of siccing an *Audubon* reporter on their monthly meeting. Oman, who was to give a presentation, merely had provided me transportation at my request; and the fact that we made it through the door indicated progress in Communications. When Brockman had hosted the meeting he'd ordered Oman out of the house.

But all that was office dirt, and now Don Oman was smiling and enjoying the crisp air and the breathtaking scenery of Rock Creek Canyon. We drove north as sunshine spilled over the canyon walls— up into cougar range and high desert, past brushy slopes trimmed with dark bands of mountain mahogany, along clean, exuberant Rock Creek and its wild rainbow trout, beside lush stands of alder and willow and towering cottonwoods glowing with the first shades of autumn gold. A boy strung his fishing rod by the side of the road, and here and there men and women picked ripe elderberries in their national forest.

Oman stopped the truck at a new beaver dam, and we dismounted.

Below the pond the stream was protected from erosion by a heavy growth of sedges and willows. Now there were no washouts or vertical cutbanks. Keeping cattle out of places like this is a constant battle, Oman explained. "They love the water and the shade, and they'll just lie down in here on the bottoms where the gentle ground is."

The ranchers, Oman told me, are doing better this year just about everywhere on the district, and there seems to be much less cheating. I asked him if this could be because the count had scared them. He conceded the possibility.

At 6,500 feet above sea level the only native trees in the South Hills are aspen, lodgepole pine and alpine fir. The range is coming back here, too, but there are vast areas of devastation. We passed a defunct beaver lodge in a dry, cattle-blasted creekbed. "If this whole drainage was in good condition, you wouldn't have all this compaction," remarked Oman. "Instead of soil being cut out and carried away by runoff it would be building back up. You'd have your sedges catching sediment and building soil. That's the way it was. A creek like this would be running water year-round. There'd be trout here. The only chance we have to improve riparian areas, short of fencing, is to move the cows through the system and give riparian areas a chance to rest."

We hiked into another defunct beaver pond, this one with about two acres of water. The desiccated earth around the pond was plastered with cow pies, and the beaver-cut willows weren't regenerating. Dragonflies patrolled the broken, muddy shoreline; a snipe whistled by. Despite the hideous damage, it was obvious that the place was bursting with potential. Even as we stood there a Forest Service crew was busy stringing new fence; and, save for a narrow watergap (a compromise worked out with the ranchers), Oman had excluded cattle from the far bank. Two beavers had been released the week before, and more were due in today.

We drove on to the South Fork of Shoshone Creek. Before cattle converted the watershed to semidesert, the stream had held four-pound cutthroats. Now I saw only dace, though Oman told me a few thumb-size cutts survive. They'll grow in the new beaver ponds. Cow-free for the past two years, the stretch above the wooden bridge still looked bare and abused but considerably better than the 1988 photo I held in my hand. Sandbars had stabilized; banks were regreening. "The potential for these areas to recover is just amazing," said Oman. "New growth traps sediment. You build up your stream bottom that way. The stream channel tightens; willows shade and cool the water. Trout habitat improves. And, gradually, you raise your water table. The sagebrush dies out and sedge meadows return. The beavers return . . . ." He sounded like a man who loves his work.

Next, Oman showed me a spring that he had fenced off. Now, instead of wallowing around in the pool, the cows drink mud-free water from a pipe-fed trough. Inside the split-rail fence the growth was green and luxuriant. Outside there was no growth, just desert. The ranchers hate such exclosures because they teach the public that cattle are the scourge of the earth. Bill Brockman reportedly complains regularly to Oman's bosses about his exclosure lessons, but when I attempted to interview Brockman on this and other subjects he declined to speak, referring me instead to the Idaho Cattle Association.

Oman's pride and joy is the pond and surrounding meadow that he, the Izaak Walton League and the Idaho Fish and Game Department excluded from cows in the spring of 1989. The pond had been built in 1986 "for wildlife," which on the Sawtooth used to mean cows and domestic sheep. Oman handed me a two-year-old photo that showed three cows wading in a mud hole embraced by bare, compacted dirt. I lifted my gaze from the photo to the pond, now rimmed with greenery and full of ducks and grassy nesting islands. We climbed over the fence and walked into the 27-acre oasis. Everywhere flax and aster were in blue and purple bloom, and thousands of willows, some waist high, were sprouting around the pond's perimeter. We pushed on toward the dike through Great Basin wild rye—the native bunch grass that lapped the stirrups of the pioneers. A year ago the dike had been naked. Now it was filling in with western yarrow and small burnet, a good wildlife staple. Killdeer screamed, a marsh hawk wheeled and dipped, redwings rustled through the cattails.

On the far side of the exclosure there is a 500-acre riparian pasture. When it recovers, in about two more years, Oman will let the ranchers graze cattle there again, but only on a limited basis. This way the cattle will get more and better grass, the land and streams will maintain their natural vitality, and fish and wildlife will flourish. Oman says he's not anti-cattle and that grazing is a legitimate use of public rangeland. "We'll probably graze in here two years out of four," he told me, "and only early in spring."

With all Oman's talk about how much better the ranchers are doing, I wondered if the old guard in the Forest Service hadn't converted him a little. Might it be that he had bent in the hard wind, maybe lost some of his toughness?

"Do you really think the ranchers are going to cooperate and keep their cows out of here in summer?" I inquired.

United States Forest Service Ranger Don Oman took the bait but didn't stiffen or change the soft tone of his voice. "Well," he said, "either they will do that or we'll have a nice 500-acre exclosure."

UPDATE

Don Oman continues to stand tall in defense of fish and wildlife. And now he has Bill LeVere—a tough, young forest supervisor made from the same stuff he is—to back him up. W.B. Whiteley has died. The ranchers on the Rock Creek allotment have calmed down a lot. But the ranchers on the Goose Creek allotment are worse than ever. When Oman hit them with a 15-percent suspension of their grazing privileges for gross and continued permit violations, the former supervisor refused to let him enforce it, placing the ranchers on probation instead. During this probation the ranchers continued to cheat, and now Oman has reinstated the penalty. LeVere is supporting him.

Congress is attempting to emasculate the Forest Service with one hand and pick its pocket with the other. Legislation has been introduced that guarantees ranchers ownership of their grazing permits and forbids Forest Service personnel from entering onto public land without rancher permission. Meanwhile, budget cutbacks have created chaos and despair. "We have been going through death throws in reorganization and downsizing," one of Oman's staffers told me. "Right now the budget that we're working with is 75 percent of last year's."

But good things are happening on the ground. Oman's pride and joy—the fenced-in pond that looked so great in 1991—looks even better today. The field behind it has recovered to the point that Oman can allow cattle to graze it for 10 days in the early spring. There has been an enormous increase in willows around the pond. Now the South Fork of Shoshone Creek is a chain of beaver dams, and the water table is so high Oman has had to send crews in to build up the road. This and other streams in the district have recovered to the point that the state is considering restocking them with redband trout—a sensitive species.

Don't Worry, Plant a Tree

Cluster-bombing the planet with seedlings

Audubon, May 1991

ONLY GOD can make a tree, but any environmental illiterate can plant it in the wrong place. All of a sudden, Americans are rushing around the country like Johnny Appleseed on applejack. We need to slow down and think about what we're at before we do more harm than good.

As of old, the nation's mood can be read on the pages of *Life* magazine. "A vista without a tree," it reports, "is missing something indispensable." Is it? I have never thought so. Most of Earth's terrestrial ecosystems are treeless, and planting trees degrades them. "Where trees are absent there is a desert," says *Life*. Usually not; and what's wrong with deserts anyway, provided they aren't man-made? "It seems the mind cannot do without [trees], that the image of a tree is embossed on our thoughts, on our ideal vision of the world." True, but that's our problem, not nature's.

All the tree-planting groups appear united in their devout belief that lots of trees equal a forest and that "planting" or "replanting" a forest is both admirable and possible. The general public believes this, too. So cherished is the superstition that *Business Week* recently served it up not as opinion but news: "Weyerhaeuser is doing better than Mother Nature," it reported. "Its forests are uniform green rows of straight Douglas firs with no leafy trees or rotting logs." According to Weyerhaeuser, "even the animals like the idea" of slash-and-plant forestry. But this remains unconfirmed by the animals, especially tree-nibbling beavers and porcupines who get rubbed out for rushing the harvest.

The timber industry, which started the replanted-forest superstition, makes hay from it. "Every day that dawns we renew our partnership with the land by the planting and seeding of 250,000 new trees from Maine to California," proclaims Georgia-Pacific, as if it were undertaking some public service. Michael Kellett, of the Wilderness Society, hasn't gotten very far in his efforts to set the record straight: "When I talk to people about clearcutting they say, 'Yeah, but don't the companies replant trees after they do that?' And I say, 'Yeah, they do in some cases, *and that's bad*. If they have to replant, they shouldn't be cutting there.'"

Citizen tree planting, on the other hand, is harder to dissect. One challenges it as one might challenge truth and justice—cringingly. A statue of Julius Sterling Morton—the founder of Arbor Day—stands in the Hall of Fame in Washington, DC. Another, paid for in part by the pennies, nickels and dimes of schoolchildren from all over the world, stands in Nebraska City. Teachers and kids, clutching packets of indigenous and non-indigenous seedlings given them by the National Arbor Day Foundation, goggle up at the great journalist, politician and corrector of Divine error. On moving to Nebraska from Michigan, Julius Sterling found he didn't like the way God had made it. Therefore, he called forth—as he put it in 1870 and as the National Arbor Day Foundation proudly reported in 1991—"a grand army of husbandmen . . . to battle against the timberless prairies."

Call me a curmudgeon, but my hero is Ansel Adams, who helped run the Boy Scouts out of California's Marin Headlands by declaring: "I cannot think of a more tasteless undertaking than to plant trees in a naturally treeless area, and to impose an interpretation of natural beauty on a great landscape that is charged with beauty and wonder, and the excellence of eternity."

It's not that tree-planters don't do lots of good by frequently planting trees in the right places, and it's not that they aren't nice people who mean well. It's just that, in their innocence, they are an environmental menace. They are so *vulnerable*, so easily manipulated by special interests.

They are the sort who go around reciting and reprinting Joyce Kilmer's wretched ditty, "Trees." Or, as in the case of the Arbor Day Foundation, unfacetiously giving "Joyce Kilmer Awards." And they are the sort who run the Wichita, Kansas, organization Trees for Life. "Staff members," reports the *Wichita Eagle*, "begin their day with hugs. They join hands and pray, expressing hope that they will be proper instruments of a higher power. They sing: 'Spirit of the living

God, fall afresh on me.' Then they begin the business of saving the world."

Consider TreePeople, of Beverly Hills, California—the group that organizes citizen tree-planting parties and puts out a handsome, helpful volume entitled *The Simple Act of Planting a Tree*. Since trees sequester carbon dioxide from the atmosphere and reduce the need for air-conditioning, they retard global warming, explains the book. True. "Every tree planted is another step forward in the battle to save the planet." Not true.

On my copy of *The Simple Act of Planting a Tree* there's a green sticker that says, "Free tree seed coupon included. GEO." The "O" of GEO has longitudes and latitudes through it, as if it were Planet Earth. Is GEO an environmental organization? A plant nursery? A born-again magazine? No; it's a car made by the bloated US automaker that led the successful fight to sabotage fuel-efficiency legislation—the single short-term measure that would have done most to retard global warming. But now General Motors has turned over a new leaf and found beneath it magic seeds from trees that may or may not belong in your area.

Then there are the tent-caterpillar-like "national partners" of Global ReLeaf, the massive tree-planting program sponsored by the American Forestry Association. Among them: Arco Foundation, Conoco, Baltimore Gas and Electric, Edison Electric Institute, Metropolitan Edison, Octane Boost Corporation, Pennsylvania Electric, Texaco and Keep America Beautiful (the front for the energy-intensive throwaway container lobby). Why all the fossil-fuel extractor-burner types? And might some of these have had a hand in hatching the American Forestry Association's "Energy ReLeaf," which supposedly "is designed for electric utilities, to help them develop tree planting-and-care programs as part of their energy conservation and peak load-demand reduction strategies"?

One can't help wondering how many polluters will sign up with Global ReLeaf or Energy ReLeaf out of genuine desire to help the public consume less of their products and how many will sign up to divert the public so they may continue to spew greenhouse and tree-killing gases. "Plant a tree and cool the globe," instructs the American Forestry Association. Too bad it's not that easy.

Applied Energy Services has gotten into tree planting on its own in order, it says, to offset the annual slug of 387,000 tons of carbon from its new coal-fired powerplant in Uncasville, Connecticut. Steered by the World Resources Institute, the utility has allocated $2 million to help CARE plant 52 million trees in Guatemala. Probably, it deserves lots of credit. The idea of planting trees to help deal with carbon overload is sound. Furthermore, the timber will improve the unhappy lot of impoverished farmers and take pressure off the dwindling rainforest.

On the other hand, the project is rife with disturbing messages and dangerous precedents. It is not, as the World Resources Institute advertises, "reforestation." A little more than half the trees are slated for "agroforestry plantations," the rest for "woodlots." And included in the species mix will be aliens like eucalyptus and temperate-zone pines. Worse, the scheme of planting foreign carbon sinks is so typically *American*. It teaches that the United States—by far the grossest greenhouse polluter on the planet—doesn't need to change its lifestyle. Instead, it can just pay the Third World to clean up after it.

This eat-all-you-want diet appeals particularly to George Bush, sire of an ambitious initiative called "America the Beautiful," by which $175 million a year was to be spent to plant 10 billion trees during the next decade. For Ronald Reagan, trees were polluters. For Bush they are cover for polluters—a thousand points of shade conveniently obscuring real issues.

"Those who think we're powerless to do anything about the Greenhouse Effect are forgetting about the White House Effect," boasted candidate Bush. Since then, as they say on the Hill, he's been giving us the "Whitewash Effect." Fortunately for biological diversity, America the Beautiful—now trimmed in the tree-planting department to $75 million—cannot possibly get 10 billion seedlings into the ground by century's end. But even if it managed to do so, US carbon dioxide pollution would be reduced by no more than 5-percent annually.

Bush figured on spending a dollar each to plant some of the trees in cities. But you don't just jam an acorn in the sidewalk and amble down the street. You must start with a robust sapling, then water, fertilize, spray and prune. And by the time you're done—especially if you're working in the North, where air-conditioning isn't much used—you likely will have burned more fossil fuel than the tree will save, in which case you will have proved Reagan right.

Even when you don't count maintenance costs, the planting of urban trees is enormously expensive. Despite volunteer labor and help from city employees, TreePeople managed to spend $325 on each of 400 Canary Island pines it planted in Los Angeles to celebrate

Martin Luther King, Jr.'s birthday. Maybe the $130,000 would have been better invested in lobbying the town fathers to make Los Angeles safe for trees by cracking down on air polluters. According to a report by the World Resources Institute, the average big-city tree survives seven years, and for every one that gets planted, four die.

If the President is genuinely worried about global warming, why did his administration help Detroit nix fuel-efficiency standards? And why is America standing alone among rich nations in refusing to commit itself to near-term reduction of greenhouse-gas emissions? "The old White House position was this isn't a problem and we're not going to do anything about it anyway," remarks Environmental Defense Fund scientist Michael Oppenheimer. "The new position is yes, this is a problem, but we're still not going to do anything about it."

A more effective means of greenhouse postponement than planting trees is not cutting them—at least when they are very old. The ancient forests of the Pacific Northwest are the most efficient carbon sinks on Earth. In Oregon, for instance, their liquidation results in 17 percent of the state's total carbon dioxide pollution. Roots, bark and branches are burned or oxidize quickly. And from the machine-ravaged soil which is suddenly exposed to rain and sunlight, stored carbon surges back into the atmosphere. The President's unpared tree-planting initiative conceivably could have sequestered 165 million tons of carbon by the year 2000. Old-growth logging at current rates will *release* 220 million tons.

But weaning clearcutters of old growth or even getting them back on sustainable yield is unthinkable to the Bush Administration and to the timber industry, which, naturally, is all excited about America the Beautiful. Recently, the Oregon Legislature passed a bill that required state agencies, via diverse "advisory committees," to explore ways of reducing Oregon's greenhouse-gas emissions by 20 percent. One option the transportation committee came up with was a state-wide ban on driving cars. A radical alternative, to be sure. But they considered it, stuck it into the computer and looked at the numbers. The advisory committee for forestry couldn't even *talk* about not cutting ancient forests.

No one has more experience in tracking the timber industry through Washington, DC than Brock Evans, of the National Audubon Society. When I asked him for an assessment of the President's tree-planting proposal, he responded as follows: "I thought it was as phony as a three-dollar bill because there wasn't any new money to plant trees. All it did was take money that had already been earmarked for tree planting, stick it in a special program, give it a new name and call it 'a new initiative.'"

Global ReLeaf excites the timber industry even more than America the Beautiful because, in a way, the American Forestry Association is the timber industry. AFA represents forestry as an art and a science rather than an excuse. It's a place for foresters to talk about "wise use," although some of the uses that get talked about are pretty foolish: Clearcutting, for instance, which AFA misidentifies as "a [sometimes] necessary harvest method." And "even-aged management," which it defines as just another "silvicultural system."

There are notable exceptions, but AFAers appear singularly unconcerned about how their industry replaces complicated and diverse communities with make-believe "forests" of the sort America loves to plant—clone monocultures in chalk-lined rows. As Weyerhaeuser vice-president (and AFA director) John McMahon proudly puts it, "We're getting away from relying on the uncertainties of natural reseeding."

AFA is the oldest citizen's conservation group in the country, and one of the most sedentary. It hasn't moved much from the days when Gifford Pinchot wrote about it. Nor even from the days, 20 years back, when it fired Mike Frome from its currently well-edited magazine, *American Forests*, for defying an official decree "not to write critically about the US Forest Service, the forest industry, the profession, or about controversial forestry issues." In the opinion of a noted professor at the Yale School of Forestry and Environmental Studies, it was the noncontroversial nature of tree planting that tempted AFA to launch Global ReLeaf in the first place. "AFA," he says, "is a group that's sort of moribund, that should have grown along with everyone else and didn't. And they're struggling to find something to put them back into the limelight."

But where, other than under the limelight, does Global ReLeaf intend to go? It appears bereft of any direction, other than cluster-bombing the planet with trees of whatever sort are handiest. In 1990 it awarded 42 grants totaling $753,732 to 40 communities. Some of the money was used to preclude natural succession in South Carolina's Francis Marion National Forest by planting 137,500 trees in the wake of Hurricane Hugo. For $5 you can call a 900 number and get a Global ReLeaf tree planted in your name, except you don't get to choose species or location or even talk with a real person. By 1992 AFA hopes to have 100 million trees in the ground, who knows what kind or where.

One Global ReLeaf report gushes about this manic tree planter who, admirably enough, "aches to see vast forests [of the planted variety] cover old clearcuts" but also "aches to see them cover burns, deserts, and even remote spots that have not known trees for tens of thousands of years." He takes Boy Scouts into Washington's Gifford Pinchot National Forest to replant the area "devastated" by the 1980 eruption of Mount St. Helens, thereby teaching them precisely the wrong lessons. And he "honors" dead soldiers by planting "Canadian maple trees" in Kentucky.

Most tree-planting groups boast of working closely with Global ReLeaf. And many, such as "Trees for Tucson," are more appropriately thought of as appendages of Global ReLeaf.

I first learned about Trees for Tucson by attending one of its presentations at the annual convention of Keep America Beautiful. The mission: "to plant 500,000 desert-adapted, low-water-use trees by 1996." Participate and you will "save money, save the world!" A few problems here. First, tree growing in Tucson tends to be difficult and energy intensive because most of the city proper is naturally treeless. Nature and/or God didn't just forget to put trees in Tucson; other, better-adapted vegetation evolved instead. Second, two of the trees the group is pushing—southern live oak and South America thornless mesquite—are not only alien to the state but allergenic to people. Tiny-capsuled eucalyptus and Chinese pistache, also recommended, are alien even to the hemisphere.

The 20-year-old National Arbor Day Foundation—which selected Global ReLeaf for one of its "Arbor Day Awards"—has committed itself to "covering America with trees." Annually, the foundation distributes some seven million not necessarily indigenous seedlings to more than a million members, exhorting them to plant the trees because "helping to neutralize today's ominous new climatic forces is the single greatest contribution you can make to the future of your loved ones, mankind, and the Earth itself!" Last year taxpayers kicked in when the US Department of Agriculture awarded the foundation grants totaling $291,518. Before that the department had left public tree planting in the not-so-able talons of Woodsy Owl, who in 1980 tried to sell the bird-brained idea that Americans should rush out and plant 75 million trees to celebrate the US Forest Service's 75th birthday.

Among the "public services" rendered by the foundation are what it refers to as "plant-trees-to-fight-the-greenhouse-effect" announcements by honorary trustee Eddie Albert "on hundreds of TV stations across the nation." Albert has experience in this sort of thing, having starred in a piece of Weyerhaeuser ecoporn entitled "To Touch the Sky," in which, standing beneath old-growth conifers, he proclaims: "This forest is dying. The enchanted forest of yesterday is being replaced [here the camera pans one of the company's clone plantations] by the fast-growing forest." Albert then effuses about "remarkable" machines that fell a tree with "one bite" and explains that each American consumes a ton of wood products per annum. At this point a bird chirps.

After Yellowstone's 1988 fire season, America turned out to "replant" the forest. At least 25 companies and hundreds of individuals volunteered their services, among them the governor of New Jersey, offering pines native to his state. The National Park Service thanked everyone, then patiently explained that nature would be handling all the replanting in the park. The truth about the fires—that they were both inevitable and necessary—soon appeared in virtually every magazine that dealt seriously with the outdoors. Even newspapers eventually stopped interviewing sources like Joe the Guide and tuned in to fire's vital role in the dynamics of real forests.

Somehow the National Arbor Day Foundation missed the news. As recently as January it was reporting that the fires "devastated the Greater Yellowstone area," that "much more needs to be done to restore the forest so that it can once again provide food and cover," and that "millions of trees must be planted." Accordingly, it has taken over where Woodsy Owl left off, teaming up with the US Forest Service and enlisting public and corporate support in "replanting" the area's national forests, beginning with the Gallatin in the vicinity of Cooke City, Montana.

The Forest Service—which has disappeared Woodsy because he vaguely resembles a spotted owl and therefore offends clearcutters— is enthusiastically supervising the project. "Wildlife Habitat Enhancement Reforestation" it's called because, supposedly, it will benefit grizzly bear, elk and moose. Everyone with something to sell is climbing on board: *Country Living*, Crest, Beatrice/Hunt-Wesson, Bristol Myers, Moore Business Products, Wing Industries, New Antiques, Le Jardin Academy, Waldenbooks and Sunrise Productions, which, together with the Fit for Life Foundation, will plant a tree in your honor if you buy a copy of *Delicious Vegetable Entrees*.

Why, I wondered, would the Forest Service feel it had to manipulate vegetation for grizzlies, elk and moose? Grizzlies weren't affected by the fires one way or the other and their numbers are increasing. Moose are fine; and, if anything, elk are too prolific. Arbor Day Foundation personnel could comment only on grizzly management, explaining that among the trees to be planted for this purpose are whitebark pines, whose cones are an important food source for Yellowstone-area bruins. But this, too, seemed strange because I knew that it takes decades for any pine to produce cones.

So I contacted US Fish and Wildlife Service biologist Chris Servheen, who leads the interagency task force for grizzly recovery in the Greater Yellowstone area. Servheen said he hadn't heard of any tree planting for grizzlies near Cooke City or anywhere else. "Does the management of grizzlies call for planting whitebark pine?" I asked.

"Not that I'm aware of," he said. "It's 70-plus years for a whitebark pine to produce any cones, and the probability of survival is pretty low with trees planted that way. The trees are normally coming in by themselves all the time. If there's any tree planting for wildlife going on, Jack Lyon [of the Forest Service] would know."

Dutifully, I phoned Lyon—who has research going on elk and grizzly all the way from Yellowstone to Montana's Flathead National Forest. But he hadn't heard of any tree planting for bears either. When I asked him if the Forest Service was planting for moose or elk, he said: "As far as I know they're not. Tree planting is a timber management thing. Habitat for elk, for example, is a function of tree growth and succession, but there wouldn't be any particular point in planting specifically for elk. Same thing for moose."

What, then, could be the motive behind the Arbor Day Foundation/Forest Service venture? Hard to say, but one learns from a Forest Service report that: 1) "Timber management for fiber production" is the other part of the "co-dominant objective" for the planting area; and 2) that the area qualifies under the "Watchable Wildlife Program" owing to the "unique opportunity for viewing wildlife based on a comparative rarity of moose and the close proximity of the habitat used by the moose to the roadway."

In other words, moose will benefit from tree planting to the extent that motorists can remain seated while watching them.

One group that does not "work closely" with either the National Arbor Day Foundation or Global ReLeaf is the National Audubon Society. Dede Armentrout, vice-president for the Southwest region, politely declined when Global ReLeaf offered her chapters 10,000

Afghan pines to hand out at the malls. "They're garbage trees as far as wildlife goes," she told me.

When Global ReLeaf contacted David Northington, executive director of the Austin-based National Wildflower Research Center, he said his group would participate only if officials guaranteed that no alien trees be used. No one got back to him. "Every time I turn around, someone from Global ReLeaf hands me an Afghan pine," he laments. "I say, 'Thanks but I don't live in Afghanistan.'" They don't understand, so Northington accepts the gift and discreetly euthanizes it by jerking it out of the tube and leaving it in the Texas sun.

Another organization that has tried and failed to reform Global ReLeaf is Health & Habitat, of Mill Valley, California. It would have joined except that it couldn't extract a promise to promote only indigenous species in areas that used to have trees. "I have trouble talking to these people who have this wonderful enthusiasm for planting trees," declares Health & Habitat's president, Sandy Ross. "You don't want to say no because it sounds like you're anti-conservation. But most of them don't have any idea of site endemic situations. 'We're gonna plant trees!' And I'll ask what kind. And they'll say, 'I don't know; they're in little pots.' I think there's a greater danger in planting the wrong trees than not planting trees. Mill Valley doesn't need a tree-planting program. It needs a *tree-removal* program."

But try selling this to Ross's busy neighbors, the "Friends of the Urban Forest," who propose to plant 1.8 million trees in San Francisco, thus tripling the number in the city and further endangering the grassland-wildflower community on which it squats.

"Planting trees 'wherever you can' sends chills down my spine," comments Jacob Sigg, president of the San Francisco chapter of the California Native Plant Society. "Civic-minded leaders thought it would be an improvement to plant 'barren' hills with trees. The trees chosen were of only three kinds and not native to San Francisco. They were imposed on the land and did not carry with them the complement of biological organisms—the seed-eating birds and squirrels, the insects and larvae which chew on leaves and burrow in bark and seed, the bacteria and fungi that are part of the recycling process." Today San Francisco's make-believe forests are, in Jacob Sigg's words, "biological wastelands, monotonous and uninviting—and expanding."

One such wasteland is Angel Island, in San Francisco Bay, like the city itself chock-a-block with blue gum eucalyptus from Tasmania, the most pernicious and invasive alien of them all. "Wonder tree," Californians used to call it before they tried building with it and before it caused the extinction of the Xerces blue butterfly, reduced Raven's manzanita to a single bush, swamped whole ecosystems and made the state smell like a cough drop.

Three years ago, when the California Parks and Recreation Department released a plan to restore native flora and fauna by razing a patch of Angel's eucalyptus monoculture, it found itself confronted by a group called POET (Protect Our Eucalyptus Trees). POET called the project leader a "plant Nazi" and charged that the department was trying to "eradicate history" in that the trees were very old and had been planted by the US Army. Further, POET maintained that wildlife positively doted on eucalyptus.

So Parks and Recreation contacted the University of California at Berkeley and signed up Michael Morrison, associate professor of wildlife, to do a study. "Basically," says Morrison, "we found that very, very few species of wildlife use eucalyptus. That was no surprise to us because none of these species evolved with eucalyptus. When I said killing non-native trees is not immoral, they [POET] said: 'The next thing we're going to hear from you is getting rid of all non-native people is okay.' And I said, '*Where did you get that?*' These people forced Parks and Recreation to spend well over $100,000 in research funds and hundreds of thousands of dollars in employee time to justify removing 30 acres of eucalyptus. I thought that was obscene."

At the moment the department seems to be winning. But POET has a powerful new weapon—a poem lovely as an alien tree. It quotes the persecuted eucalypti as they cry out against arboricide:

> *We love our home*
> *Here on the isle*
> *We love our fellow trees, plants, animals*
> *And people*
> *We would love to*
> *Continue living*
> *But we have no voice*
> *As trees*
> *Because we are eucalyptus*
> *And we are not native*
> *Therefore, we must be*
> *Destroyed.*

POET's great contribution to the environment is the lesson it teaches (or should) the nation—that the best time to make the land right by getting rid of wrong trees is before tree-planters try to fix the world with them.

UPDATE

Now even the Republican Party is saturation bombing the earth with trees. "Tree Planting" is the title of an "action item" in a dress-up-like-an-environmentalist manual it has mailed to all GOPers in the US House of Representatives (see "How Green Was My Party," page 227): "This exercise provides members with excellent earned media opportunities. When participating in tree planting programs you should include both children and seniors."

Meanwhile, neem, a fast-growing tree from India whose significant potential for damaging semi-tropical ecosystems hasn't been adequately investigated, is being peddled around south Florida as if it were Dr. Kickapoo's Elixir for Rheum, Ague, Blindness and Insanity. According to Marc Ketchel, who grows and sells neem seedlings, this "amazing tree" exudes compounds that kill bacteria, fungi, viruses and human sperm, prevent tooth decay, gum disease and malaria, ease diabetes, reduce cancers and, perhaps, "assist in the treatment of ulcers, inflamation and AIDS."

Zion:
The Movie

With Nature on the Big Screen, who needs reality?

Audubon, November 1991

"IN YOUR NATIONAL parks nature runs the show," proclaims the sign at the Visitor Center of Zion National Park, in southwestern Utah. Such humility seems appropriate given that the National Park Service and the rest of humanity arrived at the theater about a quarter-billion years late.

The show started before there were people, birds, or even large reptiles—when a vast, featureless plain covered the space between what is now central Wyoming and southwestern California. Volcanoes laid down ash. Quartz sand swept in on southerly winds. An ocean appeared, bearing lime that filtered into the sand and cemented it together. Gradually, the flood receded, exposing sedimentary rock. Sediments poured in from adjacent highlands. Again the ocean rolled in, and again it retreated, leaving fields of sandstone, much of it stained red by iron oxide.

The planet's last dinosaur had been dead 40 million years when forces deep within the earth pushed the ancient sea bed two miles into the air. Rivers quickened, slicing down through the soft sandstone and leaving formations that tower out of the old desert like decayed canine teeth and broken molars.

About 21 million years after the first major upheaval, humanoid primates rose on their hind feet. Four million years later, in 1988, a band of *Homo sapiens* known as World Odyssey, Inc. arrived in Springdale, Utah—a "city," as it often calls itself, of 300 souls surrounded on three steep sides by Zion National Park. World Odyssey acquired the 11-acre meadow abutting the park's Watchman Campground and south entrance where the Virgin River—Zion's main sculptor—keeps the grass lush and green through the brutal desert summer. Here visitors would be able to see Zion National Park on a giant, wraparound movie screen.

This show, shot entirely in 70-millimeter, IMAX-like format, would last a full 30 minutes. It was going to be breathtaking and spectacular. A large conventional movie screen is merely 18 feet by 36 feet and flat, but this one would be 58 by 78 and curved. World Odyssey explained that its Ultra 70 process would actually be more breathtaking and spectacular than IMAX and that it would "make you feel you are more than there."

Even those offended by major developments hanging lampreylike from the flanks of our national parks agree that the film, tentatively entitled *Treasure of the Gods*, will be a technical marvel. It is to be produced by Kieth Merrill, a founder and owner of World Odyssey, who in 1974 won an Oscar for his documentary, *The Great American Cowboy*. Such is Merrill's reputation as a filmmaker that one Park Service official rose at a public meeting and unwaggishly declared that, at least for many viewers, the movie version of Zion will overshadow the real thing, rendering park visitation superfluous. While even World Odyssey's partner Doug Memmott thinks this is stretching it, he does expect that his company "will eliminate some of the pressure on the park." And Merrill goes so far as to claim that reducing park pressure is part of World Odyssey's motive. Along with the movie theater would be a row of stores, a 275-car parking lot, a restaurant and an 80-room motel unit.

Instantly, the Springdale business community took on the spiral-eyed countenance of an Appalachian chicken farmer who's just hit three pineapples on his first pull on a Las Vegas slot machine. "Within 20 years we can have gold-plated sidewalks," effused the mayor to the Associated Press. World Odyssey flew members of the Springdale Town Council and the Springdale Planning and Zoning Commission to the south rim of the Grand Canyon, the better to view it in an IMAX movie Merrill had directed and which is said to attract 600,000 people a year at $6 a pop. All hands agreed that the Grand Canyon, as seen in the film, was breathtaking and spectacular. According to Merrill, the elderly and handicapped weep with gratitude after they see the Grand Canyon in his theater.

Louise Excell, the English professor who then chaired Springdale's planning commission, was not so overwhelmed by the show that she failed to notice the blockish building in which it played. "Grotesque," she called it. So Excell and her fellow planning commission members implored World Odyssey to make its Springdale development fit the decor of Zion. After all, the Town Zoning Ordinance requires development to be compatible aesthetically with the National Park. Eager to establish itself as a good neighbor, the company did its utmost to comply.

Apparently inspired by Zion's many natural stone arches, World Odyssey architects drew up an enormous arching bridge that ran from the highway down into the project. The inspiration for the theater itself was to be Zion's rock formations, in particular a flat-topped monolith, sans iron oxide, that soars above a raging sea of red peaks. In 1916, notes a Park Service plaque, one Frederick Fisher intoned: "Never have I seen such a sight before. It is by all odds America's masterpiece. Boys, I have looked for this mountain but I never expected to find it in this world. It is the Great White Throne." Accordingly, the architects designed the building to be light in color, flat topped, and to soar six stories up from the canyon floor.

Still, the planning commission didn't like the design. It urged World Odyssey to forget about mimicking the Great White Throne and instead go "park-a-tecture"—that is, use rock and timbers to mimic Zion Lodge. World Odyssey complied, making change after change— 22 in all. Originally, it had planned to remove a hill so pilgrims approaching Zion's gate might better spy the theater. The hill is said to offend former meadow owner and project partner Steve Heaton, who is quoted by the *Los Angeles Times* as calling it a "dumb hill" and "completely out of place." Merrill does not agree that the hill is dumb. He maintains that it is "ugly," and although he fervently believes "it ought to come down," he and his associates are so environmentally sensitive that they're going to leave it right where the Virgin River discarded it. As for the meadow, it strikes Merrill as a "dumpy horse pasture," but even so he vows to preserve a major portion of it. Not only this, but World Odyssey has miniaturized its parking lot to accommodate just 169 cars. And finally, it has promised not to build any motel units, at least for awhile.

For those unschooled in Springdale politics, the city's comprehensive plan might at first make even the scaled-down theater complex appear unwanted. According to the plan, the "big fields" near the Virgin River are to be preserved in order to retain a "village" experience and keep Springdale an "oasis in the desert." Further, "the 'village' scale and character can be achieved, along with a feeling of being 'in the park,' if development maintains a harmonious visual character, and is concentrated in the valley." And, further still: "The Virgin River is to Springdale (and Zion Park) what the Nile is to Egypt, and it would be a great mistake for the town to continue to turn its back on this prize possession."

Nevertheless, on June 12 all four members of the town council and the mayor voted to approve a conditional-use permit for a 55-foot-high building, circumventing a zoning-code provision that limits building height to 35 feet. The permit—under court challenge by the National Parks and Conservation Association, the Southern Utah Wilderness Alliance and the Wilderness Society—strives to mitigate damage to the park experience by stipulating that "nature trails will be provided."

Although Merrill avers that his environmental sensitivity is obvious to anyone familiar with his work, this does not mean he likes environmentalists. As he puts it: "It's very difficult to work with environmentalists because their view of the world is very, very different than normal people—er, than average people .... There's a point at which you can't deal logically with a person whose view is that rocks and trees and bushes are as important to human beings as progress."

Just such illogical people, according to World Odyssey partner Memmott, are those who publicly caterwaul about the choice of sites. He guesses there are only five of this ilk left in Springdale, and he knows about one upstate: Robert Redford, of Provo Canyon, who writes that "the light and noise generated by such a development is not conducive to such a serene location."

Guilty also of this illogic are 19 members of the House Interior and Insular Affairs Committee and the National Park Service itself, all of whom have written open letters to World Odyssey asking it to select another location. One veteran park official refers to it as "an analogue of reality at the doorstep of reality." Other park officials wish that the theater complex would pull away visitors but fear that it will cause traffic jams instead.

Last year a record 2.3 million people visited Zion. If use increases at just 5 percent per year (and the figure hasn't been below 6.1 percent since 1980), there will be three million visitors in 1995, nearly four million in 2000. Marcel Rodriguez, who leads interpretive hikes and volunteers at the visitor center, reports that on weekends the trail to Zion Narrows is so crowded "you simply have to pace yourself" with the masses ahead of you. "At the visitor center people are irate.

One guy came in and told me he waited for two hours to park and hadn't been able to and that right now he was double parked in front. He wanted his money back."

But somehow World Odyssey officials have figured out that their development will *alleviate* traffic jams by giving tourists a place to pull off the highway until rush hour ceases, at which point they will hop back in their vehicles and continue into the park. The company no longer maintains that its movie will reduce crowding by reducing visitation, perhaps having been discouraged from this argument by a supermarket tabloid that published a widely and gleefully quoted exposé on the venture entitled "Vacations for Couch Potatoes."

It is appropriate that most visitors who fly to Zion National Park land first in Las Vegas. Viewed in conjunction with natural shrines, there is a certain verisimilitude about the city. It provides perspective, a sense of humanity's real and imagined significance and, possibly, renewed appreciation for what has not yet transpired three hours uphill to the northeast. Those drawn to places like Las Vegas and those drawn to places like Zion generally are two different sorts. For me the single pleasing sight in all of Las Vegas was the ramp onto Route 15 heading out of town.

And yet as I pulled into Springdale I saw little patches of Las Vegas grafted onto the future course of the gold-plated sidewalks. The most noticeable was a 27-foot-high neon sign advertising Indian Village. According to Larry McKown, of the Springdale Alliance for Responsible Development, the sign is "illegal" because it violates a city ordinance. But Terry West, who owns the sign, maintains the ordinance was passed when his sign was already under construction.

West, 56, one of the most successful and aggressive businessmen in Springdale, has redeveloped and revitalized the central part of town. When I finally caught up with him he was trotting toward one of his new gift shops, clutching a jug of ice water, long sideburns matted with sweat, brown eyes blazing under a forelock of thick, silver hair. At first he seemed miffed about having to talk with another reporter, but he warmed quickly to his subject. Soon he was slashing the air and braying into my tape recorder.

"The guy has a right to do it," he said of Heaton's land-use scheme. "It's the park's plan that's out of step because the city was here first. The park comes in and builds their campground next to the city and then turns around and says, 'Hey city, don't utilize your land.'"

When I told West about my interview with Louise Excell he snorted and said, "She loves to have interviews," and that "she opposes every-thing." As I was leaving, West expressed astonishment that I'd been sent all the way from Massachusetts to write about the park-side theater, that it wasn't a big story at all. I told him he was right.

The story isn't about World Odyssey's little atrocity in Springdale, Utah, which, viewed on a national scale, is lost in a Las Vegas of atroc-ities, many uglier and many perpetrated by the Park Service itself. The story is about how parks lose in the push-and-shove with gate-way communities, about our superstition that parks are ecological islands unto themselves and about America's hermetic insulation from wild things and wild places.

World Odyssey's Springdale project is a symptom of our "desire for instant gratification," declares Doug Kimball, an educator with the Massachusetts Audubon Society. "We don't want to go out and watch a bird build a nest. We want to see it on TV where we're right in the nest with the bird, watching it lay the eggs, incubate them, hatch them, feed and fledge the young. All in four minutes."

Springdale mayor Robert E. Ralston, 69, resents the way his neighbors have cast him as the story's villain. "Everybody blames the mayor for everything," he sighs as he places his hands behind his tight-fitting "Disabled American Veterans Life Member" cap and stretches out his arthritic legs. But Mayor Ralston is not dispirited, even though his administration is being investigated by the county attorney. In his voice is bemused resignation, and on his face is a perpetual smile as if he has seen the folly of human existence and risen above it. He bought this house and property in 1964, and, he says that "they're not gonna get rid of me because I bought a lot in the cemetery."

Now, as cool evening pours into the canyon, the day's first zephyr stirs the heart-shaped leaves of the mayor's California popples, and hummingbirds buzz around his cactus garden. High overhead the top of Watchman Mountain burns ocher under a fierce sun that set on Springdale 40 minutes ago. "When I get through telling you, you're gonna see why they call it the Watchman Mountain," Ralston announces. "You see the highest part of the mountain and you come down and you see a little tree? And you come over to another bump. Now right below that bump is a red surface. That is the profile of a man looking up into the canyon. He's got a pompadour haircut and a mustache. That's the watchman."

Those who condemn the theater complex soon to be built at the Watchman's feet are grievously deluded, says Mayor Ralston. "They don't realize that the more business you have here the better it is for everybody. This town is a business." He explains that the malcontents who are trying to shut down the theater are the very ones trying to shut down his pal Terry West. "They've done everything they can to try to stop the man. They've accused him and me of being in cahoots."

The push-and-shove between national parks and gateway communities is visible on the west side of the mayor's house, where he contracted some unauthorized excavating of Bureau of Land Management real estate and the habitat of the threatened desert tortoise.

Ralston, who maintains that he was digging on public land merely to save himself from a landslide, harbors great bitterness about being ordered to cease and desist. He says he's told the feds not to cross his property with their "damn trucks" and to "build yourself a road." Moreover, he was going to plant trees for them on their land, *but not now*. As he put it at a recent town council meeting: "If everybody obeyed all the laws, we'd all be closed up."

Not far from where he was digging, but on his own land, the mayor alleges that the antigrowth faction buried sun-triggered firebombs. Luckily, he was planting trees and discovered them in time.

Having agreed to give me a guided tour of the theater site, the mayor rises and walks slowly to my rented car. Five minutes later we swing off the highway and cross the Virgin River, now flowing barely faster than the amusement-park water slide on the road from Vegas, whose owners recently suggested an identical facility almost next door to World Odyssey's Springdale property. "You see in the paper where this is a 'pristine' meadow," says the mayor. "The only thing pristine about it is those little piles of manure that horse has dropped down there. And the only reason they're pristine is that nobody wants to disturb them."

Watchman Campground is immaculate and not especially crowded. Here, at least, the people are not irate. They are laughing, playing ball, hauling water, setting up tents and cooking supper. Above us stands the Watchman, still lit by the long-gone sun.

Briefly, we emerge from the car. The mayor is used to the scenery, but to a Yankee flatlander like me, it is breathtaking and spectacular. My eyes pan the chartreuse band of cottonwoods, box elders and big-tooth maples along the flood plain, then swing up to sage and pinyon pine on the desert foothills, up farther to cedar-flecked talus slides, and finally to sandstone peaks and arches beyond which, like the halls of Olympus, stands an unseen subalpine forest of Douglas fir and

Ponderosa pine—the dwelling place of mule deer and mountain lions. I feel as if I am standing in the middle of an Ultra 70 movie.

"The park built their damn gates too close to the town," interjects the major. "Their damn traffic backs up into our town. They built their campground right across from the river and now they tell us we can't use our land? No good, baby. We just got through with a little war over in the Gulf. What was basically behind that? Some people wanted to tell other people what to do with their land and their property. Same thing here . . . .

"Somewheres this crap has got to stop. They took all the damn land from the owners, and they built a campground across from the town; and the town grows; and now the town is wrong . . . . This is a Springdale matter; it's not a national matter. Hell, you could drop an atomic bomb right on this damn town and it ain't gonna ruin the park."

From Watchman Campground we drive into Zion and climb to the wide, yellow meadow across from the visitor center, where the Mormons used to hold Easter pageants. Zion's a big park, but most of the acreage is vertical. Grasslands are at a premium, and this one provides important forage for deer. Park Service biologists have used it to acclimate desert bighorns before release, and they may have to use it again because the reintroduced bighorn population appears too small to be viable. The meadow lacks water or shade, and large sections are regularly bombarded by falling rocks.

Abruptly, the mayor gets back to the push-and-shove. "All of that," he pronounces, sweeping his hand down toward the present campground, "could be moved up here . . . . You could have the most beautiful campground."

Terry West, his 31-year-old son and employee, Larry, and Mayor Ralston are at war with Springdale's antigrowth faction. Larry, who is a member of the planning commission, recently saw fit to break the nose of a member of the Springdale Alliance for Responsible Development, then convinced a jury that he hadn't committed a crime. The victim, says Larry, "was upset because I didn't have a building permit. He came down with an ax to grind and stuck his nose in someone else's business and got it broke."

One of Terry West's buildings has been "red-tagged" by District Fire Marshal Al Bench for fire-code violations. A red tag is a stop-work order, but on-site construction continues. Bench charges that West "tore down the red tag within minutes of me posting it" and that

West physically restrained him from testing a hydrant. Moreover, the fire marshal is put off by West's hippie jokes and has complained to the city in writing about the way Larry unceasingly gives him "the finger."

Bench, 45, wears his auburn hair in a ponytail that falls about two inches below his waist—a length made all the more impressive by his six-foot, three-inch frame, which he keeps lean and hard by running through the park. He speaks eloquently, peering down over a crooked nose with intense hazel eyes. After he got out of the Air Force in 1966 he promised himself he'd never take another order and started making sandals on a California beach. Now, because his job as fire marshal is a volunteer position, he ekes out a precarious living fashioning Indianesque art pieces from silver, turquoise, leather and bone. Even pro-growth boomers—excepting the Wests and Mayor Ralston—acknowledge that he's a top-of the-line fire marshal.

Bench lives in Steve Heaton's old house, now owned by World Odyssey, and the horse who deposits the pristine road apples belongs to his daughter. Part of the rental deal is that Bench doesn't flap his gums about the theater complex, but everyone knows what he's thinking. All he would tell me was: "I would like to see them take all the money and give free helicopter rides over the park to the really handicapped and ban all other flights."

In their conflict with the preservationists, the Wests and Mayor Ralston have thermonuclear capability. Terry West is a member of the Utah Bar and can file lawsuits without having to pay attorney fees. So together, in one sweeping action, they are suing the opposition. They are suing Louise Excell. ("She said it was government by terrorism and that I was the terrorist," Terry West explains.) And they are suing Al Bench. ("He stood up at a public meeting once and libeled and slandered me," explains Larry West.) And they are suing the Wests' next-door neighbor, Lillian Baiardi (who "has apparently conspired" with Excell, Al Bench and the former building inspector "to continue this slander and liable [sic] campaign to accuse me of felonies," writes the mayor). And they are suing members of the volunteer fire department. And they are suing some of Louise Excell's relatives.

It may not be government by terrorism, but the opposition clearly is terrified. Baiardi had agreed to an interview but changed her mind when I showed up at her door, informing me that she didn't dare speak because of the ongoing litigation. And local reporter Sandi Graff says Terry West has twice sued her newspaper, *The Daily Spectrum*, so that it now has to be "very careful about using his name."

Thirty people—about 10 percent of Springdale's population—are seated in the little cinder-block building at 9:30 AM on Thursday, August 1, 1991. They are here for the weekly meeting of the town council, an increasingly popular spectator and/or participatory sport. Mayor Ralston, now in a clean blue shirt, sits behind the council table, clutching his gavel. Without his vet's hat he looks like a bald LBJ. He asks the sheriff's deputy, who is there to prevent contact sport, to lead the congregation in the Pledge of Allegiance. Mayor Ralston asks that we pay special attention to the words.

Presently, planning commission Chairman Eric Bonner rises to report that a developer who seeks to build the "Zion Fun Center" (consisting of a miniature golf course and video arcade) has been instructed to pursue a conditional-use permit just like World Odyssey. And further, the commission would like to see the city attorney—who has represented Terry West and the mayor—replaced because of conflict of interest. This incenses the mayor. He says he won't listen to such talk, but Bonner says he has to because it's in the minutes.

After Bonner sits down, Terry West—now wearing three large silver rings, a thick silver bracelet and an enormous turquoise-and-silver belt buckle—passionately defends his post-red-tag construction, then backs the mayor in an abortive attempt to remove Al Bench from office by suggesting that Springdale withdraw from the fire district. Bench isn't rolling over for anyone.

Bench: "The town can revoke Mr. West's business license, if they have the fiber to stand up to him . . . ."

Mayor, voice rising to a scream: "Can't you use a little discretion and say, 'If you correct these things within a certain length of time' instead of saying, 'Boom, you're shut down . . . .' *Who's going to be targeted next?*"

Lillian Baiardi: "I don't trust town officials. And I won't as long as you're in office."

Mayor: "You heard it; it's all my fault . . . . "

Someone interrupts.

Mayor: "We've got some sick minds in this town. You're damned right we have. When people try to burn me out with incendiary devices . . . ."

Someone interrupts.

Mayor, yelling: "I'm talking. When a board member's car is trashed. When chickens' heads are cut off and thrown into my car and the blood is all over . . . ."

Someone interrupts.

Mayor, shrieking: "I'm talking. You keep quiet!"

Someone interrupts, complaining that this has nothing to do with the agenda.

Mayor: "Yes it does . . . . A rock was thrown at me and it hit my car . . . ."

Someone interrupts.

Mayor: "Go ahead, say that louder . . . . Call me all the names you want."

So goes the thrust-and-parry between Springdale residents and their government, and so goes push-and-shove along the southern border of Zion National Park.

When the town council meeting ends I head for Zion. I'd hoped to do some hiking. But this is my last day and I have but two hours. And, since the temperature is pushing 100 degrees, I seal myself into the car and turn up the air-conditioner. The motorized tour of Zion Canyon takes just under 90 minutes.

On the way out I dismount at the Great White Throne and try to envision all the parts of the park inaccessible by car that I'll be able to see next year on Ultra 70 film. As Merrill has stated, about 80 percent of all national-park visitors "have no opportunity" to hike the canyons. And, at least for the moment, I am one of them.

The next question is why do they have no opportunity? Certainly 80 percent of all park visitors aren't handicapped. Most have basic hiking equipment—functional eyes and feet. The answer is that since childhood they have been conditioned to seal themselves from the natural world. This is why World Odyssey's giant, wraparound, air-conditioned theater on the little meadow next to Watchman Campground will be a smashing commercial success. And this is why the company is talking about building up to 100 more such facilities (not all abutting national parks) in the next 10 years.

Treasure of the Gods will be very entertaining, and it will be educational as well. It will teach that nature is something passive and prepackaged that one goes indoors to see. And, if everything about the analogue of reality is breathtaking and spectacular—as it surely will be—then many young viewers are going to find the reality disappointing and probably not worth protecting.

Now there are video walkmen—little portable TVs you carry on nature trails to see all the wildlife you missed because you were staring at the screen. A Park Service consultant predicts that within this decade they'll be available at national parks and that you'll be able to reserve one by car fax. If you switch it on during the movie credits—as you shuffle from the theater into the real park—you always can feel you are more than there.

UPDATE

The theater got built. Mayor Robert Ralston is out of office, and the new guy seems downright sane. So far, Springdale has not acquired "gold-plated sidewalks."

Though gross, the development could have been worse. The motel units didn't go up, and the building is lower than originally planned. The National Park Service is, as Tom Rush sings, "makin' the best of a bad situation" by trying to use the new parking lot as a staging area for tour buses.

Elsewhere in the nation the commercialization of our national parks continues.

To Be Chosen by Phoebes

Maybe you're not a blight upon the living Earth

The Living Bird Quarterly, Winter 1991

DIRECTLY ABOVE the glowing, green monitor of my ancient Apple and two feet beyond the open window is a long, scraggly pine bough—the favorite perch of my camp phoebes. The female alights there with an enormous dragonfly held crosswise in her mandibles. I had watched her flutter out over the calm lake surface, wheel and hawk it as it hawked gnats.

Now she is so close I can see the flycatcher whiskers around the base of her dark bill. As she puffs her elegant gray-and-white plumage and struggles with her meal, her slightly larger but otherwise identical mate touches down on a higher branch, assumes his jaunty, erect posture, raises the crest on his oversize head, pumps his tail and chirps. At this time of year he sings mostly in the predawn, and on occasion she does, too.

Their harsh, raspy *fee-bee* pales beside the chickadee's sweet, plaintive rendition. But as my fellow Yankee curmudgeon Robert Frost put it, "we love the things we love for what they are." I am never sure if my phoebes wake me or if I wake to hear them. In any case, they are always the first birds I notice, if you don't count whippoorwills and owls. Twenty years ago I had shown their great-grandfather—or maybe great-great-grandfather—where I wanted the nest by nailing a board under the eaves above the outside light socket, and he (like all his male issue ever since) had shown his lady by hovering and chattering.

Such scenes are infinitely more interesting to me than what is happening on my computer screen. They remind me how important my camp phoebes are, and how they helped straighten the rambling worm trail of my life.

Phoebes held no fascination for me in 1954 when, at age eight, I helped build the camp. Part of my job was fetching bricks, in the wooden rowboat, from the ruined mansion of New Hampshire's first governor, Benning Wentworth. Maybe these artifacts from the wild, forgotten north end of the island helped the phoebes choose the new camp or, more likely, they had nested in the dilapidated one it replaced. Whatever drew them, their acceptance of the raw, unweathered building was a monumental compliment to my grandparents.

To be chosen by phoebes . . . now I understand what it means. Phoebes never choose the vinyl-sided houses lit by blue moth zappers ("homes," the chop-and-plop developers prefer to call them) that sprout in clearcuts along the mainland shore and are named after what they have destroyed—"Lakewood Estates," "Hemlock Heights." They choose instead the spare, non-multiplying Yankee camps on Governor's Island—always (save in my grandparents' case) after the pines have bulged around the hammock hooks, raised the shingles with their discarded needles and provided enough shade and dampness to rot the sills a little, after the false lily of the valley has marched beyond the pumphouse, after wintering red squirrels have gnawed the window mullions and at least two generations of boys have traced bass, pickerel and trout on smoke-stained cupboard doors.

More interesting than how phoebes react to humans is how humans react to phoebes. My grandmother—Grammy—was repulsed by the droppings on the porch steps and, as a rite of spring cleaning, brushed the nest from the light. To the matron of the camp it was just a mass of mud, moss, grass and pieces of my fishing line, but to the matron of the eaves it was a masterpiece that sometimes took two weeks to sculpt.

It's not that Grammy and so many of her contemporaries didn't love and appreciate nature. It was just that they were products of another age.

Yet it never ceases to astonish me how that age could have stockpiled so much information about individual species and so much tommyrot about the way they interact with each other. In 1927, for example, the celebrated ornithologist Edward Howe Forbush was able to write in *Birds of Massachusetts and Other New England States* that the phoebe's "only known harmful trait is the occasional destruction of a few fish fry. It [therefore] well deserves all the protection it usually receives at the hands of man." From this it follows that the ospreys, loons, cormorants, mergansers, herons and kingfishers, all of which dine almost exclusively on the ever-prolific fish of Big Island Pond and all of which make my fishing joyful and meaningful, deserve to be excised from the planet.

When Grammy became too old to clean, the phoebe nest no longer was removed. Instead the eggs got hardboiled when people forgot to leave the light turned off. In the spring of 1970 the nest crashed to earth after I had broken the bond by loosening the bulb. That's when I nailed up the nesting platform and hid the bulb in the darkest recess of the cellar, where it reposes to this day. "Stolen," I truthfully told Grammy when she asked me where it was.

Now the first thing we do when we arrive at camp—even before unloading the car—is check on the progress of nest or clutch or hatchlings. Once, when we arrived on a fine, gusty afternoon in mudtime, the nest was empty. The next morning, at first light, there was one egg. And one more each morning thereafter until the clutch was complete at five. It's impossible to see the eggs from the porch steps, even if you stand on tiptoe, but I can feel them, and I do see the empty shells. The eggs are pure white, although a few (usually the last laid) have brown spots on the large end.

Even without cats there are tragedies. One summer when the blueberries were ripe and the soft lakeside air was heady with the fragrance of sweet pepperbush, I found the second brood dead on the steps, each tiny, naked corpse swarming with red mites. I removed the infested nest and sponged the board, but "Mrs. Phoebe," as the kids call her, didn't rebuild that year. And once, in the tumult of his youth, Ruggles the Brittany spaniel broke point and gummed to death a brace of fledglings. Still, the board is solid and secure, a relatively safe nesting site. When the first dab of mud appears we lock the south door and use only the north door until the second brood has taken wing. From my porch cot—in those last, delicious minutes before I rise and stumble with my fly rod to the canoe—I love to watch the busy parents helicoptering up and into the nest and listen to the greedy shrieks of their young.

Sometimes when I cut the brush that tries to reclaim the camp as if it were Sleeping Beauty's palace, or when I trim back the clutching hemlocks that rot our sills more than just a little, I feel the phoebes watching me. I think that maybe this time I won't pass inspection and they will choose someplace else.

I was sure that I had failed five years ago, when I arrived for the first time since ice-fishing, alone and late. I pulled Grammy's old leather chair up to the governor's reassembled fireplace, touched off the dry pine logs and contemplated the framed, autographed passage on the wall. The words were composed by friend and mentor John Voelker (aka Robert Traver), author of *Anatomy of a Murder* and the superior work from which they were taken, *Anatomy of a Fisherman*: "I fish because I love to; because I love the environs where trout are found, which are invariably beautiful, and hate the environs where crowds of people are found, which are invariably ugly . . . because only in the woods can I find solitude without loneliness; because bourbon out of an old tin cup always tastes better out there . . . ."

"How true, John, how true," I said, taking a long pull on my third cup of bourbon. With that, my thoughts turned to the camp phoebes. I wondered if they had an egg yet, so I walked unsteadily to the porch, opened the door and felt around. To my horror, Mrs. Phoebe already was on the nest, incubating. When I touched her silky back she cried out and fluttered onto the porch and thence into the living room. At least I had the presence of mind to throw the screen over the fire.

She did not fling herself hysterically against the windows and walls, as so many birds will do. Instead, she fluttered and hovered, soundlessly, like a moth. I ushered her out onto the small back porch, closed the kitchen door and caught her in my cupped hands against the screen. She didn't struggle, scream or peck, but her eyes were quick and wild and her breast heaved.

I took her out into the cold, black night and held her a long time against the pine needles, stroking her crest, waiting for a shaft of moonlight through the clouds. Peepers jangled from the swamp across the lake and toads trilled from the fire pond on the hill. At last the moon broke through, racing over our rippled cove, up into the lacy birch catkins, onto the roof and, finally, to the tops of the sentinel pines. I left her then and retreated into the camp, where I spent a long and restless night.

But at dawn she was on her nest. Even in the face of such an insult I remained the undeserving recipient of her trust and approval. I felt the way I had in the spring of 1969 when, after reading none of a dozen books and having gone fishing and drinking for the previous three days, I passed my advanced philosophy final because the single question had been, "Explain your own philosophy."

Every spring I can't quite believe it when our phoebes choose us again. They are spirits that waft out of old, stonewall-laced forests to hover around old waterside buildings of precisely the right sort. Maybe they are the spirits of dead fishermen who drank and laughed and played cribbage there and who loved the lake or stream. Anyway, I thank God that there still are plenty of phoebes. Without them our place would be deprived of memory and magic, and we would be disowned. To be chosen by phoebes means that you are not a blight upon the living Earth, that, finally, you are almost decent and acceptable, and that, even considering your species, there is hope for you.

UPDATE

We are still chosen by phoebes. But now they always nest on the platform off Scott's room. I wish they'd nest on the porch as well. But for some reason we only get one pair. Maybe the camp is smaller than a phoebe's territory.

One of the problems about writing pieces like this—especially after three cups of bourbon—is that sometimes what sounded smart and funny when it went into the computer sounds petty and mean when it appears in print. Getting chosen as a friend by Betty at the Point and her fabulous daughters and son is even better than getting chosen by phoebes. And, like getting chosen by phoebes, I can't quite believe it. That they tolerate me in the fashion my phoebe did when I stupidly flushed her off her nest and then stupidly pontificated about a similar mistake shows that they understand my nature (crude, rough and careless but not mean—at least not intentionally). And it shows there is hope for me.

Anyway, this improved version is for you, Betty. And by the way, I've sworn off bourbon forever. Now I drink only scotch. See you in summer. Love, Ted.

Canned Hunts

Killing isn't necessarily hunting

Audubon, January 1992

"DON'T JUDGE US BY TODAY," declares the woman with the straight black hair as I peel out three tens and a five, which, along with my $25 deposit check, will entitle me to join the circle around the pheasant tower at Lido's Game Farm, in Taghkanic, New York. Usually, she tells me, they throw 200 birds for 40 guns, but with the long weekend and all . . . well, only 13 guys signed up. Already, in my coverts back home, hillside popples are smoky gold, bracken burnt with frost, apples on the ground . . . . Already Wilton, the new Brittany, has left his milk teeth in my sock and pointed his first woodcock wing. Already the 1991 upland bird season is two weeks old, and I haven't been out once.

This is a morning made for hunting—bright and cool and still, with fog hanging in the river bottoms and flights of geese blowing like black crepe across a cobalt sky. How I wish I could hunt today. But I am here, to participate in my first "tower shoot," as part of my research for this column.

Inside the clubhouse, Lido—undershirt and gut protruding through an unbuttoned camouflage shirt—leans on the bar. On his right a gray squirrel with wings sprouting from its withers clutches a varnished stick. On his left a crudely mounted whitetail buck chews a tuft of hay the way Lido chews his Italian cigar. Lido lays his cigar on the edge of the bar and lectures us about safety and etiquette: "Don't shoot no cranes," he commands. "And don't shoot no deer. Lotsa guys up here been spraying deer and cranes and beavers. Only shoot what you're supposed to. You know the rules."

George, who has brought a group up from the Bronx, announces that this time he wants a good spot. With that, he snatches a station ticket. "Hold on, now," exclaims the woman with the straight hair. Later I hear Lido whisper to a guide: "If he don't rotate, stop the hunt right then. If he pulls that shit again, I'm not letting him back here."

I follow Lido outside, past the owlproof pens where professorial pheasants strut about with plastic, nontransparent glasses wired to their upper mandibles—pink for the hens, blue for the roosters. (Without their vision blocking eyewear, game-farm pheasants would attend to their own defeathering.) At the tower, guide Arthur hitches the crates of pheasants to the rope while guide Dave hauls them by pulley to the release platform. On the way up, each crate exudes copper and buff breast feathers that hang in the morning air like milkweed silk. Dave, who will be throwing for us, allows that he's been lucky—he's only been hit twice, and each time he's been able to pick out the lead with his fingers.

Presently Lido resumes the lecture. "Actions open, guys," he says. "Every five birds you will rotate to your right. Everyone will have chances at birds, so don't worry about that. Keep your gun in the air. Don't shoot the tower . . . . What else?"

"Tell 'em about the cranes," someone hisses.

"Oh, yeah. Fellas, don't shoot cranes. Don't shoot nothing you're not supposed to shoot. The guys see a deer, they shoot the deer for no reason. That's a sin. Have a good time, guys."

You find the shooting stations at Lido's by looking for the plastic shell casings. There are thousands of them, in a rainbow of colors, most from past years. I load up at Station 18 as Dave holds a fat rooster aloft in his right hand and walks around the platform four times. "Awright," he hollers. "Ready, guys. Keep those shots up high. Here we go." He hurls the bird skyward. "Open up now. Open up now. Open up now." A dozen muzzles bark and the bird somersaults into the birches, trailing feathers. The next bird crumples after just two shots. One rooster orbits the entire perimeter, drawing unspeakable fire, the shots building in volume as he approaches from my left. I never see him go down because I am holding my forearm in front of my eyes, but finally Dave calls: "Good shooting, guys."

Four times Dave throws birds that are apparently injured or diseased, for they crash to the ground before anyone can touch off a round. Once someone shoots while Dave is still holding the bird.

"Hey, what are you shooting at?" he screams. "Don't never play games with me!"

Spent shot rains around me on at least half the releases. Once I am struck painlessly on the left shoulder. Another pellet hits my gun barrel, but it too is spent. A hen sculls over my head, and I miss on all three shots. The next hen flutters like a woodcock, and my load of number sixes catches her cleanly. In all I burn nine shells, assisting on three kills.

When the last of the 75 birds has been thrown, we open our actions and filter through the brush, eyes to the earth. I do not pick up the single kill I find because it is from a previous season and lacks meat. Of the 50 or so pheasants that clearly took shot, we retrieve only 22. Later there will be a walk-up hunt for MIAs. Lido says he hopes we haven't hidden any birds.

As habitat shrinks and posted land proliferates, "canned hunts," as they are being called by their detractors, are catching on everywhere. There are more than 4,000 shooting preserves in the United States (predominantly for birds but also for mammals), only a few of which do a decent job of simulating natural hunting conditions. In Florida, state officials estimate that there may be as many as 40 establishments where, in pens ranging from 100 to 600 acres, you can run your hounds on coyotes or foxes that are supposed to get away but sometimes don't. That's about twice as many as in the mid-1980s. In Texas, where canned hunts for exotic big game are a major industry, there are just under 500 "game ranches," where you can kill the trophy of your choice in the enclosure of your choice. That's up from about 380 eight years ago.

"No Kill—No Pay Guarantee" proclaims the brochure of the Priour Ranch, in Ingram, Texas. Indeed, major effort is required to find a big game-shooting preserve in any state that doesn't guarantee success. At the "No Game—No Pay" Texoma Hunting Wilderness, in Norman, Oklahoma (recently shut down by the state), you could shoot a "Texas elk"—a cross between a European red stag and a North American wapiti—for $2,895 and a "male African lion with good mane" for $5,995. The case against Texoma, said the district attorney, had nothing to do with illegal hunting, only with "the deplorable state of the animals' housing."

At the 777 Ranch, in Hondo, Texas, you can check out one of the Iranian red sheep and, if you find it to your liking, kill it for $6,500. If you get an invitation to the annual celebration at the Y.O. Ranch, in

Mountain Home, Texas, you can dine on wild boar shish kabob, roasted Botswana eland, young nielgi cabrito on a spit, frog legs, rattlesnake, caviar and "tons of ribs"; watch "huge fireworks"; enjoy an "almost-overkill of dancing, eating, carousing, western fashion watching, schmoozing, and so forth"; eat breakfast at midnight; drink at the bar till dawn; be kept "corralled and peaceful" by "uniformed constables on horseback"; then go out and kill any or all of 20 varieties of game, including three genetic concoctions engineered by Y.O. breeders: white Corsican ram, black Corsican ram and Y.O. ibex. "No Game/No Pay."

A much less fancy game ranch, also in Mountain Home, Texas, is Rancho de Dios. "We have an elk we're going to kill this year," manager Royce Rodgers told me. "And a couple of real nice axis. One might go 34 inches [as measured along the main antler beam]. The brow tines got a real nice curve to 'em, measure about 12 inches. He costs a thousand. If you don't like him, you don't pull the trigger."

I forgot to ask Royce if his 34-inch axis had a name. But I did learn some of the names of the African lions who have been shot in Texas. Even in adulthood, just prior to being "harvested," Rachel, Bathsheba, Paul, John, Matthew and dozens of other pet lions raised by private breeders would amble over to you and lick your hand. One operation charged $2,500 for old, toothless specimens, $3,500 for younger cats with better dentition. Canned-lion-hunting outfitter Larry Wilburn, of Dayton, Texas, ran afoul of the law, but only because he left a brace of skinless, headless lions on land managed by the US Army Corps of Engineers. Ticketed for littering and running a commercial venture on government property, Wilburn paid $125 in fines.

And then there is Dr. Sonny Milstead, an orthopedic surgeon from Shreveport, Louisiana, who made national TV news this past September when the Fund for Animals obtained a videotape of his canned cat hunt at a game ranch near Fredericksburg, Texas. After riding out to the lion pen in a pickup truck, Dr. Sonny approaches the trophy as it reclines trustingly on the ground. Dr. Sonny is protected by backup gunners. When Dr. Sonny shoots, the lion leaps to his feet, clawing dirt. You can see a divot fly from his flank as the heavy bullet slams home. Dr. Sonny fires twice more; the lion dies. Nothing in the least illegal about that.

But the tape also shows Dr. Sonny shooting a penned Bengal tiger, an endangered species, as it rests beneath a tree. At the first shot the big cat gets up and runs to the right, dragging its shattered hindquarters.

When Dr. Sonny shoots again it somersaults three or four times. Dr. Sonny cautiously approaches, prods the dead trophy with his gun barrel, then flashes the thumbs-up sign.

Along with Milstead's exploits the networks aired a video of a canned cat hunt set up by nationally known outfitter Dan Moody on a ranch 75 miles west of San Antonio. A little black leopard—surrounded by eight or nine frenzied dogs, each as big as it is—cowers in a cage. When it emerges from the cage it attempts to hide under a pickup truck, then runs into the open, where the dogs maul it. Enter Ty Bourgeois, of Lake Charles, Louisiana, brandishing a scoped pistol, desperately trying to find a hole in the spinning dog flesh. The cat, a declawed pet, isn't fighting back. Finally Bourgeois dispatches it. The canned hunt cost him $5,000—$3,000 for the outfitter, $2,000 for the federal government as a fine for killing an endangered species without a permit.

California Ram Hunt, a game ranch in Lockwood, California, got into illegal cat hunting during the spring and summer of 1990. The cats—tigers, jaguars, leopards and cougars—were fed chickens. When it came time for them to be shot some were reluctant to leave their cages and were ventilated while still inside, then dragged out for the obligatory hero photos. One customer paid $10,500 to kill a leopard, a cougar and a Bengal tiger. Before the tiger left its cage Bwana fainted and had to be taken back to the ranch to be revived—whereupon he returned and killed all three animals. At least one tiger had been a pet; his name was Tony. "Well, sure, we had a little business going there," proprietor F. Lester Patterson told *The San Jose Mercury News*. "What's the difference if they put the thing to sleep in a zoo or if somebody wants to mount it on the wall and appreciate it?"

Finding the source of canned-hunt trophies is like finding the source of crack cocaine. The legal market and the black market suck them out of dark, dirty places littered with everything save paper bearing a return address. The Texas exotics industry is largely self-sustaining. In fact, many of the state's 123 alien species—such as aoudad sheep from northern Africa and nilgai antelope from India—have escaped and are breeding in the wild, to the detriment of native fauna. Except to acquire new species of hoofed stock, most Texas game ranches don't need zoos and perhaps could get along without private breeders.

Canned-cat-hunting operations are the exception. US Fish and Wildlife Service special agent Jim Stinebaugh says there are at least six legal sources in Texas and scores of breeders who lack permits to sell; he says he could pick up the phone and set up a cat hunt in 40 minutes. "I don't know anybody I respect in the cat-raising business." he told me. "They tell you they love the cats and they only place them in good homes. That's bull. If someone comes up with $3,000, they've got a cat."

A jaguar and a leopard supplied by Mickey Sapp, of San Antonio—who claims to have bred cats longer than anyone in Texas—wound up getting shot in their cages by Jimmie Weir, of Eunice, New Mexico, apparently for their hides. In media interviews Sapp observes that there are no guarantees in life and professes such love for his cats that he serves one of them beer.

Major zoos supply few cats and probably only a small percentage of the hoofed stock. But then, most zoos are not major. Of 15,000 animal exhibitors in the United States, only 160 belong to the American Association of Zoological Parks and Aquariums (AAZPA), the zoo-industry trade group, which claims to proscribe the sale of animals either at wildlife auctions (which frequently supply game ranches) or directly to the ranches themselves. "Our association would not tolerate any of our members contributing to this abhorrent slaughter of wildlife," pronounces AAZPA president Steve Taylor.

Yet last September Lisa Landres, a former elephant keeper at the AAZPA-certified San Diego Zoo and now with Friends of Animals, released documents proving that two sika deer from the zoo had been sold to the Priour Ranch, in Ingram, Texas, and that three mouflon sheep had been purchased by a New York game farm that supplies ranches.

Both transactions were mistakes, explained the zoo. But less than two years earlier CBS had caught it, along with the Oklahoma City Zoo, in another mistake—selling animals to dealers who then brought them to a wildlife auction in Missouri.

The CBS report was unfair, avers zoo spokesman Jeff Jouett. But he says he's come to expect such coverage because of "the Thirteenth Canon of Journalism," which, in a speech to the annual AAZPA meeting (delivered the day after Landres went public with her investigation), he defined as "Never let the facts stand in the way of a good story." Further, he informed his audience that certain animal activists were "vultures" and "low-class, no-class slimeballs," who would "tap-dance on the graves of your friends if it suits them."

But Landres told me this: "Most of the big zoos have been dumping animals for years. So what we did in San Diego is expose the tip of the iceberg. The big problem is that there is no paper trail." Indeed there is not. This is because the Animal Welfare Act of 1966 requires zoos to share their transaction records only with the US Department of Agriculture, and the documents aren't available under the Freedom of Information Act. Further, no law prohibits zoos from selling directly to auctions and game ranches.

For a variety of reasons—not the least of which is that the public loves to see cute babies cuddling with their moms—zoos produce a flood of surplus animals (1,200 last year from San Diego alone). Of those that can't be placed in other collections, the lucky ones get euthanatized or knocked off at game ranches. The rest wind up living hideous lives in cramped cells well insulated from public view.

What astonishes about the "hunting fraternity," as we like to call ourselves, is our eagerness to take on the role of thrown pheasant. There are nearly 14 million hunters in America. And then there are roughly 500,000 shooters who patronize game ranches and preserves. You'd think hunters, fretting as they do about their image, would be leading the charge against stop-n-pop game shopping. Instead, they've left the battle to the ubiquitous "antis," who are enjoying a tower shoot of their own. "The good news, if any is to be found in shooting tame animals, is that the growth of canned hunting marks the beginning of the end of all hunting," reports the Animal Rights Network in its magazine, *The Animals' Agenda*. "Canned hunts strip away the pretense that hunting is about anything other than killing."

The hook-and-bullet press, which scarcely can draw breath between rambling harangues on the wickedness of antihunters, has turned into a billboard for canned hunts. "Is A Ranch Elk Hunt For You?" inquires the cover story in the September 1990 *Sports Afield*. Could be; among other "pros" cited by the author: "Success runs 100 percent . . . . The hunting is less competitive . . . . Less time is required."

Professing to set the standard for big-game hunters everywhere is Safari Club International. Club rules stipulate that in order for a trophy to make it into the *SCI Record Book*, "it must be from a breeding population . . . that is self-sufficient where it lives, except for occasional supplemental feeding; it must not have been taken while closely confined." Yet the *SCI Record Book* contains page after page of trophies killed inside game-proof fences, and "occasional" seems to be loosely defined.

For instance, of 17 entries in the category of introduced North American wild boar, all 17 are from a game ranch in Nova Scotia called

Shangri-La. At Shangri-La you do your "hunting" in an enclosure that averages 75 acres, and the "wild boars" are fed commercial hog grower all winter. As an SCI member, Baron Carlo Amato accounted for two of the 17 records, including the number-two boar, and he has guided SCI members to five more. He owns Shangri-La.

SCI has an especially big presence in the Gulf states. The 777 Ranch, in Texas, advertises that it "supports Safari Club International and recommends the *SCI Record Book*." Kevin Christiansen, who with his father owns and operates 777, chairs SCI's Trophy Records Subcommittee for North American Exotics—on which watch he recently relieved Louis Schreiner, general manager of the Y.O. Ranch.

Also representing big-game hunters in the Gulf states is (or was) a canned cat shooter from Louisiana you may have seen on TV last September. He's the former president of SCI's Ark-La-Tex Chapter—Dr. Sonny Milstead.

Lido's Game Farm was recommended to me by the National Shooting Sports Foundation, a "nonprofit, educational, trade-supported association" dedicated to shooting sports and "practical conservation." Such poultry processors are, according to the foundation's Directory of Hunting Resorts, "conservation showcases" and "the ultimate in game management." Moreover, "Sportsmen now say: 'The only difference in open hunting and hunting on a quality hunting resort is that you practically set your own seasons and bag-limits—and you know the birds are there . . . .' Aldo Leopold, the 'father of wildlife management' in the early 1900s, recognized the fact that private landowners were the custodians of public wildlife." Other commentary by Leopold, which the foundation didn't get around to quoting, includes the following: "The recreational value of game is inverse to the artificiality of its origin."

On the wall at Lido's hangs a framed certificate revealing that it has "fulfilled all the requirements" for accreditation by the National Rifle Association. I can't help wondering what you have to do to flunk.

After the tower shoot I walk up the hill with George's young friend Miguel, who hadn't hunted before except once, unproductively, for deer. Sixty dollars was a lot for him to spend on pheasant shooting. Has the experience been worth it? "Oh, yes," he effuses. "It's nice, you know. Everyone gets a chance to shoot." He tells me how wonderful it has been to get out of New York City and come hunting in this beautiful, clean place.

"They do this here every weekend?" he inquires.

"Yes," I say.

As we reach my truck, at the brow of the hill, Miguel pauses before joining his buddies. He looks at my shredded brush pants. "You been out hunting lots this fall?" he asks.

Ten years ago, when I used to believe that you could teach by lecturing, I would have told him what hunting was and what it meant to me. Instead, I just reply, "Not even once."

UPDATE

Canned hunts are as ugly as ever and, if anything, even more popular.

After the piece appeared I got a call from a special agent of the US Fish and Wildlife Service who'd heard from my fishing buddy George. George had noticed the sign for Lido's Game Farm while motoring through New York State and, having just read about the establishment in *Audubon*, had stopped in to say hi. He was sitting at the bar having a beer and chewing the fat when one of the staffers suddenly launched into a tirade about all these goddamned pheasant-eating chicken hawks he had to shoot. Alas, I was unable to provide evidence for the investigation.

In summer my son Scott works at a game farm where pheasants are mass-produced for Massachusetts' put-and-take stocking program. Since he stands 6 feet, 8 inches, one of his jobs is to pick "hangers."

"How many hangers didja pick today, Scott?" I ask him each night when he comes in.

"Thirty-two," he may say. "Only had to kill four."

Hangers are dumb, even by game-farm-pheasant standards. They fly up and get their plastic blinders caught in the wire, and there they hang until Scott rescues them. If they have seriously injured themselves, he wrings their necks. Manure clusters around the feet of hangers and non-hangers alike, rotting their toes. So pulling off pheasant toes is another of Scott's jobs. He also burns off the sharp part of their beaks with a hot iron so they won't pluck each other.

Last summer, when Scott got suspended by the pants as he was jumping down from his truck, the rest of the staff yelled "Hanger, Hanger!" They love him at the game farm, but a few of the big bosses still splutter about the nasty things his father used to write about this kind of "wildlife management."

Killer Fish Farms

Farmers are blasting away at America's birds

Audubon, March 1992

ON THIS, THE SECOND DAY of our stakeout, we took the field at first light. Special Agent Roger Gephart peeled off his jacket, strapped a 9mm SIG Sauer semiautomatic under his shoulder, then passed me the binoculars. We moved through a land of stark contrasts—beautiful and ugly, fertile and barren. Surging from the broken, herbicided earth were lush plantations of olives, grapes, pistachios, plums, nectarines, almonds, oranges—all in rows straight as the high-tension towers that goose-stepped through them and off into the hazy, snow-capped Sierra Nevada.

It had been a cold night in California's San Joaquin Valley. Behind us in the orange grove, the frost-dispersing fans sounded like a formation of Apache helicopters, drowning out most sound. Still, we made out gunfire—single reports, not the double pops characteristic of nonlethal "cracker shells."

"Hey, look at this," said Gephart as he swung the spotting scope to focus on the gray Ford pickup that had just bounced onto one of the fish farm's bare, earthen levees.

Gephart—a trim man of 40 with hazel eyes, thick mustache and a boyish mop of brown hair—is precisely the sort of guy you don't want on your case if you've been knocking off avian varmints without a "depredation permit" from his agency, the US Fish and Wildlife Service. Like all the special agents I know, he is smart, tough and tenacious. You have to be in his business, because no law enforcement branch anywhere is so overburdened and underfunded, and no kind of police work, including drug interdiction, is more dangerous.

Two hundred feet ahead of the gray pickup, California gulls and great egrets peeled away like plowed snow, then settled beyond effective killing range. Above us, at staggered elevations and backlit by the crimson sun, great blue herons sailed in from all compass points, set their wings, uncoiled their pterodactyl necks and spiraled out of a windless sky. Other farmers had probably moved them off their ponds. Wildlife habitat is almost nonexistent in this irrigated desert, and fish farms provide most of the open water. They serve as magnets for fish-eating birds—sources of life, sources of death.

For birders like me such scenes call to mind a *World of Audubon* special. For fish farmers like the one we had under surveillance (Mort, I'll call him), they bring to mind an Alfred Hitchcock movie. Understandably enough, Mort finds it painful to watch his profits slide down the gullets of wild animals. But Mort's legal options—and even his illegal options—are limited. For instance, the Fish and Wildlife Service's Pacific region generally gives a farmer just one depredation permit, good for a year or a few dozen birds, whichever comes first. After that he's expected to implement such largely ineffective "nonlethal" controls as electric fences, pyrotechnics, scarecrows, balloons and wires. According to an informant, Mort had made a long-term commitment to lethal control instead; yet that, too, is largely ineffective.

Gephart's investigation hadn't been getting anywhere; but now, as the sun's heat shut down the fans and two more vehicles appeared on the levees, both of us sensed a major break might be at hand. Presently the gray pickup disappeared behind the metal building, and we heard a shot. A hundred yards away a flock of egrets billowed into the air. Then the pickup reappeared, stopped and disgorged a man carrying a firearm that he steadied on the hood and shot into the flock of egrets. Ten minutes later he jumped from the truck and fired into a circling flock of gulls.

Wanting more evidence, Gephart wouldn't make his move today. As he glassed the gunner, I saw another truck headed our way. There was not a shred of cover to hunker into. "I think we got picked off," I whispered.

"Pretend we're doing something," he said, fading into the orange grove and inspecting trees. I snatched an orange and professionally scrutinized the frosted skin. The man dismounted from his truck and walked over to us. "Good morning," he intoned.

"Hi," chirped Gephart. "We're from the Department of Agriculture." Suddenly the man seemed friendlier, and slowly, artfully, Gephart steered the conversation from frost to oranges to dogs to dove hunting to windstorms to fish farming to bird predation.

American aquaculturists have a monumental bird problem, which is intensifying in direct proportion to their fish production. Currently they raise 860 million pounds a year. By century's end it is estimated they will produce *2.2 billion* pounds of fish annually. In the Southeast alone the number of depredation permits has increased from one in 1986, with no reported kills, to 103 in 1990, with 5,414 reported kills. (Reported kills constitute a tiny fraction of real kills because the Fish and Wildlife Service lacks the manpower to check limits.)

The permit system was designed to provide applicants with short-term relief until they could set up nonlethal controls. "But this objective has been ignored by fish farmers and the service alike," complains Randall Snodgrass, wildlife policy director for the National Audubon Society. "Permits must be renewed annually, yet no effort is made by the agency to force compliance. Thus, bird depredation is a never-ending, ever-increasing problem."

Aquaculturists can't blast their way to success. Even if open season were declared on winged piscivores, the cost of bullets, shotgun shells and gunners would quickly surpass the cost of lost fish. And any hunter who has twiddled his thumbs in a duck blind the morning after opening day understands how quickly migratory birds learn to avoid getting shot. On the other hand, such nonlethal measures as propane cannons, "screamers" (whistling rockets) and cracker shells (shotgun-launched salutes) mainly disturb the neighbors.

As I interviewed one fish farmer he fired a cracker shell at a passing egret, who looked at us indignantly when it exploded off his starboard beam, then described a lazy circle and came back. Another farmer told me the herons sit on his propane cannons until they hear the click of the timer, at which point they hop to the ground, cock their heads, wait for the explosion and hop back on. Yet another farmer engaged the enemy with a radio-controlled model airplane until a collision with a cormorant proved fatal—for the plane only. When farmers constructed deep, steep-sided ponds and set up electric fences on the banks, egrets and herons learned to hover and dive like ospreys.

After losing three-quarters of a million trout a year from a production of 1.5 million, the state of California saw fit to wrap chain-link fence and nets around and over its San Joaquin trout hatchery. Now the place looks like San Quentin Prison. There's no way I could break in, but every morning en route to breakfast two great blues lift the weighted nets under the door, then scold the managers who shoo them out. Before the screening went up, a mannequin rode up and down the raceways on cables, toting on its shoulders trout-scouting herons.

The farmers say that fishermen should hate the birds too. "I'm a cormorant. I'll have your lakes bare of fish in three years . . . [unless you] call or write your Senator or Congressman this week and ask them to protect our fish from THESE WORTHLESS BIRDS!" screams a newspaper ad in Oklahoma.

You can hate birds, curse birds, haze birds, even kill birds; but if you set the table for them, you can't get rid of birds. Still, fish farmers who never engage in illegal bird control appear to be about as common as truckers who never speed. Even the secretary of the California Aquaculture Association turns out to have a record. George Ray, who is also the association's past president, owns Fish Producers of California, in Brawley. When he applied for a depredation permit in 1989, special agent Ben Perez and a state game warden drove out to inspect his operation.

"We started seeing dead birds all over the place," recalls Perez. "We picked up about 80 carcasses. Mostly Caspian terns but also two [endangered] brown pelicans . . . . We came by a week later with a search warrant, and in addition to what we'd already picked up got about 145 more carcasses, along with five or six hundred empty shotgun shells. And they'd cleaned up since we first came."

Ray was fined $14,500 and, for violating the Endangered Species Act; his company paid $25,000 restitution to the Salton Sea National Wildlife Refuge. When I asked Ray who, other than himself, could tell me about avian predation, he directed me to former goldfish farmer Marvin Carpenter, who Ray said had been "run out of business" by the birds.

There was a FOR SALE sign in the driveway at the Carpenter place, in Merced, California, and most of the ponds were dry and full of tumble weeds. Marvin, 59, with Spock-like eyebrows sprouting from dark glasses, was draining the water pump on a bulldozer. I shook his greasy hand, told him who I was and asked if the birds had really ruined him.

Birds and feds, he explained. The Fish and Wildlife Service had closed down part of its Kesterson refuge and "driven" the birds onto him. "They give you a permit for 50 a year. What the hell. It's like trying to put out a hotel fire with a garden hose," Carpenter said. "All fish farmers shoot birds. I'm bitter. When you work 36 years and people say you're done, that's not fair. Fish farmers are *producers*, and the government is knocking us out. The environmentalists have [the government] right by the nose." He'd been forced to take action, he explained. Then Roger Gephart's associates had brought in this backhoe and excavated his dikes . . . .

Later I watched a video of the dig, shown to me by San Joaquin Raptor-Wildlife Rescue Center president Lydia Miller, who had tipped off the special agents. With every scoop, mortified birds hung from the backhoe's bucket like gray noodles. About 700 carcasses were recovered, but some government witnesses estimated the total kill at 20,000.

"If it flies, it dies," was the battle cry at Carpenter's, according to investigators. Even non-fish-eaters like avocets, stilts, willets, gallinules and red-shouldered hawks were splashed if they violated company air space. As many as 200 night-herons would expire in a single evening after consuming cyanide-soaked goldfish scattered along the banks. One former employee reported regular use of 300 beaver traps, which splintered heron legs like fly rods dragged through a revolving door. In 1987, when Carpenter hired "Rambo," a survivalist-type college kid who prided himself on dispatching birds with a rifle, the annual purchase of .22 cartridges rose from 550 to 6,350. From 1983 to 1987 the company spent $14,949.73 on shooting supplies, mostly ammo.

Carpenter, who is awaiting sentencing for Migratory Bird Treaty Act violations, says he's "very proud" of getting his Lacey Act convictions (for "receiving" and "acquiring" migratory birds) overturned. He did this, he maintains, "for future fish farmers and myself." But the Carpenter case inconvenienced fish farmers, too. It made the Fish and Wildlife Service's Pacific region uniquely stingy with depredation permits.

Six years ago, when cormorants, egrets, herons and such were first changing their foraging areas to take advantage of lavish new food sources provided by modern fish farms, livestock interests got Animal Damage Control (ADC) and its predator killing operations moved out of the Fish and Wildlife Service and into the Department of Agriculture. The main business of animal-damage controllers (gopher chokers, as they are unaffectionately called) has always been killing wildlife. At least they were under professional supervision when part of Fish and Wildlife, whose mission is *protecting* wildlife. The mission of the Department of Agriculture, on the other hand, is promoting agribusiness.

So now Animal Damage Control documents fish-farm depredation (basically, by interviewing farmers) and tells Fish and Wildlife, now under orders from its director to accept the information at "face value," what sort of permits to issue. "There was a study out of Texas," says one special agent, "that said the only advantage of killing the birds is that it makes the fish farmer feel better. Right now you can almost turn it into a party, and I'm sure if they're killing that many birds, it is a party. You get a bunch of rednecks out there shooting birds. It chaps my butt just a smidgen."

Monty Halcomb, the special agent in charge of the southeast region, reports that the service is considering moving the permit process from its Division of Law Enforcement into its Migratory Bird Office. "We agents should be enforcing the law, not making biological determinations," he told me. "Right now the division is responsible for receiving the applications, issuing the permits, enforcing the permits, revoking and suspending permits. We're the judge, jury and police."

In Arkansas ADC goes so far as to prepare the permit applications for fish farmers. It asks the farmer what birds cost him (always, the figure is astronomical) and which birds are bothering him (usually the white ones, sometimes the gray ones and always the "cranes"). With that, ADC types up three or four pages of technical mumbo jumbo, then prevails on the farmer to inscribe his signature and mail the application to the Fish and Wildlife Service's southeast regional office, in Atlanta.

Thurman Booth, ADC's man in Little Rock, notes that fish farmers do not excel at bird identification. He's got a good point. Consider the aspiring birders at Levert St. John fish farm, in St. Martin Parish, Louisiana—where an annual loss of 540,000 pounds of channel catfish is attributed to avian predation. On December 12, 1990, the Fish and Wildlife Service issued the company a violation notice for killing great egrets and Forster's terns sans permit. Two months later special agent Frank Simms caught employees illegally shooting great blue herons and yellow-crowned night-herons. (By this time ADC had "documented" all sorts of predation, and the company had permits for about everything except herons and white ibises.) When Simms came calling yet again, in June, they were shooting white ibises and herons. After a plea agreement in which Levert St. John was sentenced to a $1,500 fine, the company invited Simms to come out to its headquarters and teach a bird-identification class. He did.

And consider the case of minnow farmer Dewey Walker, of Jena, Louisiana—who claims that birds cost him $50,000 a year, and this on top of bleak market conditions. "Jigs [artificial lures] has drove us way down," he says, "and minnows is selling for very little more than they was 25 years ago." He used to set out rags to decoy the big white kind of birds within shotgun range (not exactly what ADC had in mind), until Fish and Wildlife busted him. "We had the pond down low, and the cranes decided they was going to come on in anyway," he told me.

"What kind of cranes?" I inquired.

"That was, er, them egrets or cranes or herons. The boys, they killed a couple of cranes, and this game warden come upon 'em. He claimed that they had killed species that they shouldn't have killed. I got to studying up on it, and there've never been any of them kind of birds around here. He just said that for protection of himself . . . . It was a white bird. I don't remember now what they called it, but it's got thwattles kinda like a turkey."

Terns keep masquerading as gulls at Lake St. Anthony's catfish farm, in Mecca, California, where both species—along with pelicans, herons and egrets—supposedly make off with "a couple hundred thousand dollars' worth" of produce each year, according to owner Rick Lewis. Before Lewis bought the place a year ago, one of the help got cited for trying to fill the gull permit with common terns. (They were big and white and looked just like gulls, he explained.) After Lewis moved in, the same employee was cited for the same offense— the terns still looked just like gulls. Now Lake St. Anthony's has a tern permit.

ADC's stated and straight-faced solution to the farmers' deficiencies at bird identification is to recommend permits for one of everything they might shoot by accident. In the Southeast, for instance, it recommends permits for such rare fish-farm visitors as ospreys, anhingas, white ibises, eared grebes, horned grebes and pied-billed grebes. And it has been trying, unsuccessfully, to get permits for insect-eating cattle egrets, or "cow birds," as the farmers call them.

Elsewhere around the nation fish farmers have been issued permits for such often incidental marauders as snowy egrets, American bitterns, green-backed herons, tricolored herons, coots, eiders, western grebes, loons, old squaws, ring-necked ducks, hooded mergansers, lesser scaup, common goldeneye, mallards, ravens, magpies, grackles and crows. Permits are commonly issued for white pelicans, which in dim light are difficult to distinguish from endangered brown pelicans.

And common and Forster's terns, legally shot at many fish farms, resemble the endangered interior least tern.

State hatcheries are responsible for some of the most draconian control. For example, in 1990 the Utah Division of Wildlife Resources, with an unlimited permit, reported killing 209 black-crowned night-herons, 37 Forster's terns, 69 great blue herons, 22 belted kingfishers and 10 snowy egrets. The same year the Wyoming Game and Fish Department, also with an unlimited permit, reported killing 52 great blue herons, 15 black-crowned night herons, three common terns, six belted kingfishers and 35 mallards.

One of the best birding spots in the Southeast is the world's largest minnow farm, in Lonoke, Arkansas; but don't argue with owner James Neal Anderson about how many birds he feeds. When Tom Wittenberg, then president of the Audubon Society of Central Arkansas, publicly expressed doubt that Anderson really hosted 1,000 great blues, the society temporarily lost its birding privileges. "He called me a liar," explains Anderson. "His comments were so foolish and so unnecessary, we just told them if that's the approach they're going to take, they didn't need to be out here in the first place."

Anderson, who may have actually underestimated the number of herons, has forgiven the Auduboners; but his Louisiana employees might have benefited from hobnobbing with folks who knew their birds. "We found that the people who were doing the killing had no idea how to identify species, just shooting indiscriminately," reports special agent Joe Oliveros, who investigated the company's operation in Mangham, Louisiana. Anderson himself—an important industry leader—speaks of the vile and ubiquitous "green-backed night-heron" (a species known only to himself) and wrongly complains that the great blue heron, little blue heron, snowy egret and even the shockingly prolific double-crested cormorant are now on the endangered-species list. Even with lethal control, Anderson says birds cost him in excess of $200,000 a year. He is sorely tried by what he calls the "liberal bleeding hearts" who don't like bird control. "It's not a bit different than you having mice and roaches in your home. 'Because I like mice and roaches I don't want you getting rid of them. You got to let them eat till they die.'"

"So what's the ultimate answer?" I asked.

"Poisoning the rookeries," he said.

So what *is* the ultimate answer? Obviously, it is not chemical war. The public will not abide it. Obviously, the sort of conventional war currently being waged doesn't work; and while the public abides it now, it may not for long. In a synopsis of a recent multiagency meeting on fish-farm depredation, Bill Vermillion, of the Louisiana Department of Wildlife and Fisheries, warned that the National Audubon Society had been snooping around the Fish and Wildlife Service with Freedom of Information Act requests. He described the situation as a "potential 'powder keg' waiting to explode should other environmental groups become involved." As I write, the Izaak Walton League is getting involved.

To avoid being pariahs and criminals—and indeed, to stay in business—fish farmers need the best nonlethal controls possible. And these are? Well, no one knows because there has been no major research. Nothing will work perfectly; but some combination of tactics will work best. This is why the National Audubon Society is pushing for legislation to fund a one-year study to discover what this combination might be and to establish low-interest loans or tax incentives to help farmers implement it.

"Ludicrous" is how the current system strikes Audubon's Snodgrass. "We have to pay the Fish and Wildlife Service to issue permits to kill birds that we are paying it to acquire habitat for." He tells me the society is going to fight this one till the last bell.

UPDATE

"Nothing has changed," reports Randy Snodgrass who, alas, has left the National Audubon Society. The Fish and Wildlife Service has a director's order providing for *short-term* bird-killing permits at fish farms. But fish farmers are coming back year after year, collecting "short-term" permits instead of investing in long-term solutions. "The Fish and Wildlife Service is violating its own order," says Snodgrass.

Shortly after the piece was published, Snodgrass joined the fight to save the Endangered Species Act. He didn't have time to deal with fish farms, and no other environmental organization picked up the slack. No one is working on the issue at the national level. No one has even filed a Freedom of Information Act request to find the number and species of birds that have been killed. A great project for some environmental intern would be to compare these new stats with Snodgrass's, which still are in his old office at the National Audubon Society.

The Last Bluefin Hunt

Or perhaps not. There still may be time to

save the giant bluefin tuna

Audubon, July 1992

CAPTAIN TOM MORRISON spotted them from the flying bridge—six giants, streaking through Hemingway's "Alley" off Bimini on their spring migration to the Gulf of Maine. He didn't have to holler; he just gunned the engines. The *Huntress* reared up and galloped over the turquoise ground swells, sending Jim Hunt, commodore of the 1980 Cat Cay Tuna Tournament, scrambling out of the cabin and into the fighting chair. Soon we were ahead of the pod, and Hunt was free-spooling the big Fin-Nor reel, dropping the weighted mullet onto the nose of the lead fish—a sleek 600-pounder.

She surged and took, slamming the rod down level with the transom. Then we veered toward Miami, racing her to the blue water so she wouldn't cut us off on the shallow coral shelf. Beside me, first mate Ray Waggener poured fresh water on the smoking reel as hundreds of yards of waxed Dacron line sizzled into the sea. Thirty minutes later, as Hunt wrestled the creature up from the depths, it seemed to me impossible that any fish could be so big, or so beautiful. Her silver, almost slimeless flanks were washed with blues and greens, and all the little finlets behind her scythelike ventral and rear dorsal fins glowed neon yellow.

Among bony fishes only marlin are bigger and faster, and not by much on either count. Bluefin tuna can hit 55 miles per hour, at which speed pelvic, pectoral and front dorsal fins retract into slots. Even in relation to body weight, their hearts are immense.

The gills of bluefins are immense, too; and instead of pumping water through them like lesser fish, they reverse the process, pushing their gills through the water. Always they swim with mouths agape, supercharging their blood-rich muscles with oxygen after the fashion of a ramjet engine; and like aircraft, they have horizontal stabilizers protruding from the base of their hard, sickle tails. Restrained from swimming, they suffocate and drown. They can live for more than 30 years and attain weights of at least 1,500 pounds. These elk-size pelagic wanderers, among the most advanced of fishes, are warm-blooded, at times maintaining body temperatures 38 degrees above that of surrounding seawater. They are, as Pliny the Elder wrote 19 centuries ago, "specially remarkable." Yet before 1992 virtually everyone, even most environmentalists, thought of them not as wildlife but as a commodity.

I remember when they weren't even thought of as a commodity. By 1980 the Cat Cay tournament was releasing all fish, but only a few years earlier giant bluefins taken at major tournaments had been hoisted by the tail, written upon, photographed, then dumped off the dock. Hemingway, exhibiting as much about the mindset of his age as about his own personality, would get drunk and use them for punching bags.

Then in the early 1960s four West Coast purse seiners steamed east and opened a major commercial fishery on Atlantic bluefins. Targeting juvenile fish for the canneries, they killed 5,000 metric tons' worth in a single season. Concurrently the Japanese arrived to mine the giants (defined in the trade as fish weighing more than 310 pounds) everywhere they could find them, including the Gulf of Mexico—the only known spawning area of the genetically distinct western Atlantic population. In 1962 they set 12 million nautical miles of longlines festooned with baited hooks, enough to girdle the globe 500 times. By decade's end it was clear to anyone paying attention that the resource was in trouble.

In 1976 the California-based tuna industry—whose vessels were regularly seized by foreign governments for violating exclusive fishery zones and which regularly relied on US taxpayers to make bail—lobbied all tunas out of the purview of the Magnuson Fishery Conservation and Management Act, which had been passed that year to control foreign fishing within 200 miles of the United States.

As the 1970s ended, a brash, ingenious Boston fish dealer named Gerald Abrams pioneered a giant-bluefin export market in Japan, where the fish had long been relished raw as sushi (with rice) and sashimi (plain), but where Western stock had been largely unavailable because no one had figured out how to get it there fast, fresh and cost effectively. Abrams knew the secret: When the Japanese decide something is beautiful or delicious no price is too high. By 1986 giants were fetching $12 a pound. Last winter a single fish sold in Tokyo for $68,503—$95.65 a pound. Raw bluefin, arranged in beautiful flower patterns, can retail for as much as $350 a pound. The Japanese claim they depend on it, that it's vital to their culture and diet.

Such demand has rendered even sportfishing for giants a deadly serious pursuit. In his recent book, *The Atlantic Bluefin Tuna*, Captain Al Anderson of Wakefield, Rhode Island, describes what it's come down to: "A large pod of fish erupted, busting on the surface, and the race was on. Boats converged en masse from all directions . . . . We were close enough to see outriggers clash, then bend, trolling daisy chains hastily deployed almost immediately cut clean off, harpoons launched as well as wheelhouse glass shatter with the affronting pulpit bent askew." Among unpleasantries exchanged by participants were numerous death threats. In more peaceful settings, reports Anderson, some of his fellow charter skippers deliberately give anglers wrong advice when they hook up and then, when they inevitably exhaust themselves, order an experienced crewman to take their place in the chair. This way the boat gets to sell the fish.

Perhaps the pithiest summation of the influence of big money on conservation ethics in general and sportfishing in particular is the following reply to a plea for moderation in tuna killing—heard on the marine radio by, Dr. Carl Safina, of the National Audubon Society's scientific staff: "No one left any buffalo for me."

Genuine sportfishing still exists for the smaller juvenile bluefins, which the Japanese don't want and which persist in at least catchable numbers now that the purse seiners have redirected their efforts to brood stock.

Charter captain Dave Preble, of Narragansett, Rhode Island, who no longer sells giants and whose eloquent objections to the last buffalo hunt may have something to do with his master's degree in marine physiology, was fishing the Nineteen Fathom Bank off Nomans Land when a helicopter appeared, disgorging chopped fish like a Mixmaster. Within seconds the glistening hull of the *White Dove*—the largest of the purse seiners, half of whose bluefin catch is handled by Abrams—popped out of the sunset, bearing down on the boat of John Martini, who was working on a big school of fish a few hundred yards away. The captain of the *White Dove* got on the bullhorn and told Martini to haul anchor and leave or he'd set the net around him. Martini, whose boat measured only 20 feet, didn't argue. When Preble returned to the spot next morning he found the *White Dove* butchering the last of her catch. "The water for an enormous area was still red with blood," he says.

While the United States has moved the Japanese out of the Gulf of Mexico (to the chagrin of Japanese scientists, who claim they need to kill giants there in order to see how many are left), the National Marine Fisheries Service (NMFS) permits US longliners to take one giant per trip as "incidental bycatch." The rule is you've got to land 2,500 pounds of other species before you can bring in a giant. So fishermen collect things like ocean sunfish—big, slow grazers of comb jellyfish with virtually no commercial value—and then kill bluefins incidentally on purpose. "They're going out under the pretext of catching swordfish," one NMFS official told me. "But they target bluefins." About 85 percent of the bluefins hooked come up dead because they've been restrained from pushing water through their gills. After the one-fish limit is filled these are cut off and left for the crabs.

Environmental writer and activist George Reiger, who in 1974 alerted *Audubon* readers to the "skyrocketing" price of bluefins ($1.20 a pound that year, up from a nickel in 1973), has organized a no-kill tagging tournament to encourage catch-and-release. No way could he or anyone's army convince an angler to throw back a fish worth more than his boat and tackle, especially since giants often fight to the death, literally burning up their muscle tissue and blowing out their great hearts. So Reiger's tournament concentrates on young fish. Last year a dozen vessels caught zero. The Cat Cay Tournament still happens, but the boats don't come in at noon to unload their giants as in the old days. Instead, the entire fleet accounts for maybe one a week. Another NMFS official told me that when a recent billfish tournament out of Bimini accidentally extracted a giant from Hemingway's Alley—the cradle of bluefin-angling tradition—no one knew what it was.

Soon it may be impossible to catch bluefins even by accident. Since 1972, when the population already was depressed, the number of spawning adults in the western Atlantic has decreased 90 percent— from an estimated 225,000 to fewer than 22,000. Presiding over this crash has been a multi-national management body called ICCAT— not an acronym for International Commission to Catch All the Tuna, as conservationists have suggested, but for the International

Commission for the Conservation of Atlantic Tunas. One of the three US commissioners—the chief—plays sock puppet to the fish-industry's right hand, one is a fish-industry lobbyist and one is a recreational angler who lets himself get pushed out of the way by the other two.

ICCAT has a long-standing tradition of ignoring its own scientists. In 1981 they classified western bluefins as depleted and recommended that catches be cut "as close to zero as possible." Instead, ICCAT aped Japanese whalers, establishing a "scientific catch for monitoring purposes" of 1,160 metric tons a year, to be shared by the United States, Canada and Japan.

As generous as this seemed, it so outraged Gerald Abrams, the bluefin exporter, that he called an emergency meeting of tuna traffickers at the New England Aquarium, in Boston. Dave Preble recalls being thoroughly impressed with "the masterful way he worked the crowd" and how he seduced even recreational anglers to fund his crusade for the "American interest" in tuna, though later they reneged when it became evident that the East Coast Tuna Association (the group hatched that night) was to be nothing more than a paid lobby group for the seiners.

Abrams, the new president of the new association, hired an industry consultant to vet ICCAT's data. Lo, the consultant found flaws (none of which changed the basic graph of population decline). The Japanese found flaws, too, so the following year ICCAT raised the quota to 2,660 metric tons. Here it remained until 1991, when this "scientific catch for monitoring purposes" represented 50 percent of the breeding stock. ICCAT scientists warned that such removal was nonsustainable and recommended that the quota be halved.

This made sense to NMFS director Bill Fox, a decent, competent man committed to conservation and the public good. So last November he sent the American commissioners to the ICCAT meeting in Madrid with instructions to ask for the 50-percent cut. For the first time in its 26-year history the US delegation had negotiating plans in writing. But it started backpedaling even before the meeting began. When the Canadians caterwauled, the Americans meekly agreed to a 10-percent cut instead.

The Canadians had argued that just a few surviving open-sea fish can rebuild a population. Often, this is so. As far as is known, humankind has failed to extirpate any of the pelagic fishes. They are mightily prolific, blitzing the planktonic zone with spawn. Biological extinction would take an awful lot of doing. And yet in 1991—considering population trends and fishing pressure, which was up 2,200 percent from 1970 and rising—a future without bluefins seemed possible. The old rules, by which commercial extinction ends the killing, no longer apply. In the 19th Century the last few buffalo were spared because tracking them down didn't make economic sense; one animal wasn't worth a house or even a horse. But given Japanese sashimimania, it just might pay to track down the last bluefin. As it is, boats are willing to stay out two weeks to kill one.

These fish pulse north in units. Very likely there's a population threshold, below which they can't function, migrate or mate. "Maybe we're already below it," suggests Michael Sutton, of the World Wildlife Fund. "Look at the right whale in the western Atlantic. That population is still at about 300 individuals. That's since commercial whaling stopped on that species in the early part of this century." Depletion of the gene pool may increase vulnerability to pollution, global warming and extra ultraviolet radiation associated with ozone loss. Finally, competitors like yellowfin tuna and albacore appear to be expanding into the bluefin's niche. If this continues, the bluefin may wind up like the once-abundant Atlantic halibut, pounded so unmercifully in the 18th Century that it was permanently squeezed out of the food web and can't recover after a century with no directed fishery.

Even if ICCAT weren't run by fishmongers and politicians it would have trouble managing bluefins, because 75 percent of tuna-killing nations aren't members. To ensure the safety of the species, something else had to be tried. NMFS suddenly seemed the perfect vehicle, in that Congress had patched the loophole procured by the tuna industry in 1976, thereby giving the agency management authority for tunas as of 1992. But Abrams and his export lobby executed a brilliant end run, winning an amendment that prevents NMFS from setting a quota lower than ICCAT's. So National Audubon's Safina turned to the 112-nation Convention on International Trade in Endangered Species (CITES).

On behalf of the society, Safina formally requested that the US Fish and Wildlife Service recommend the western Atlantic bluefin population for CITES's Appendix I, a listing which prevents all export. When the service declined, the society—now allied with the World Wildlife Fund, Center for Marine Conservation, National Coalition for Marine Conservation and the Council on Ocean Law—made an end run of its own, asking Sweden to offer the proposal. Sweden, sympathetic because its own bluefins had been mined out years earlier, agreed. The tuna miners went ballistic.

Abrams explained to me that conservationists are whoring for sport-fishermen: "The goal of these élite recreationalists is to make the bluefin tuna a rod-and-reel-only fishery. We've described these people as trick birthday candles—you blow them out and they keep coming back on again. Audubon I guess was looking for something to spread their wings into, birds not being enough to be able to compete with the larger environmental groups. So they latched onto this with Safina . . . . This does not have a blessed thing to do with conservation. This is the most illegitimate crusade, the biggest hoax that's ever been perpetrated on people who pick up the newspaper."

Something smelled fishy. The aroma of fried, baked, smoked, raw, broiled and spoiled samples wafted through the Hynes Convention Center last March 18, at the Tenth International Boston Seafood Show. Bonefishlike, I ghosted through more than a thousand displays, snarking such bait as squid, tilapia, oysters, crabs and salmon. At the booth of Phillips Seafood, of Barnegat Light, New Jersey, I struck up a conversation with an affable young buyer named Dennis Gore. He told me the CITES initiative was "ridiculous" and that there were "many, many bluefin tuna, more bluefins than people realize." The boss, Saul Phillips, declined to speak other than to inform me I was "an environmental terrorist" and that "next year, we'll have the show over at the aquarium, with you guys floating around."

Later I found Robin Alden, publisher and executive editor of *Commercial Fisheries News*. She explained that she'd been brought up as an Auduboner and a naturalist, that environmentalists and commercial fishermen had so very, very much in common. She struck me as someone you could reason with; someone who would favor management over mining, especially when made to see that a fully recovered bluefin stock would yield US fishermen 11,000 metric tons a year instead of the meager, nonsustainable 1,387 tons they take now. Then she gave me a copy of her newspaper, in which she had commented on the CITES initiative: "Elite sportfishing organizations are joining forces with conservation groups to target commercial fishing . . . . Very simply, they want the fish for themselves, as they now have ducks and much game. For opportunistic conservationists, branding fishermen the enemy is a fund-raising gimmick cloaked in good deeds. Fish have become the newest incarnation of the save-the-whale movement and fishermen the latest industrial rapists." So goes the dialogue.

And so it went last March at the CITES convention, in Kyoto, Japan, when the bluefin proposal was hastily withdrawn by Sweden. The Swedes were astonished at what they had stirred up. Clouds of Japanese delegates—50 in all—buzzed around them like hornets. They were hounded by the press. Japanese chefs and seafood dealers waved placards that said: "Down with Sweden," chanted invective, served bluefin sushi and told all who came to eat that if bluefins were listed in Appendix I, all the sushi bars around the world would be forced out of business.

Seiji Masuda, of the Japan Tuna Fisheries Cooperative, called the attempted listing "an outrage aimed at Japanese fish-eating habits." Minoru Tanba, one of Japan's top Foreign Ministry officials, proclaimed that "it is ridiculous to equate bluefin tuna with the coelacanth [an Appendix I fish thought to be extinct until discovered in 1938]." Sweden and other nations were reportedly threatened by Japan with trade sanctions if they voted the wrong way. Delegates from small countries told Safina they would have backed him if the ballot had been secret. The export lobby, led by the Canadians, shut off all debate.

"Very disappointing," says Safina.

"Politics dominated over science," says World Wildlife Fund's Mike Sutton.

"We lost," says Roger McManus, of the Center for Marine Conservation.

True enough. Yet for the first time since the 1960s the future of the bluefin tuna is looking brighter. Recently Abrams lamented to me as follows: "We're only flyweights. You guys are heavyweights. You've got the referees and the judges, and horseshoes in your gloves." He couldn't be more correct; there are approximately 100 Americans who make more than a third of their income catching or exporting giants, and at most Abrams represents 75 of them. What's more, the first tentative left jab by the environmental community produced stunning results. The specter of CITES so terrified Japan, which gets less than 20 percent of its bluefins from the western Atlantic, that at last November's ICCAT meeting it actually supported the 50-percent quota cut aborted by Canadian bluster and American timidity. ICCAT itself is terrified, and by the time you read this there's a good chance it will have upped the cut to at least 25 percent.

If meaningful action isn't taken within two years, there's always the next CITES meeting—to be held, appropriately, in Washington, DC. And there's Bill Fox's NMFS, itching to shed the quota yoke placed on it by Congress at Abrams' bidding. And there's the US Endangered Species Act . . . .

Now, as Safina says, "the bluefin tuna is clearly on the same playing field as the charismatic megafauna of the wildlife conservation movement"—the stuff with legs, fur, flukes and flippers. Now ICCAT is accountable to someone other than Abrams and the East Coast Tuna Association. Now, finally, environmentalists are awake.

UPDATE

My friend and National Audubon Society colleague, Dr. Carl Safina, helped get ICCAT to vote a 50-percent cut in the allowable catch of giants. But between the time ICCAT agreed to the new limit and the time it would take effect, the tuna industry demanded an outside review from the National Resource Council—"a big rush job," says Safina, "with lots and lots of problems, errors and inconsistencies." The review alleged that the population hadn't really declined 90 percent—just 80 percent. The industry used this to lobby Congress, which, in turn, got ICCAT to overturn the 50-percent cut. Then, under pressure from Japan and the industry, ICCAT increased the old quota by 10 percent.

Meanwhile Safina and a bunch of sportfishers successfully petitioned the National Marine Fisheries Service to ban the sale of small bluefin. Now there's a 70-inch minimum size, which corresponds to roughly 230 pounds.

Two years after my piece appeared in *Audubon* I went bluefin fishing off of Rhode Island, landing and releasing nine from 60 to 80 pounds. I felt like I'd played in the Super Bowl without pads.

When I interviewed Safina for this update he'd just visited a sushi bar on Long Island. The owner announced that he had some really great bigeye tuna from Ecuador. Safina, playing dumb, asked if bluefins were being overfished. "Oh, yes," said the owner. "Very overfished. We don't get any here because good stuff go to Japan; and if it not good enough for Japan it terrible." Then he said that the bigeye population is starting to falter. "I think in five or six years no more tuna for sushi."

Safina told me he couldn't believe he finally had met someone who was more pessimistic about bluefins than he is.

No Dogs Allowed

The prairie dog is still denied its rightful place

in the American West

Audubon, September 1992

OUT WEST there are dogs and there are dogs. It's considered quite normal for Jon Sharps, the wildlife biologist who ran South Dakota's endangered-species program until he quit because of "low pay and rancher politics," to count the first kind among his closest friends. His English setters bound around his yard, knowing better than to even look at the loose hens. They point songbirds, "whoa" on command, then "kennel up," leaving contrails of dust along all compass points as they dash exuberantly to their clean, spacious quarters. It's even considered normal for Sharps to engage his dogs in conversation. "Owww, owww, owwwwww," he declares, tilting back his head. "Tell me yo-o-o-our troubles, Speck." And Speck does.

Where the big, powerfully built bachelor of 57 gets his reputation for weirdness is the fact that he also has befriended prairie dogs—ground-dwelling squirrels that, according to more than a century of ranching gospel, compete with cows for forage and so are classified as pests. If you have them on your land, you're expected to poison them off. Refuse and the county weed and pest board can do it for you, attaching the cost to your tax bill.

On public land, poisoning is attended to by the South Dakota Game, Fish and Parks Department, the US Forest Service, the Bureau of Land Management (BLM) and even the National Park Service. If the ranchers have it right, there would have been even more bison, elk, deer, bighorn, antelope and the like two centuries ago had these agencies been around to look after the prairie-dog-infested grasslands that confronted the pioneers and that, even in their "neglected" condition, were several times richer in wildlife biomass than the most productive African savannas.

You count dogs not by the nose but by the acre—as in "700 million acres of dogs." That's how many there were in 1900. Bombing, gassing, flooding, shooting, even germ warfare, reduced dog populations but failed to deliver the nation from the presumed pestilence. "Death to the Rodents," an article by W.B. Bell that ran in the 1920 issue of the *Yearbook* of the US Department of Agriculture, pronounced that prairie dogs cost ranchers $300 million annually by "selecting the most productive valleys and bench lands for their devastating activities." In the same year, the government launched a grand chemical assault on prairie dogs, as 132,000 men festooned 32 million acres with 1,610 tons of poisoned grain.

Today—despite giant vacuum cleaners that suck dogs from their burrows more or less alive—poison still works best. The agent of choice is zinc phosphide, which is quite selective. To establish trust among the dogs you do a "prebaiting" with raw oats in late fall, when food is scarce; wait till they're hungry again; then deliver the spiked grain. When zinc phosphide hits saliva, it produces a phosphine-type gas that attacks the respiratory and nervous systems. "They don't go into convulsions like with strychnine," explains one South Dakota Animal Damage Control officer. "They just lay there in a relaxed state, blinking their eyes, and slowly die."

Now there are but two million acres of dogs nationwide. Still, that's too many for ranchers who graze private cattle on public land. "Eliminate 'em," is what Jack McCulloh, executive secretary of the South Dakota Stockgrowers Association, would like the state and federal governments to do, even though he concedes it's not possible. "Humans look for the best possible position," he told me, "and the best possible position for a prairie dog is to be croaked. How would you Boston guys like it if Boston was full of sewer rats, running all over?"

"It is," I informed him.

"Well, that's just what we're talking about. Hell, we don't like the bastards."

On the fine, gusty morning of May 16, 1992, Jon Sharps and I hike in to a 90-acre dog town in Badlands National Park, kicking up lark buntings and orange-winged grasshoppers. Wildflowers are bursting everywhere, and the prairie grasses are green and dancing in the wind. In a brushy draw a bull bison full of spring and hormones raises his tail at us and we ease past, eyeing the nearest cottonwood. Beyond the draw the prairie is washed with impossible shades of blue and purple. It spreads out into infinite, rolling hills where dark clumps of Rocky Mountain juniper sprout from the moist northern slopes. Along the southern horizon the Badlands dirt formations stand against the azure sky like snow-clad peaks.

Soon the dogs start barking at us, a constant house-sparrow-like chipping. They are black-tailed prairie dogs, the most reviled and widely distributed of the five species. Doglike in behavior, too, they sit erect and wag their black-tipped tails, wrestle like puppies and exchange "kisses" with jaws agape. They are lighter in color and more slender than the Yankee woodchucks in my back meadow. We sneak to within 20 feet of one, and Sharps snaps a photo before it ducks into its burrow. Finally, we settle into a fragrant field of yellow clover under a windbreaking bluff. Gradually the barking subsides, and the citizens of this sleepy, sun-drenched town resume the business of being prairie dogs.

The town is bordered on the east by a little creek that curls through towering cottonwoods and serves as a natural barrier. But in all other directions the dogs are free to colonize new turf. So why haven't they? Why have they squatted on these 90 acres for decades? Why is everything save the relatively bare core area so lush? Why does the prairie wind make waves through the luxuriant expanse of mid-grasses bordering this town? Why are there so many bison droppings? What attracts all the kingbirds, flycatchers, mourning doves and lark sparrows? These dogs have not been affected by the periphery poisoning program—roughly 100 acres every three or four years—that the Park Service agreed to undertake as part of an out-of-court appeasement of the local ranching industry. How is it that they haven't taken over the world?

At another dog town in the park we flush four antelope. Surely it hadn't been idle curiosity that drew them to this alleged ground zero. And why is Sharps suddenly so worried about rattlesnakes? "You don't go walking into a dog town without foot protection," he announces, waiting for me to haul on a set of his cowboy boots.

As we hike through the barking, scurrying, diving townsfolk, I notice that the core area only looks bare. It has pretty much been abandoned and now is coming up in diverse forbs favored by diverse wildlife. According to the federal government (in this case the BLM, which evidently doesn't read its own literature because it hasn't veered from massive poisoning), 10 species of amphibians, 15 of reptiles, 101 of birds and 37 of mammals use black-tailed prairie dog towns.

On the way out we pause to read a Park Service sign. "Prairie dogs," it says, "make the prairie rich. Prairie dogs turn up new soil and fertilize it with their droppings, encouraging prairie plants to grow. They eat the plants, converting grass into prairie dog flesh that feeds snakes, hawks, badgers, swift foxes, coyotes, and black-footed ferrets, an elusive, endangered species not recently seen in the Badlands . . . . Without prairie dogs the prairie could support fewer plants and animals."

At yet another dog town, this one in the cow-blighted Buffalo Gap National Grassland, tended by the US Forest Service, Sharps and I encounter close-cropped, diverse vegetation bombed with cow pies. Like wildlife, cattle prefer dog-town forbs over rangeland grass—at least until early July. "No one forced these cows to come here," comments Sharps. "They know something the cowboys don't."

Even the Forest Service knows as much as the cows. A study conducted on this very area found that plant-production values "where the cattle plus prairie dogs grazed were generally higher than those for areas grazed only by cattle and the ungrazed area." The same study referred to a University of Oklahoma finding: "The influence of prairie dogs on the forage crop did not significantly reduce steer weight gains during either year."

What we have stumbled upon is a "leave town"—a backward term revealing backward priorities. A leave town is a tiny area of public prairie-dog habitat that isn't poisoned off the map, a contrived gesture by the Forest Service or the BLM to prove that ranchers aren't completely in charge of public land. Out West, as Sharps likes to say, "multiple use means multiple cows, and wild animals can have all the grass they want provided it goes through the cows first." So leave towns are "created" not where they are most ecologically significant but where they are least politically offensive.

Like many leave towns, this one is relatively small and very remote, with no stock dam nearby. Unfortunately for the diminutive swift fox, which used to abound in the West and which depends on prairie dogs and species associated with them, this town is perched on a hill and surrounded by rough breaks—ideal coyote habitat. Coyotes eat swift foxes. So do the hawks and eagles drawn to the updrafts created by the steep slopes. "Swift foxes really don't have a chance to make it here in my opinion," says Sharps, who has petitioned the Fish and Wildlife Service to list the species as endangered.

We climb back into the blue Ford pickup and bounce on through our national grassland. Long-billed curlews stalk the damp sinks, and grasshoppers clatter through the open windows, striking us in the neck and cheeks. "We're heading into a town now that has been poisoned out by the Forest Service even though it had a sighting of a swift fox, a state threatened species," says Sharps. The Forest Service had hired him to confirm it, and he had. But the area was scheduled to be poisoned, and schedules are schedules.

Apparently, the Forest Service doesn't read its own literature, either. Agency studies make it clear that prairie dogs are to the Great Plains what sockeye salmon are to Alaska, that they fuel the whole energy flow. In its own three-year-old environmental assessment for prairie dog "management" in the Nebraska National Forest (which includes Buffalo Gap National Grassland), the service states, "Prairie dogs act as ecosystem regulators by altering plant species composition and reducing the standing vegetation, thus maintaining a short-grass plant community. Prairie dogs manipulate the soil, increase plant diversity, and increase animal diversity. Prairie dogs in the mixed-grass prairie create habitat patches characterized by altered species composition [and] lower standing crops of plants, but higher forage quality. Wildlife species and domestic livestock preferentially feed on these prairie dog colonies."

Students of plains ecology agree that prairie dogs are vital to wildlife and, with proper grazing practices, at worst harmless to cows. So why the massive, expensive poisoning? The science behind it is precisely the science behind the theory of spontaneous generation (life from inanimate objects), advanced by Aristotle and successfully tested in the early 1600s by Belgian physician Jan Baptista van Helmont, who placed wheat in a sweaty shirt. Lo, in 21 days it generated adult mice. Denuded range is seen where prairie dogs exist. Ergo, prairie dogs generate denuded range.

But prairie dogs are a symptom, not a disease. To check out predators, they require a clear field of vision. Create one by overgrazing, and you get prairie dogs. Remove one by letting grasses push sunward several inches, and you get rid of prairie dogs. During the drought of the 1970s dogs increased in cowless Badlands National Park from 2,500 acres to 3,200 acres. In the Buffalo Gap National Grassland—stocked with cattle to twice carrying capacity—they increased during the same time from 2,000 acres to 30,000 acres.

"It used to be we had range conservation planning," recalls Erling Podoll, a retired wildlife biologist who worked 36 years with state game and fish agencies, including South Dakota's. "You reduced your herd in dry years; it was just part of the game. Now if they have to reduce herds, they call it a disaster. But that's the way the plains are. If you don't want the high population of dogs, you have to cut down on your number of cattle. We've gone through a century of by-and-large overgrazing. It's become such a way of life that it's accepted."

"Why do managers permit it?" I asked.

"Managers don't really manage," Podoll replied. "Politicians and ranchers manage. It's management by politics."

Out West prairie dog defending isn't considered weird at all, provided you also enjoy blowing them up with high-powered rifles. A 1989 survey in South Dakota revealed that 21,700 recreational dog shooters spent 122,400 days a year pursuing their sport, thereby injecting $4 million into the state's economy. The International Varmint Association, publisher of the now-defunct *Varmint Hunter International* Magazine, which evolved from *Prairie Dog News*, has 3,000 members. "We want to support anything that has to do with good conservation," asserts President Mike Comstock. "IVA has stopped dog poisoning twice before. We've saved tens of thousands of animals . . . . The masses out there don't understand, but we love the animals we hunt. We'll do everything we can to preserve them. We're no different than Ducks Unlimited or the Safari Club."

IVA member and Varmint Hunter International writer George Butland describes a day afield with his AR-15 assault rifle: "I turned the scope's power ring down to 12X, lined up two in a row, and squeezed off my first shot. Then I pulled off two more rounds in quick succession. Wow! The dogs that were flying up were meeting the ones on their way down. I nailed all five of them in under three seconds! What a thrill."

The IVA seeks "IVG." "That's the 'Instant Visual Gratification' of being able to actually see the bullet strike its mark and watch the target disintegrate in the scope," explains Butland. Essential to IVG is the cloud of dog blood that hangs in the prairie air. Nosler bullet company even passes out "Red Mist Society" T-shirts to sales reps and outdoor writers who participate in its annual dog shoot. Because the dog shooters told me their sport is the one viable alternative to chemical warfare and that I could never understand it merely by reading about it, I arranged an expedition with the most famous dog shooter-outfitter in South Dakota—Rich Grable, of Kadoka.

Grable is a short, effervescent man of 56 called Mr. Dog by his neighbors and his license plate. He meets me and two clients—Guy Smith and Ralph Sievert, of Appleton, Wisconsin—at the Sundowner Inn, which he owned until earlier this year and which this weekend has rented 18 rooms to dog-shooting parties. On a ranch out by the Rosebud Sioux reservation we get Guy and Ralph started on "The Prairie Dog Pedestal II," a customized Kawasaki Mule painted in desert camouflage. Guy, manning the bottom 180-degree gun turret, drives; Ralph takes his position on the top turret, which swivels 360 degrees. Stenciled on the ammo box are the words PRAIRIE DOG CONTROL WITHOUT POISON.

I stay in the truck with Mr. Dog, who steadies his heavy-barreled, bolt-action Remington .222 on a Styrofoam window rest melted by clients who let their barrels get too hot. Excitedly, he passes me his dog journal: "Nov. 12, 1991. Dogs were all about 100 yds. and thick as flys. I killed 75 straight once before missing! This might be a record to beat. Shot 494, killed 452; 91 percent. Nov. 13: Can't believe I can shoot so well . . . . Killed 395. Shot 427; 92.5 percent. 7,652 [dogs killed year to date]."

Last year Mr. Dog shot up this town pretty well, and grassy, vacant burrows—rich, loose and moist—stand out like limes on a brown tarpaulin. But there are plenty of survivors; on all sides of us they are barking and sitting erect on their dirt mounds. Mr. Dog bisects a target, sending its hindquarters spinning five feet into the air. "Dead," he announces, punching the kill button on the dashboard-mounted device he made from the counter on a hay baler. The dogs are astonishingly cooperative, seldom flinching even when bullets, traveling at 3,300 feet per second, part their fur. Mr. Dog fires and swings, fires and swings. Two babies stand on their burrow, one with its paws on its sibling's back. Mr. Dog squeezes the trigger, and they both explode in red mist. Last year he killed five with one shot.

On this day the prairie wind is even stronger than it was on my outings with Sharps, but Mr. Dog knows how to allow for it. He is a stupendous marksman. Most of the dogs explode or are cut in half. Bang. "Can ya hear it go plop?" he cackles. Bang. "Dissolved him! Ha, ha." A few dogs wobble drunkenly around town or dive into their burrows minus a lower jaw or a shoulder. "I done somethin' to him," shouts Mr. Dog. "I done somethin' to him, too."

In his alliance with the dog shooters, Jon Sharps has borrowed the philosophy of Winston Churchill, who, when chided for teaming up with Stalin, declared: "I have only one purpose, the destruction of

Hitler, and my life is much simplified thereby. If Hitler invaded Hell, I would make at least a favorable reference to the Devil in the House of Commons." Sharps has plenty of opinions about dog shooting, all of which are irrelevant to the work at hand because the sport does no lasting damage to prairie ecosystems. Prairie dogs are too prolific, and when the law of diminishing returns converts sport to work, the shooters move on. Rich Grable's ammo-box graffiti notwithstanding, dog shooters do not and cannot control populations.

What disgusted me more than dog shooting was that the International Varmint Association, inspired by Grable and Comstock, is one of but two organizations that have supported Sharps in his crusade (the Black Hills Group of the Sierra Club contributed $600) and the only organization that has done so consistently, stridently and in print. Local environmentalists have other priorities—such as fighting expansion of Mount Rushmore's parking lot.

Like Churchill, Sharps has the disposition and tenacity of an English bulldog, taking such decisive if impulsive action as twisting the ears of loud anti-environmentalists who pontificate in bars, stabbing confrontational ranchers in the chest with his forefinger at hearings until they run out of floor and hit the wall with their butts, getting his nose broken in fights and having his hand lacerated by a swift fox who hates politicians even more than he does, while testifying to the state legislature on the ecological significance of prairie dogs. Most recently, he has filed suit against the US Forest Service.

"The prairie dog advisory group, of which I was a member, settled on 19,000 out of almost three-quarters of a million acres that would have prairie dogs on it," he told me. "And then the Forest Service reneged, said 11,000 of those 19,000 acres would be poisoned every three years. I said, 'No, that wasn't what we agreed to.'" The suit is draining him financially, but his dream is to set a precedent nationwide. "There are laws that require federal agencies to manage for wildlife, too," he says. "They're as plain as the ass on a goat."

Indeed they are. "Fish and wildlife habitat shall be managed to maintain viable populations of existing native and desired non-native vertebrate species," proclaims Forest Service Rule 36 CFR 219.19. "The national forests are established and shall be administered for outdoor recreation, range, timber, watershed, and wildlife and fish purposes," proclaims the Multiple-Use Sustained-Yield Act. "All federal departments and agencies shall seek to conserve endangered species and threatened species," proclaims the Endangered Species Act.

It's not as if Sharps is asking for the moon. All he wants is the public's prairie dogs back on 10 percent of the public's prairie-dog habitat. Within a year black-footed ferrets may be reintroduced to the
Buffalo Gap National Grassland. If they reproduce, where are the
young supposed to go? This was one of the questions asked by
Sharps and Grable, both of whom sat on the local coordinated-
resource-management group for ferret recovery before it dissolved
because of rancher intransigence. One reason prairie-dog control is so
popular out West is that it also is ferret control: Poison off the prairie
dogs that ferrets eat and you don't have to worry about the federal
meddling associated with endangered-species management. Jack
McCulloh, whose South Dakota Stockgrowers Association has signed
on with the Forest Service as an amicus curiae against Sharps, says it
best: "We've got nothing against the little critter, but we've got a hell
of a lot against what can happen to you and your property rights. We
didn't develop the country and live out here to have some son of a
bitch take it away from us."

On my way back to Rapid City I spy prairie dogs and pull off the highway. It is a delight to watch the engaging little creatures romping in
this little roadside leave town—part of 6,500 to 8,000 acres of the
Buffalo Gap National Grassland that the Forest Service has agreed
not to poison. Meadowlarks sing from the fence posts, and a red-tailed
hawk hangs in the cloudless sky as if from a diorama wire. It all looks
just like multiple-use management.

Here the Forest Service has erected a handsome wooden sign
explaining that prairie dogs inhabit "about 20,000 acres" (the real figure is 12,000) of Buffalo Gap "as part of the multiple-use management of this national grassland" and that killing some of these prairie
dogs will "return the grassland to a satisfactory ecological condition."

Another case of Forest Service employees not reading Forest
Service literature. But then, I suppose it might be argued that the sign
itself is Forest Service literature. Once engraved in wood, such words
and figures are believed. They give taxpayers a warm, tingly feeling
about the future of their land and their wildlife.

UPDATE

Black-footed ferrets—the most endangered mammal in North
America—have been reintroduced to Badlands National Park, and
they're reproducing. But there isn't a lot of habitat for those ferrets to

expand into, and if they don't find prairie dogs for food and prairie-dog burrows for shelter, they're doomed.

The Buffalo Gap National Grassland would be fine ferret habitat, but the federal government continues to poison prairie dogs there. When this piece appeared in *Audubon*, the Forest Service (which counts poisoned dog towns as active because it never gets a 100-percent kill) claimed that prairie dogs inhabited "about 20,000 acres" of the grassland. The real figure was about 12,000 acres. Today the real figure is about 5,000, and the dog towns are stressed by heavy varmint hunting.

I wish some environmental group would give my friend Jon Sharps a national award. He lost his lawsuit after a gallant effort that left him broke. Then, with help from the Biodiversity Legal Foundation, he petitioned the Fish and Wildlife Service to classify the prairie dog as a Category II species (to be studied for threatened or endangered status). When that effort failed he succeeded in getting his beloved swift fox listed as a Category I species (waiting to be listed). But the Fish and Wildlife Service has assigned a low priority to such action.

"People don't realize how many species depend on prairie dogs," Jon Sharps told me the other day. "Upland plovers, ferrets, raptors, swift foxes . . . . And they're all being sacrificed for surplus cows. All the public land in the West produces just two percent of America's beef. The cry among the ranchers out here is: 'My granddaddy went broke, and my daddy went broke, and by Gawd I got a right to go broke.'"

Hard News on "Soft" Pesticides

EPA-approved pesticides are killing fish and wildlife

Audubon, March 1993

THE PESTICIDE-INDUCED FISH kills that routinely occur in southern Louisiana have been deemed news by the local media for each of the past two growing seasons. Conservative estimates place the 1991 loss at one million fish—largemouth bass, yellow bass, striped bass, bluegill, perch, warmouth, crappie, ladyfish, menhaden, flounder, freshwater drum, mullet, shad, bowfin, gar, carp, buffalo fish and mosquito fish. Crabs, crawfish, shrimp and smaller invertebrates sank to the bottom without being counted.

The 1991 poisonings were among the most massive in US history— 10 times the numbers killed the same summer by a chemical spill that annihilated 40 miles of California's Sacramento River and dominated the news for a week. Still, the national media buried the Louisiana story. And the national environmental community—mainly concerned with pesticide dangers to humans—paid virtually no attention.

Modern "soft" pesticides break down rapidly, as do dead fish in Louisiana's semitropical heat, so investigators from the Louisiana Department of Environmental Quality (DEQ) frequently arrived on the scene too late to establish anything. Still, they were able to prove that azinphos-methyl (AZM) was responsible for 15 separate kills in 1991. The state Department of Agriculture and Forestry (DAF), to which the US Environmental Protection Agency has delegated responsibility for enforcing federal pesticide regulations, disagreed right up until it was politically impossible to do so. And later it said the kills had been "acts of God," because heavy thunderstorms had followed the AZM applications.

But God had been doing this fairly regularly in Louisiana at least since 1974. And He did it again in 1992, when, explained the DAF, "thunderstorms [also] caused a runoff of the chemical." In a separate statement the agency asserted that "the unpredictable nature of thunderstorms in south Louisiana this time of year makes the possibility of runoff likely."

As with many other short-lived poisons, AZM came into wide use about 20 years ago as an alternative to DDT and its persistent cousins—the chlorinated hydrocarbons. So giddy were environmentalists about their victory in controlling the food-chain biocides that they accepted the relatively light, one-shot mortality associated with soft pesticides. In southern Louisiana AZM took the place of endrin in protecting sugarcane—the state's second-biggest crop, after cotton—from a slender moth larva called the cane borer. Farmers eventually embraced AZM. Environmentalists spoke of a new age of cooperation with agribusiness, then joined other battles.

AZM and its many relatives short-circuit an organism's nervous system, binding with an enzyme that controls electrical impulses at synaptic sites throughout the body. Muscles contract in random sequence, and the victim usually dies of respiratory failure. In fish the symptoms are unmistakable; you find them just vibrating on the surface or dead with their pectoral fins thrust forward. That's how DEQ biologists found them in 1991, in the bayous around the cane fields hours after spraying. Dissolved oxygen levels were normal, and prominent among the dead were species most tolerant of oxygen depletion. In 14 of the 15 cases, traces of AZM were found in the water. Still, DAF Commissioner Bob Odom blamed low oxygen, a common cause of fish mortality in hot weather.

"DAF just would not give any information," recalls Helen Vinton, a trained biologist based in New Iberia who was then a member of the Louisiana Pesticide Advisory Commission. "What we knew was only what they would put out. They kept saying, 'We do not have the tests back yet, but we will inform you as soon as we do.' There was a spirit of 'Hide everything, go to the bunker.' I kept writing to Odom and the other commissioners. I'd say, 'We need to have a public forum.' There was no answer; that was their method of dealing with it."

Under intense public pressure, Odom set up a "blue-ribbon panel" to investigate the kills, packing it with pesticide apologists and excluding the DEQ. Even so, the panel criticized him for failing to report an eyewitness account in which, on the eve of the big kill at

Bayou Lafourche, a biplane was observed spraying the bayou as well as adjacent sugarcane.

When the DAF withheld documents on crop duster violations, Maureen O'Neill—then chief of the DEQ's water-quality office—marched into a panel meeting and towed a DAF official into the hall, where a confrontation ensued. The DAF's response to the fish kills outraged her. "I could not believe this was going on," she told me. "When it became clear to me that Agriculture was not going to deal with this, I decided I would. Somebody had to."

The DAF kept withholding information, and the farmers kept spraying. Eventually, when the cane borers were no longer much of a threat, Odom suspended the use of AZM and replaced it with cyfluthrin (also deadly to fish) under the emergency exemptions of the Federal Insecticide, Fungicide and Rodenticide Act (FIFRA). But the Environmental Protection Agency, charging that the DAF had "abused" the statute by failing to prove the ineffectiveness of gentler alternatives, revoked the exemption.

Louisiana pesticide infractions are considered by the state Pesticide Advisory Commission, which then recommends enforcement action to the DAF. But Odom had also packed the commission with pesticide apologists, including its chairman, a sales rep for Mobay Corporation (now Miles, Inc.), which manufactures formulations of both AZM and cyfluthrin. When a pilot was cited for spraying in the rain, the Mobay representative cast the deciding vote to drop the charges.

The only significant enforcement action associated with the fish kills of 1991 was a $25,000 pollution fine imposed by O'Neill on a flying service she caught killing fish, crawfish, turtles, snakes and at least one duck by washing AZM tanks in a drainage canal. However, after incoming governor Edwin W. Edwards replaced O'Neill, the fine was rescinded on grounds that clemency would foster good will between the DEQ and the DAF.

The local media were more casual in their scrutiny of the six AZM fish kills of 1992. For one thing, poisoned fish were old news. For another, Hurricane Andrew killed many more fish by choking waterways with oxygen-depleting vegetation. Once again the DAF went to the bunker. And once again Odom suspended use of AZM when the cane borer ceased to be a major threat.

"Before the 1992 season DAF and the extension service held one meeting for something like seven counties," reports Wilma Subra, who runs her own chemistry lab and environmental consulting firm in

New Iberia. "I went and sat on the back row, and they were telling the farmers how last year everyone got in trouble and there was a lot of misinformation going around, and that this chemical was completely harmless; if we apply it right, everything will be fine. They never leveled with the farmers. When we had the fish kills in 1992 one of the farmers even held the runoff water in a holding area for twenty-four hours [AZM's half-life], then discharged it and caused a massive fish kill. DAF hadn't told him that 'half-life' means that half the stuff is still poisonous."

When I interviewed Odom at his Baton Rouge office last December he claimed everything was copacetic, especially now that the DEQ wasn't attacking his agency. "We were being sabotaged by a young lady by the name of Maureen O'Neill with DEQ. She had a vested interest in seeing [regulation of] pesticides moved over there." I asked if he'd ever had any reports of human health problems related to AZM application. "We have not had any health complaints," proclaimed DAF Commissioner Odom.

FIFRA—enacted in 1947—is a reasonable law capable of protecting species not targeted for pesticide control. How is it that the new generation of soft pesticides registered under this statute and applied according to instructions on the label is killing fish and wildlife? I didn't find the answer in Cajun country. Louisiana's Department of Agriculture and Forestry isn't the problem; it's just a spot spawned by a pox infecting the EPA and contracted from a society that believes ardently in a quick chemical fix for everything from chinch bugs to insomnia.

The basic tenet of FIFRA is that a pesticide may be used only if benefits outweigh risks. But that standard isn't applied. For instance, last summer—over the strident objections of its own Ecological Effects Branch, as well as of the US Fish and Wildlife Service—the EPA granted California an emergency exemption for fenamiphos, a cousin of AZM long known to be deadly to fish and wildlife when used as directed. Supposedly, benefits to broccoli and cauliflower outweigh risks to migratory birds and endangered species.

But when I obtained the benefits analysis under the Freedom of Information Act, I learned that the EPA had merely asked California officials what they thought: "Conversations with knowledgeable experts in the state indicated that the other nematocides that are currently federally registered on broccoli and cauliflower are unsatisfactory." That was it!

Biologists employed at the EPA's Ecological Effects Branch are bashful with the press, so I found one who had quit. "What needs to be exposed," declared the biologist, "is that people are misled because they think there's this big federal apparatus safeguarding the environment. I often talk to homeowners who use pesticides and come up with dead birds, and they're just shocked. Farmers the same way. They want to do right. They feel that the material is there for them, and if they use it correctly, everything will be fine. That's not the case at all. The whole pesticide-registration system is a sham.

"If one looks at the records, one finds a constant pattern of scientists saying this stuff is positively *nuclear.* You follow that chain of paper through to what the agency tells chemical companies, and the advice is, 'Don't worry, be happy.' "

When William K. Reilly took over as administrator in 1989, the EPA at last began to act—but never fully or swiftly and only after a media flap had generated political pressure. A case in point is the settlement on granular carbofuran negotiated on May 14, 1991, with registrant FMC Corporation of Philadelphia, 19 years after the first documentation of a bird kill caused by this nerve poison. So toxic to wildlife is carbofuran that ranchers use it illegally to kill coyotes and eagles. Eagles have been found dead with their heads still in the gut cavity of carbofuran-poisoned coyotes. Vultures and magpies have succumbed after scavenging the eagle carcasses. In Virginia, where the poison is now banned, dead birds had turned up on 10 of 11 treated farms surveyed.

"This is nasty stuff, the black plague of pesticides," comments Paul Nickerson, endangered species chief for the Fish and Wildlife Service's northeast region. "In my opinion it should not be put in the environment in any formulation, in any circumstances, at any time. We hammered EPA. Every time we had a dead bird we'd write them another letter. We laid it on them hard, and finally they negotiated with FMC."

But the deal permits FMC to export granular carbofuran, to sell it domestically until September 1, 1994, to keep selling it thereafter for "minor" uses (about five percent of the previous volume), to keep selling liquid carbofuran—which also kills wildlife—and to appeal each step of the phaseout. It's like granting Sunday furloughs in Central Park to Son of Sam.

The EPA has signed off on a similar belated, inadequate settlement with the various companies registering parathion, another nerve poison that under normal label use causes widespread mortality in shorebirds, raptors, songbirds, and waterfowl in the prairie-pothole region of the Great Plains, where it poisons ducklings directly and deprives survivors of their invertebrate prey. In September 1991 the EPA canceled "most uses" of parathion, but not most parathion; roughly half the past volume still can be applied to nine major crops. The news release announcing the partial ban elated environmentalists because parathion regularly kills people and because the EPA promised sweeping action on applications not yet outlawed: "The Agency remains concerned that these uses still may result in unacceptable avian and aquatic risks, in addition to any remaining human risks. Therefore, EPA is preparing to issue a notice of intent to cancel the nine remaining parathion uses."

Exactly 14 months later I asked Al Heier, the contact person listed on the EPA release, how cancellation was going. It wasn't. In fact, he didn't think cancellation was in the cards. "We don't have the data to do that," he said. I asked him about the reams of shocking, incriminating data supplied by the Fish and Wildlife Service, which, in its words, "indicate 'unreasonable adverse effects' "—FIFRA's canon for cancellation. "Not adequate," he said.

But an internal memo by Robert Zendzian, of the EPA's Health Effects Division, suggests that even back in 1988 the EPA had sufficient data to cancel *all* uses of parathion. "We are held up by a refusal to act on the bird-kill data, which looked good enough in March 1988 and April 1991," he wrote last year. "Another stall has been proposed: Let's have a public meeting 'to gather information.' This should take about a year, during which we will get a new Assistant Administrator (and a new Administrator) and we can start all over again. Four more years!"

The nerve poison diazinon is peddled by supermarkets and lawn-care companies as if it were Dr. Kickapoo's Elixir for Blindness, Baldness and Brown Grass. More than 150 bird die-offs caused by diazinon application have been documented by the Fish and Wildlife Service.

When I asked Al Heier why diazinon was still legal on lawns, he explained that there wasn't enough evidence to ban it, that "it's hard to find dead birds."

"But shouldn't the registrant be required to prove that it *doesn't* kill birds?" I persisted.

"Once it comes on the market, it becomes the government's obligation to prove that it is a problem," he averred.

Politically perhaps; not legally. According to the Code of Federal Regulations: "The burden of persuasion that a pesticide product is entitled to registration or continued registration . . . is always on the proponent(s) of registration."

While these proponents are fully aware of what their products do to wildlife, applicators are not. The Fish and Wildlife Service now is prosecuting applicators of diazinon and other poisons who are left liable by the EPA's pesticide-registration system. WMI (Waste Management, Inc.) Urban Services, then doing business as Tru-Green, says it was following the directions on the label when it trustingly applied diazinon to the lawn of Sun Lakes Condominiums in Indianapolis. Still, it killed 47 mallards and last November pled guilty to violating the Migratory Bird Treaty Act. As part of the plea agreement the company was fined $4,700.

Homeowners who use diazinon can also be held legally accountable for birds they kill. And they assume that because the stuff is registered, it must be safe around the home. "I was in this store," says Fish and Wildlife Service environmental contaminant specialist Dan Sparks. "There was a mom, and she had one kid in the cart and one kid walking along. She had this 20-pound bag of diazinon sitting in the cart within inches of this child. It just boggles my mind that people are so ignorant of what this stuff can do. It's sold in the stores an aisle or two over from the food."

One reason trade in wildlife-killing pesticides remains so brisk is that the chemical industry plays musical chairs with the EPA and EPA-designated state enforcement agencies. For example, before becoming Louisiana's chief pesticide regulator, Bob Odom was a "pesticide consultant"—a euphemistic job description usually meaning salesman. The doors revolve the other way, too. A former senior attorney in the pesticide section of the EPA's Office of General Counsel, Ed Gray, is now vice-president of the pesticide consulting firm of Jellinek, Schwartz, Connolly and Freshman. He warns that yanking registration of a poison might be a constitutionally forbidden "taking" of private property, and he demands that the Fish and Wildlife Service explain to him why it's in a snit about liquid carbofuran when "the number of birds known to be killed by that pesticide annually is at most a small fraction of one percent of the tens of millions of birds killed by sport hunters."

Further, companies hawking pesticides are persistent, aggressive and sophisticated. They lavish research grants on the universities that produce state and federal pesticide regulators, and they are skilled at using congressional pressure to intimidate federal bureaucrats.

Environmental groups concerned about pesticides, on the other hand, are unfocused and inconsistent. Instead of making a logical case to the EPA, they rant about such nonissues as the minuscule risk of cancer in people, thereby perpetuating the image of themselves as impractical zealots and of the EPA as a human-protection agency with no responsibility for fish or wildlife.

Not that the effects of soft pesticides on humans are insignificant. William Fontenot, public protection coordinator for the Louisiana Department of Justice, has tried—with scant success—to organize citizens on pesticide issues. "When I've found clear cases of health impacts, people were so dysfunctional from the chemical exposure that they were unable to deal with organizing," he told me. "They were either weak or unable to concentrate long enough to organize. A lot of these are neurotoxins, so you lose your normal ability to think and process information. We just don't hear from them. It's a very serious problem nationally, not just here in Louisiana."

Fontenot was skeptical of Odom's claim that the DAF had received no health complaints about AZM exposure. And Marion Moses—a doctor from San Francisco who studies pesticide poisoning and who visited Louisiana after the 1991 fish kills—describes her collection of health complaints from cane-field spraying as "a textbook of organophosphate poisoning." Finally, former state pesticide adviser Helen Vinton produced a computer printout of 27 health complaints filed with the DAF from July 10 to September 19, 1991.

On Vinton's advice, I journeyed 20 miles west of Baton Rouge, to the village of Grosse Tete, population 756, which is counted on the DAF's list as one complaint. The sweet scent of burning cane stubble hung in the still December air; as I pulled off the freeway, old cane stalks crunched under the tires. Most of the villagers are black—direct descendants of slaves who began working cane here when it was transplanted from Santo Domingo in the late 18th Century. Over the past 15 years or so they've lost their jobs to machines, but still they live beside the cane in small houses, shacks and trailers. "No drugs. No profanity. No alcohol. Violators will be prosecuted," commands the sign on the tidy playground nestled against the freshly cut cane field.

Not knowing where to start, I popped into the town hall for suggestions. Present were Shawn Washington, his sister Venecia, Catherine Etienne, Sheryl Harris, Mary Hawkins and clerk Orabell Johnson. All allowed they'd fallen sick minutes or hours after an August 1991 spraying. Reported symptoms included acute asthma, eye irritation, severe rashes and vomiting for up to two weeks.

"I was pregnant at the time," remarked Hawkins, "and I was throwing up blood. I went to the hospital, and they put a tube up my nose to pump the blood out." Hawkins carried her baby to term, but her cousin, Debra Domino, didn't.

Domino, who phoned me later from her new home, in Marietta, Georgia, had this to say: "I saw this yellow plane fly over, and my youngest son, Eric, started throwing up. I started having pains. I was five-and-a-half months pregnant, so I went to the hospital. My baby was born, and he lived a week and a day."

Behind the counter at the bank I found Ruby Blanchard, who reported that her husband had passed out during the incident and is now on medication for severe lung congestion. Her son still gets dizzy spells, and both daughters have rashes. When the yellow plane started bombing their home with AZM they'd called the police. The responding officer, Willie Harry, had been made sick too, but cured himself, he told me later, by drinking half a gallon of milk. Other Grosse Tete residents revealed they'd had the same symptoms in past years but hadn't said anything. It was just part of their lot, part of living next to sugarcane.

Woodcock were fluttering across the day's afterglow as I left Grosse Tete. With me were my notes, a stalk of sugarcane and a message for environmentalists focused on human pesticide exposure. The message is this: No one says you shouldn't worry about people first; but if you really do, you need to protect fish and wildlife. Fish and wildlife are more sensitive; they always die first. Had the national environmental community noticed the Louisiana fish kills, had the EPA acted early in the summer of 1991, the people of Grosse Tete might not have been sprayed. As Moses says, "a million dead fish is a pretty big red flag."

The last question I asked Commissioner Bob Odom was what he intended to do about AZM in 1993. "I'm probably going to allow it to be used and monitor it very closely," he proclaimed. "If we end up getting a problem with it, then I'll come by again and step in and do something."

Somehow I didn't feel reassured.

UPDATE

The public continues to douse its lawns with diazinon. Liquid carbofuran remains on the market. Bob Odom is still Commissioner of the

Louisiana Department of Agriculture and Forestry and still denying that pesticides are a major health threat. While Odom continues to permit the use of AZM, most farmers have moved away from it. There have been no pesticide-related fish kills in the state since I wrote the article.

But in Youngsville, Louisiana a sugarcane farmer was spraying his fields with a herbicide called Prowl. Somehow, he missed and hit a school, which, having sucked the stuff up into its air-conditioning system, had to be closed and cleaned. Prowl is almost a psychedelic yellow, and it got all over the children and teachers and janitors, making them sick. They couldn't sleep, and they suffered memory loss and muscle-control problems. Prowl is also vile smelling. "When parents picked their kids up, they thought they'd poo-pooed in their pants," reports Wilma Subra. They also wondered why they were psychedelic yellow.

The Tragic Folly of Mowing Down Forests

Destroying the Earth as man did not make it

Atlantic Salmon Journal, Summer 1993

"AT LEAST THEY'RE REPLANTING," declared guide Mort last September as he spun the steering wheel and sent his gear-laden truck cavorting into yet another plot of identical spruce clones goose-stepping their way to maturity. From the higher ridges we could look out over the scarlet, golden remnants of New Brunswick's mixed-hardwood forest now draped with rectangular clearcuts. They did not look like the clearcuts you see in *Sierra*.

No longer was the earth raw and bleeding. In most cases it was green and lush like the soybean fields spreading through the bottom-land forests of the southern United States. Mort is smart and woods-wise; he has worked since childhood in what lately has been called Canada's "industrial forest." He's hardly a fan of clearcutting; it's just that clearcutting has a way of sneaking up on you, and the corporations engaging in it have a way of programming your mind. On the surface it seemed to Mort, as it seems to most everyone, that "replanting" a forest is better than what is actually the next worst thing commonly done—removing it and walking away. You might even have called the clearcuts "pretty," unless you remembered what had been there before industrial forestry—the deer yards, the woodpecker nests, the grouse and woodcock coverts, the nutrients, the topsoil, the icy rills funneling salmon and trout fry to the Miramichi.

Ten years ago, when there seemed to be more time to fish and when

I believed it was possible to "teach" people things instead of merely providing them with learning opportunities, I'd have lectured Mort. I'd have told him a forest is a living system of interdependent parts that include not just trees but an endless array of photosynthesizing plants, as well as fungi, microbes, insects, fish, reptiles, amphibians, birds and mammals—all linked and functioning together in ways humans don't begin to comprehend; about how you can't "replant" a forest, just *replace* it with a commercial crop that's no more a forest than is a cornfield. Instead, I decided to let Mort take me salmon fishing, then write him an article after the season.

There is nothing modern or scientific about the practice of cutting down all the trees. It is as old as axes. By 1890 every board foot of Minnesota's merchantable timber had been razed, and in Wisconsin just 80 acres remained, spared only by a survey error in a plot too remote for loggers to profitably revisit. For half a century North Americans experimented with selective forestry, a science introduced by President Theodore Roosevelt and his chief forester, Gifford Pinchot. Then, pressured by timber demands of the post-World-War-II housing boom, we reverted to old-style forest removal—first on the sunset side of the Cascades in Washington and Oregon. This time, however, public-relations personnel wearing white smocks and yellow hardhats and calling themselves "scientists" referred to it as "clearcutting" and came up with all manner of impressive sounding explanations as to why it was necessary. As a noted forestry professor at Syracuse University, Dr. Leon S. Minckler, commented a few years later: "They make up their mind and then seem to search for ecological, silvicultural and economic reasons to support this decision. This has involved some pretty awful science and economics."

In the early 1960s computers started coming into commercial use, making it possible for black-suited executives to supervise a forest without rising from their desks, provided their underlings sheared the trees in patches big enough to be easily photographed from the air. Among the fly-bitten, mud-stained foresters who still studied trees out where they grew, clearcuts became known as "idiot blocks." In the words of one such forester—Gordon Robinson, who lived through the regression to clearcutting and the propaganda blitz to legitimize it as a silvicultural tool—"Clearcutting was practiced by most lumber companies simply because they had no intention of returning for another 'crop' of trees." Robinson tells the story of refusing to sell his company's holdings to International Paper because the deal would have violated sustained-yield policy, and how IP's representative had summed up the real motive for early clearcuttings in 24 words: "Hell, Robbie. We're on sustained yield. When we clean up the timber in the West, we'll return to New England, where the industry began."

As timber got cleaned up in both the West and the East, some clearcutters remained on their privately held sites, replacing diverse habitat with sterile monocultures vulnerable to disease and insects and therefore addicted to chemical fertilizers and insecticides. Promulgating and promoting the superstition that a forest can and should be "replanted" has been Weyerhauser Co., the multinational "tree-growing company."

According to Weyehauser, "even the animals like the idea" of slash-and-plant fiber production. But if, like Dr. Doolittle, one could talk to the animals, one would hear a different story. Beavers and porcupines, for example, get the death penalty for trespassing on company land. As one Weyerhauser official remarked, "It's not very pleasant, but what else can you do? No one wants rats in their cellar, do they?"

"Every day that dawns we renew our partnership with the land by planting and seeding 250,000 new trees from Maine to California," pronounces Georgia-Pacific Corp., as if it were engaged in some sort of husbandry rather than chemicalized, mechanized warfare against nature. The fact is that in most temperate habitats one must work diligently to render the earth incapable of naturally regenerating native trees. If a company really needs to replant, it should have been more careful or not cut where it did in the first place.

Still, the wood-fiber industry avers that it has no alternative to clearcutting. Even the American Forestry Association, allegedly a private group that espouses "intelligent management and use of forests, soil, water, wildlife, and all other natural resources," proclaims that "clearcutting is necessary as a harvest method where the desired tree and related species require full sunlight to flourish." But clearcutting, as practiced in North America, is the antithesis of intelligent management. It's a strip-mining of cellulose whereby all life, plant and animal, is removed from hundreds or thousands of acres; soil and streams are ripped apart by heavy machinery; slash bulldozed to the center and burned; and the whole site drenched with herbicides to kill off unwanted hardwoods. It has nothing to do with science and nothing to do with a quest for increased sunlight.

"Biologically, no types or species appear to require large clear-cuttings [over 10 acres] for successful regeneration," writes Jerry Franklin, chief plant ecologist at the Pacific Northwest Forest and

Range Experiment Station. And David Smith, a forestry professor at Yale and author of the standard textbook on silviculture, offers the following comment about Douglas fir—the species first said by the timber industry to regenerate only in full sunlight and therefore to demand complete removal: "It is actually fortunate that the routine of clearcutting, burning, and seeding or planting has worked at all. In most instances the optimum environment for young Douglas firs is found underneath partial shade."

Such is the pseudoscience of clearcutting. But what of its economics? The argument is that selective logging is just too expensive, too labor intensive. Is it? Who identifies the costs? Who tallies them? I put these questions to David Stearns, CEO of Lac Megantic Pulp Company, who took over from his father, Mac, who had taken over from his father, George, who had started logging southern Québec in 1888. Over the past decade the company has gotten pretty much out of pulp and timber production; but selective logging had always been a highly profitable family business, a business run on a sustained-yield basis for the next fiscal year as well as the next century. The family manages not just for wood but for other forest products as well—maple syrup, for instance, game birds, game mammals and, especially, wild brook trout. "We never got into clearcutting," David Stearns told me. "It didn't dawn on us that it was the thing to do."

Since each Stearns looked beyond his presidency and even his own life, none ever thought the company could *afford* to cut down all the trees. But today your average vice-president for woodlands of your average paper company can reasonably hope to be in office five to 10 years. "He has to make a name for himself," Stearns explains. "And what happens afterwards, well who cares?"

As Stearns observes, one of the costs of clearcutting is wild salmonids, and their worth, even in terms of hard dollars, is almost never taken into account. For instance, clearcutting on 33 sites along California's Smith River resulted in soil loss 500 to 2,000 percent over natural levels, and severe damage to trout and salmon habitat. "Downslope effects can last for years, perhaps from 25 to 100 for debris slides," reported the US Forest Service. The remains of the Smith River fishery were estimated by the Forest Service to be worth $7.8 million a year. Over the next 140 years—the time it will take to grow one harvestable crop of trees—the Smith River could, if protected from clearcutting, produce 140 harvestable crops of trout and salmon worth more than $1 billion.

The South Fork of the Salmon River was the most important

salmon and steelhead stream in Idaho. Now, however, the runs and even the strains themselves are endangered. Clearcutting on 8,600 acres of the watershed sent fragile soils cascading into the river. As one witness testified to the US Senate: "The land began to move. Along 25 miles of the South Fork the soil seemed to dissolve and run like wet concrete. Roads slumped and collapsed for great distances . . . . The forest opened to reveal swatches of naked bedrock, as dislodged trees flowed away." About 500 slides dumped 400,000 cubic yards of sediment into the river. Value of extracted timber: $14 million. Cash value of salmonids lost, estimated by both Idaho and the US Forest Service: $100 million.

"Reflect," says Yale's David Smith, "on how often one hears the judgment that a certain mode of procedure would be 'silviculturally desirable' but 'economically unfeasible.' Then consider how often these terms really translate into 'desirable from the long-term economic standpoint' and 'unfeasible in terms of the immediate objective of minimizing present logging costs.' "

In the flatter, wetter East the effects of clearcutting on wild salmonids are less obvious but no less serious. With all the other ills besetting Atlantic salmon, forest removal has received little attention. And the international support group for brook trout is relatively disorganized and non-influential. Two summers ago I returned to the Maine woods where I had fished and gone to college and worked for clearcutters, pushing their pulp logs on the last river drives. I remember catching fish until my flies fell apart and, on my way out of the dark, damp, mossy forest, drinking from springs where tiny trout and salmon flashed away from me like welding sparks. Now the springs have evaporated and the fish with them. The bare earth is desiccated for miles in all directions. Three of us fished half a dozen ponds, taking one trout in five days. What we fished in and hiked through is not a forest. It is not even an "industrial forest." What it is is *gone*.

You see the effect of clearcutting on North America's Atlantic salmon rivers, too. No longer does one get the fine angling that came with slowly dropping water levels. The clearcutters have transformed entire watersheds from sponges that filter, cool and store water to dirt parking lots that pollute, heat and shunt it. The Miramichi—the greatest salmon producer on the continent—has been made into a spate river, and in the process salmon populations have been depressed. Bill Hooper, New Brunswick's head salmon biologist, has seen a dramatic change since the advent of heavy clearcutting in the

1960s. "We have water-gauge stations all over the province," he says. "The freshets used to occur in May. But after the 1960s, freshets started coming much earlier—in April. These days you get low water periods in June and July where, before the 1960s, there was hardly any low water in summer. Back then you just had a long, steady drain-off until the September rains. Now, when we get these summer droughts, the rivers shrink to about a third of their regular size; and, obviously, habitat shrinks by that much. Something has to die.

"Ours are gravel, bedload-type streams. I've noticed in the last 20 years that we get movements of this bedload material. You'll have these gravel islands built up where none used to be. I think that this runoff is so large and so fast that it actually picks up the bedload material and places is somewhere else."

It takes a lot of thermal pollution to kill adult Atlantic salmon. Even so, clearcutters along the Northwest and Little Southwest branches of the Miramichi accomplished it during the summer of 1987. Moonscaping of the surrounding woods had shrunk the river and heated the flow to 83 degrees Fahrenheit. "Ironically, it was the rain that was the final straw," reports Hooper. "The water hit these big unshaded boulders and beaches, which acted as heat sinks. That triggered the 84-degree crisis, and fish started popping off like flies."

A few miles from these clearcuts I recently toured what, to the best of my knowledge, is the biggest entirely selective pulpwood/saw-timber operation left in eastern North America. Ever since Bill MacKinnon started logging in 1946 he has practiced Roosevelt/Pinchot-style forestry. He does this not because it is biologically and morally correct, although it is; not because he is an ardent salmon angler and conservationist, although he is; but because it is *profitable*. MacKinnon grows and harvests two-and-a-half times more volume per acre than the clearcutters that surround him. And, while the clearcutters in this region can't return to a site for 80 years, he averages 17 years between cuts.

One reason MacKinnon's neighbors clearcut is that trees can be worth more than the land itself. The owner cuts out, gets out, then invests his money in something more quickly lucrative than growing wood fiber. But MacKinnon is in business for the long haul. He and his father before him would purchase clearcut lots for $10 an acre, then nurse them back to health.

Although MacKinnon uses conventional skidders, he favors draft horses because they don't tear up topsoil or rip out seedlings or swill fossil fuel. You switch them to automatic pilot with a pat on the rump, and they strike off through the woods alone, hauling logs to the loader, lifting them to the top of the loading platform via chains and pulleys, then returning to the logger. The cut was almost complete, but the woods looked just like that—woods.

On our way out we stopped on a wooden bridge spanning a clear, cold tributary of the Miramichi. Quartz gravel the color of brook-trout fin trim covered the bottom; the overhanging banks were carpeted with lush ferns and the leathery leaves of cowslip. We watched wordlessly until we saw what we'd seen on the way in—a troutling, or maybe parr, scooting downstream into a dark, damp, mixed hardwood forest full of deadwood, decadence and disorder. I recognized it as the "enchanted forest" of my Maine youth, the kind those public-spirited "scientists" in the white smocks and yellow hardhats keep cleaning up and replacing. It is a forest that grows good trees and good fish. But according to current wisdom, it is a forest that is old and obsolete—just like MacKinnon, his horses and all who love wildness and the Earth as man did not make it.

UPDATE

Bill MacKinnon has sold 22,500 of his 25,500 acres to Doaktown Lumber Company. "They said they were going to manage the forest selectively," he says. "But they're clearcutting."

In July 1995, with much puffing about how awful he felt and how it went against his green nature, President Bill Clinton signed a rescissions bill that carried an amendment allowing Big Timber to clearcut national forestland set aside for endangered wildlife and wilderness. The new law defines "salvage" as removal of dead, dying, diseased or "associated" trees—that is, trees that are near a dead, dying or diseased tree.

"I've never met a tree that wasn't dying," declares Andy Stahl, the professional forester who directs the Association of Forest Service Employees for Environmental Ethics. As if this provision weren't bad enough, the salvage law unleashes the timber industry in green forests, and not just for phony preemptive strikes against future fire damage. It orders the Forest Service to reschedule old, illegal timber sales in the Pacific Northwest that had been canceled under court order because they jeopardized marbled murrelets, spotted owls and salmon. Some of these "Section 318 sales," as they are called, were hatched in the 1970s. So now the legal definition of "salvage logging" is *any* logging.

Twilight of the Yankee Trout

If Maine trout fishers would only stop behaving like goats

Trout, Autumn 1993

THE ANCIENT CEDAR RAFT HOVERED over Secret Pond's air-clear spring hole; Maine's endless, silent forest and its reflection above, below and all around; in my hand, a wild brook trout. The fish, perhaps three-quarters of a pound, was immense by our standards. The markings on the green back resembled grub trails on the inside of dead elm bark. Chestnut flanks were spattered with scarlet flecks, each ringed with an azure halo, bottom fins trimmed with ivory, belly brighter than a New England sunset. It was the most beautiful fish or, for that matter, creature that I had ever seen. I ran my thumb up through the gills and lanced the spine, then held the quivering carcass aloft for my Colby College roommate, Robert J. "No-Birds" Daviau, of Waterville, Maine, who was brought up to believe that the Pine Tree State rides atop a giant tortoise and that her borders fall away into primal chaos. "Eeee Tabernac," he shouted from the other raft. The year was 1966.

No-Birds, who himself knows of nothing more beautiful than wild brook trout (unless possibly ruffed grouse, whose aerial acrobatics gave him his name), had taught me that there is also no food more succulent when fried in bacon fat over dry popple and eaten with your fingers to the mad, discordant strains of loonsong. In Maine, throwing back a perfectly good trout was and is seen as sinful, akin to not cleaning your plate. In the words of life-long Mainer Bill Vail, who worked his way through the Warden Service to the helm of the state Department of Inland Fisheries and Wildlife, "Catch-and-release to an awful lot of people in Maine is an élitist, yuppie idea that comes from somewhere outside and ought to be fought at all costs. If they're not successful at defeating us at the public hearings, they go to the legislature." A case in point is the repeal last year of the lures-only law for the Kennebec River from Harris Dam to Skowhegan.

The regulation, if not quite catch-and-release, was seen as the next worst thing. It had been proposed in 1991 by Maine Trout, an 80-member group then led by chemistry professor Sam Butcher, of Bowdoin College (an institution technically in Maine but so far south as to be considered "out-a-state"). The idea was to save all the wild brook trout that would be released now that the length limit on the river has been extended from six to 10 inches and the bag limit reduced from five to two—also at the behest of Maine Trout.

Fisheries and Wildlife liked the lures-only notion, mostly because it unsnarled a morass of complicated rules. Locals had little to say one way or the other, and the measure sailed through. But when they read the lures-only notices in 1992 they bawled like mired Herefords. The kids (always it was "the kids") couldn't go worming like their fathers and grandfathers. Local culture was being flung down and danced upon by snotty, tweedy, fly-casting intellectuals probably born in Massachusetts. A phone-book-size petition was flung at the feet of the legislature, and Vail was required to hold another hearing. "I was reluctant to do it because once you start jumping through hoops on these things, you can very quickly have to change the whole damn law book," he told me. "It was one of the few public hearings where I lost my temper. I pounded the table to the point where my fist hurt, trying to get order. The only proponents for the original change were the people from Maine Trout. There were two or three of them there, and I still admire their courage. They were from 'away,' didn't even talk like Mainers." Bait was reinstated.

Maine has the only significant populations of decent-size wild brook trout remaining in the Eastern United States. With the exception of a few major streams, especially those connected to lakes, the biggest fish abide in stillwater. Four hundred and thirty-two brook trout ponds, or 43 percent of the total, never have been defiled by hatchery truck and therefore contain a priceless reservoir of genes. Each spring in these and other Maine ponds there are an estimated 1.7 million wild trout over the general six-inch minimum size limit, of which about 365,156—with a mean length of 11 inches—are caught and killed during the open-water season. Yet few people who reside in Maine—least of all the politicians—understand the significance of this resource. On those rare occasions when they look past their borders into the primal chaos, they see lots and lots of big "trout." But they need to look harder and deeper into the warm, silted water—at the gill covers that don't fit, the pinched caudal peduncles, the rounded pout tails, the matted dorsals, the pectoral fins abraded by concrete to fleshy stumps. If they did so, they might realize that there are wild trout, and there are "rubber trout"—i.e., those tame, sallow, inbred imitations, mass-produced in hatcheries. And they would realize that they are entrusted with a national treasure every bit as valuable as Alaska's grizzlies or California's redwoods.

But they don't realize. So every year Maine's wild squaretails get smaller and scarcer. Slap-dash logging and farming have heated and choked spawning streams, but Maine is unique among states in that her trout woes are not primarily habitat related. The managers will tell you that the problem is one of "access." Traditionally, the public could not use its rivers because they were reserved for paper companies to choke with logs and poison with yellow bile that had the bouquet of New England boiled dinner gone bad and that—especially on those wet, still mornings when the grouse were in the apples—you could almost taste 30 miles back from the river. When the log drives were banned in 1976, the paper companies hacked up the North Woods with a web of high-speed, permanent haul roads. The fate of Secret Pond (which, of course, is not its real name) was typical. It used to take No-Birds and me two hours to hike in and then only after we had jeeped 10 miles of rock-strewn, beaver-flooded tote roads and a rickety bridge swaying across a deep gorge. Now you can drive a Cadillac to the shore.

But access is only the facilitator of the problem, not the problem itself. One can, after all, drive a Cadillac to the shore of Yellowstone Lake, populated by Yellowstone cutthroats—arguably the one freshwater gamefish even less selective and more suicidal than brook trout. Yes, I have fished for and sworn at the troutlings, venerated by the late John Voelker, who thumb their noses with their tails from Frenchman's Pond; but these are the exception. When Yankee brook trout go on the feed, they eat like Vikings. If you live in Maine, chances are you know when these orgies happen, and because you and your buddies don't want the pond fished out by strangers, you do it yourselves. You may even obey the law. The general, any-gear-goes regulations don't work. Never have.

If you follow tradition, you will not obey the law. "You go to the barber shop in Greenville," says Vail, "and the old fellows are complaining because they used to go to Horseshoe Pond and fill a canoe, and they can only get half a dozen or so. 'What's the problem? What are you guys doing wrong?' Well, the problem is that they used to go there and fill a canoe." Maybe, as the old saw goes, a few rotten apples spoil the barrel, but we're talking here about a hogshead of fermented cider mash.

"I hardly fish brook trout in Maine anymore," says Harry Vanderweide, editor of *The Maine Sportsman*. "I can't stand it. I go to Québec. The brook trout is an anachronism; and the state of Maine is an anachronism. Time has passed them by. You want to have wild brook trout, it's really pretty simple. You can't kill them. I do not believe a naturally reproducing brook trout fishery can withstand any significant level of exploitation. Forty years ago—when everybody had a job in the mill and worked six or seven days a week, didn't have money to travel, didn't have equipment—it was different."

Certainly, there are some fine, dedicated brook trout fishermen/conservationists still extant in the Pine Tree State. One such is Warden Sergeant Dan Tourtelotte. Like all wildlife law-enforcement personnel I have worked with on stories, Tourtelotte is smart, tough and highly motivated. You don't last long in the business if you're otherwise, because no line of police work is more underfunded, none more undercut in the courts and none, including drug interdiction, more dangerous.

Tourtelotte, who has lived all his 39 years in Maine, likes and respects his neighbors; he tries not to wax cynical. Some days are harder than others.

"One weekend in 1992 I worked with two different district wardens," he told me. "Eighty-five percent of the trout fishermen we checked were breaking the law. We worked one pond and got nine. Eight boats on the water, and all eight in violation. Lures-only regs, and all were fishing worms; some were over the limit. The next day I went to a different area. I got one guy over the limit, two for littering—tossing beer cans along the trail and the case in the bushes—one guy for operating a boat under the influence. On this fly-fishing-only pond there was a fellow dressed right out of the Orvis catalog, and he was catching a few trout. 'Finally,' I said to myself, 'a guy doing it right.' He was a good fly caster, having a good time. It was kind of nice to see, so I sat down on the shore and had my lunch. I hadn't even finished it when he got into his pack and brought out a canister of worms. When he was done with it he threw it in the water, so I wrote him for littering too. You get days like that."

They weren't filling any canoes at Horseshoe Pond when Tourtelotte and I staked it out last Memorial Day weekend, and the trout we did check were runts, the sort you encounter more and more in Maine these days. We were hoping to apprehend the highly skilled "Mort," who, according to a reliable informer, had killed 40 fish the previous Saturday, thereby exceeding his bag and possession limit by 35. But low pressure had settled in. There had been heavy, cold rain, and more was on the way. Even Mort couldn't kill five trout.

"This weather's saving a lot of fish," Tourtelotte declared. He'd catch Mort later. Perhaps, as he had done the previous winter with another suspect, he would knock on his door late into Happy Hour and say, "Word is you got 400 trout in your freezer." And, as the other guy had done, Mort would bellow, "Waahden, what the hell you talkin' about? Look heah!" and whip open the freezer door, proving that he had no more than 50.

At the lovely fly-fishing-only stretch of West Branch Stream we encountered a party from Winterport angling with chartreuse and orange closed-face spinning reels terminally rigged with bobbers, spinners, radish-size sinkers and bass hooks baited with freshwater mussels. A deep-sea rod reposed against the dirty camper, an open can of corn teetered on the edge of the wooden bridge. One guy didn't even have a license.

We pressed on to Second West Branch Pond, now easily accessible by logging road. At the landing I counted 26 metal boats. Later we stopped in at Little Lyford Pond Camps, the oldest and nicest in Maine, to see our pal Bud Fackelman, the horse-doctor-turned trout outfitter. Alas, his famous goat (more about it directly) had gone to its reward, albeit after a long and lavish life. Because the two Little Lyford ponds, restricted to fly-fishing, are well off the road and Fackelman patrols them fiercely and imposes a slot limit on his guests, the fishing has held up. We met him on the path, fly rod in hand and toting litter—snelled-hook wrappers from the latest poaching, committed the previous day, when he'd been in town.

Back at the Fisheries and Wildlife office in Greenville, on the south shore of wind-tattered Moosehead Lake, I met Warden Sergeant Pat Dorian—41, thick black hair, clipped Maine humor with matching accent, an 18-year veteran of the service and another ardent advocate of wild brook trout. Recently he had checked four anglers with 110 trout over the limit. Another party of three was only 83 over. "You should have seen the look on their faces when they saw me standing behind them as they were stooped over the brook, cleaning the fish," he said.

There were five other wardens in the office, drinking coffee and coordinating the evening patrols. The subject of conversation was the new logging road—yet another—being cut within a cast-and-a-half of one of the area's most productive trout ponds. "Kiss 'er goodbye," lamented one. They spoke of other denuded trout water. Carpenter Pond, for instance—the 160-acre jewel up north of Chamberlain Lake that had produced what may have been the state's finest trouting. Dorian said he knew of two 7½-pounders that had come out of it— "squaretails, not togue"—and he had checked five-pounders each spring until the haul road went in. "They killed Carpenter in one season," he said.

Having closely observed Maine game wardens at work over the past 30 years, I have but one major complaint about them—they are too few. In other states, and especially on the federal level, wildlife law enforcement gets scant support from the public or politicians. Even the environmental community, which obsesses, with excellent cause, over "habitat issues," ignores the importance of law enforcement; this to the peril of the very creatures whose habitat it seeks to defend. Because pounded trout water in Maine is largely intact, the state has much to gain from aggressive enforcement. Yet, because it has no conception of the significance or value of its wild brook trout, no state more rashly underfunds its warden service.

Today Maine sells roughly 300,000 fishing licenses per year, an 85-percent increase from 1950. Yet there now are fewer wardens than at any time since 1950. Airplanes have been reduced from five to three. They call it "austerity" and "budget protection," but it is as sensible as trying to save federal tax money by laying off the IRS.

"Not only do we have fewer wardens in the field," comments Al Meister, erstwhile chief biologist for the Maine Atlantic Sea-Run Salmon Commission, "their quality time in the field has been reduced. They're enforcing snowmobile laws; they're enforcing ATV laws, boating laws. If a fisherman is stupid enough to go get drunk and drown, that's his problem. I don't consider it the state's problem. Back when snowmobiles and ATVs weren't invented, Maine wardens got out on snowshoes and checked ice fishermen; they got out and put a canoe in and traveled up and down some of those streams. They're not doing it now; they don't have time, and they're [generally] limited to about 41 hours a week [by budget restrictions and the federal Fair Labor Standards Act]."

One warden I met is responsible for 100 trout ponds.

And biologists are stretched even thinner. Not only does Maine refuse to protect its wild brook trout resource from poachers, it hasn't bothered to find out what it has left or what genotypes exist where. Maine hasn't even seen fit to fund a wild-trout inventory.

Fisheries scientist Forrest Bonney puts it this way: "We used to have two research biologists working on brook trout. Through attrition we've lost those positions, and now I, as regional management biologist, am trying to manage the brook trout population in Maine, too. It's not getting the attention it should. We haven't done the work on wild trout some states have because we lack the resources." Yet Maine is the one state in the East that does have the resources, if by "resources" you mean what money-spending tourists go there to fish for.

Like most state fish and wildlife agencies, Maine's operates on dedicated revenue—i.e., funds derived from the sale of hunting and fishing licenses and special taxes on sporting equipment. And like most state politicians, Maine governors and legislators regularly raid this dedicated revenue for such sustenance to the human spirit as road widening. Fending off these raids goes with the territory of any decent, competent fish and wildlife commissioner, and Bill Vail was as decent and competent as any I have encountered. There came a point, however, when even Vail couldn't fend off the raids. So last February he quit in protest. "To some extent the administration saw our dollars as a way to help balance the budget," he says. "I'd just been in the department too long, and the sportsmen had been too good to me to be a party to that. So rather than be the funeral director at my department's funeral, I resigned . . . . All we've been able to do is keep existing programs going, sometimes with just a skeleton crew. But I have always felt strongly that there should be general-fund support for fish and wildlife management. At some point there's got to be a recognition of the value of fish and wildlife to Maine's economy."

The positive note in all of this is that the trout ponds are still there and are, for the most part, physically undefiled. The spur roads into them are not unattractive—narrow, untarred and shrouded in greenery. Moreover, the recuperative power of a wild brook trout population is astonishing. I have seen Maine ponds heal themselves in two seasons when gated off or protected with special regulations.

Although the Piscataquis Chapter of Trout Unlimited is pushing catch-and-release for five ponds and a major tributary of Moosehead Lake, returning a perfectly good Maine brook trout to its element still is an idea whose time has not come. Meanwhile, the state is experimenting with what may prove to be the next best thing—two-fish limits on 137 trout ponds. The results, in the few places they've been monitored, are heartening. One of the first two-fish waters—protected in 1988—was 9,500-acre Big Eagle Lake, source of the Allagash. A 1992 study reveals that "brook trout catch rates increased dramatically, compared with the previous survey in 1987, from .23 to .43 trout per angler." and that the percentage of anglers catching at least one fish rose in those five years from 18 to 28 percent.

When the two-fish ponds are scattered among general, five-fish water, the public shuns them like two-dollar gasoline. Pat Dorian will not be pleased to read here that Tourtelotte inadvertently disclosed to me the location of the two-fish pond they both haunt during the five-week Green Drake hatch. But then, Tourtelotte had shown it to him. "I happen to fish there quite a lot," said Dorian, when he thought I didn't know which pond he meant, "and there was hardly anybody in there last year. Now we're starting to get a lot of fish back 15 and 16 inches. Last year I'd average eight to 10 trout, but that's only fishing like an hour in the evening. One night I landed 22. Biggest was 18½ inches."

I promised more about Fackelman's goat. The previous owner had hauled it into Tufts University Vet School to be put down for no apparent reason other than he'd discovered what goats are really like. But anyone, especially Fackelman, could see that it was a perfectly good goat, if such an adjective can properly modify such a noun. Accordingly, the kind doctor had rescued it from death row, keeping it chained in his yard down the street from me in Grafton, Massachusetts. Thus confined, it had chomped perfect circles in the grass around its stake. (Norman Mortimer Taft maintained that the circles had been inscribed by flying saucers.)

When Fackelman moved from traffic-choked Grafton to the wilds of Maine, there no longer was need for the chain, so he unleashed his goat in the lush meadows around Little Lyford Pond Camps. But the goat was bound by tradition; it had developed a certain way of doing things, and still it chomped perfect circles in the grass.

The story of Fackelman's goat strikes me as a parable for Maine brook trout fishermen who won't change even when there is every good reason to do so, even when they could let the resource recover and grow and make them rich as Montana springcreek owners. Even when, in the long run, they and the rest of us could have more of something most rare and beautiful.

HABITAT

Maine's brook-trout crisis is not primarily habitat related, but "not primarily" doesn't translate to insignificant. The worst damage has been done to streams that drain the tarred, subdivided southern counties and the moonscaped "industrial forests" and torn-up potato country to the north. Maine is laced with 32,000 miles of flowing water, of which 70 percent, or 22,248 miles, is capable of sustaining native trout.

If these streams were cared for properly, they would be far more productive, though only by Eastern standards. Most are freestone, sterile and naturally acidic. They need every break they can get. As it stands now, only 3,213,916 of the estimated 50,169,240 trout residing in Maine's streams are thought to exceed the general six-inch size limit.

Bob Wengrzynek, the 43-year-old fisheries biologist with the US Soil Conservation Service out of Orono, specializes in Maine trout habitat and methods of repairing it. Toting electro-fishing gear he has slogged through hundreds of streams from headwater seepage to saltchuck. "The acute effects from things like pesticides have basically disappeared," he declares. "Now we have chronic effects of siltation and sedimentation. What I've found is that the lower levels of sedimentation hurt trout, too. You get diatom and algae colonies growing on substrates. This is why the rocks are slippery. Even though the fine sediment might be flushed out, the rocks are still coated with these algae and diatoms. Trout and salmon eggs get covered over with gravel. Then, when water temperatures drop, the algae and diatoms die and decomposition sucks oxygen out of the gravel. You have streams that look good but with whole age classes missing. They produce large fish, but their carrying capacity is tremendously reduced."

The worst damage Wengrzynek has witnessed is downslope from the potato fields in Aroostook County. Pools that were deep and clear now grow cattails. "Trout can't hold their breath," he says. "All it takes is one good storm and a high sediment load when the eggs are in the eye stage, just coming out of gravel, and you've wiped out your spawn. The stream can be crystal-clear the rest of the year. People will look at it and say, 'Isn't that beautiful.'"

So Wengrzynek has designed and patented a treatment system that he is installing on farmed watersheds with the help of TU members and other volunteers. A settling pond picks up the heavy stuff. Then the runoff filters through grass, en route to a wetland full of cattails and bulrushes, thence to a deeper pond stocked with native minnows—which feed on algae and zooplankton—and freshwater mussels, each of which filters about 12 gallons of water a day. Great blue herons and kingfishers further process the runoff by eating the minnows. So do muskrats, which eat the mussels, and waterfowl, which eat colonized invertebrates. It costs $30,000 to $90,000 to treat each farm—cheap because the solution is permanent. But who pays? That's the hard part, admits Wengrzynek. "Society has to make a decision: Do we keep cheap food on the table? Or do we spend more for food so these subsidized farmers can compete?"

Because river valleys in New England are wetter and lusher than out West, bovines face a major challenge in annihilating them with teeth and hooves. But in southern Maine, trout killers who chew cuds are holding their own with trout killers who chew gum and tobacco. Cows are allowed to summer in rivers and at concentrations that would shock even the most brazen Great Plains grazing-permit violator. It's a Yankee tradition. One farmer I know of keeps 500 cows in Kenduskeag Stream, the sweet meadow brook that funnels trout and salmon fry to the Penobscot. Things fall apart; the center cannot hold. The bank sloughs into the river. The bottom is bombed with cow pies. Wherever sunlight breaks through the hardwood canopy the silted streambed sprouts blobs of algae. Another farmer keeps 200 cows in the river. Why? Because there is no law that prevents it, and fencing is expensive.

State fisheries biologist Dennis McNeish, who works out of the Augusta regional office, waxes enthusiastic about cow control: "It's not mysterious," he says. "It's not high-tech. But it costs money, and if a farmer has to pay for it, he just won't do it. People in the area are so used to cow damage they don't notice it; the good brook trout fishing we used to have here is not within their memory. You never hear them complain. But if they go up north and see that their favorite trout stream has been clearcut and there's erosion into it, they scream."

Not that there isn't plenty of reason to scream. I dread returning to my old grouse and squaretail haunts because, as often as not, they have been moonscaped, the slash bulldozed into the middle and the whole site drenched with herbicides to kill off "undesirable" hardwoods. "Even-age forest management," the paper barons call it; but it's really just cellulose strip mining. Cutting down all the trees is no more scientific in the late 20th Century than it was in the late 19th Century, when the Lake States were converted from pine woods to sand desert. But now it is justified by ad men wearing white smocks and hardhats and calling themselves "scientists." In the words of Syracuse University forestry professor Dr. Leon S. Minckler: "They make up their mind and then seem to search for ecological, silvicultural and economic reasons to support their decision. This has involved some pretty awful science and economics."

The state Land Use Regulation Commission has rules and guidelines—actually quite strict by past standards—but Maine's North Woods, the wild, diverse mixed-hardwood forest of legend, is being transformed to monocultures of planted spruce and fir that can't produce much of anything truly wild, least of all trout. Most of the stillwater is safe for the time being, but not the tiny rills that veined the once-cool, once-spongy uplands. Like the forest, they are gone—dried up and squashed in skidder tracks, and with them the clouds of trout fry that used to find their way to the ponds.

"I had a place I used to fish," recalls Warden Sergeant Pat Dorian. "Had to walk a mile and a half into it. There was a deadwater. I made me a trail in there, and the fishing was like something you'd write about. They went in and clearcut the stream that dumps into this deadwater. Both sides of it, hundreds of acres. That warmed the water up, and with the road system that came with it, that was the end."

When I complained to Champion International about the savaging it recently gave the area around Little Lyford ponds, I got the following verbiage from General Manager Robert Cope: "As you know, Champion is in the business of growing and harvesting trees over the long term in the state of Maine. We plan to continue to harvest our lands in a professional manner, following good environmental and silvicultural practices while complying with all applicable laws governing such practices."

Similar complaints from Little Lyford Pond Camps owner Bud Fackelman elicited similar gas. Finally, he wrote Senator George Mitchell as follows: "Due to the wholesale destruction of the forest, one of the best fisheries in Maine hangs in tenuous balance, the woods look like wastelands, the streams run mud, and the springs dry up by mid-July. And you complain about Borneo? I wish I could get your attention . . . . The local chamber of commerce has spent tens of thousands of dollars on experts and surveys to determine why tourists are no longer attracted to central Maine. One resultant *Moosehead Messenger* article recommended that we make the public more aware of the ugliness engineered by today's brand of mechanical harvesting and by the widespread use of herbicide—that way the good folks won't be so shocked when they get here."

Why isn't Maine studying the effects of clearcutting on brook trout? I put the question to Peter Bourque, chief of the state's Fishery Research and Management Division. "Lack of resources," he said. "We talked about warming from clearcutting as we saw it occurring, but nobody had the funds or the manpower to make a model stream and monitor temperatures and nutrient inputs and siltation and fish populations and really see. Here was this big thing going on over a major portion of the North Woods, and nobody had the resources to pinpoint an area and really study it. There were a few minor studies at the University that did show that even if you just clearcut one streambank, it could really change the ecosystem. A lot of our trout streams were marginal in summer, and the clearcutting was enough to tip them the other way."

BARSE AND OTHER ROUGH FISH

The late sage of Michigan's Upper Peninsula, John Voelker, had a word for bass, pike, perch, etc., especially when superimposed on his native brook trout water. "Unspeakable."

In Maine, the oldtimers still call smallmouths "barse," spitting the word. But newcomers who wear patch-spangled jumpsuits and steer glittery boats with their feet dote on these non-native fish, strewing them about the countryside like gum wrappers.

Wild brook trout and warmwater species don't mix. Always, the squaretail succumbs to competition and predation. In 1979, when I got skunked on Baker Lake at the head of the St. John River, it rippled with native fallfish or, as Thoreau called them, "cousin trout." (They excited him more than they do me; basically he found them "cupreous dolphin.") Today Baker Lake, Glazier Lake—and, to a lesser extent, the St. John's mainstem—is populated by muskellunge, thanks to the Province of Québec, which sought to correct Divine error in the early 1970s by stocking them in Lac Frontiére, along the international boundary. Horrified biologists in Maine had been assured by their Canadian counterparts that they had nothing to worry about because "the muskellunge is a fish of quiet water." But no one told the muskies. Imagine how many brook trout a 20-pounder packs away in a week.

Now barse are thriving in Indian Pond and seeping into Moosehead Lake, where illegally introduced white perch—certain death for wild brook trout—are just starting to irrupt. Assisted by amateur managers and bait dunkers, yellow perch have invaded Moosehead, the Rangeley Lakes and the Fish River Chain, as well as dozens of small trout ponds.

"There's no place for these fish in wild trout management," avers fisheries biologist Paul Johnson. "Each pond can produce so many pounds of fish. You add other species, and you take away from what's there. What goes first is the wild trout resource."

UPDATE

Finally Maine is waking up to the treasure it has.

When I interviewed Forrest Bonney for this update he said he'd done nothing for the past three weeks other than work on the brook-trout management plan. Progressive new regulations on almost 500 wild-brook-trout ponds include three categories, depending on a water body's ability to grow trout. For Class One waters (slightly more than 100 ponds) there's a bag limit of two, minimum length of 12 inches with only one fish bigger than 14. About the same number of ponds are Class Two (two trout, 10-inch minimum length and only one bigger than 12). The rest—about 300 ponds—are Class Three (two trout, with an eight-inch minimum).

"Over the years," explains Bonney, "people had been cropping off the bigger fish—the ones that need to reproduce if you're going to maintain the genetic integrity of the population. I did a comparison with the fish from the 1930s and '40s. Twenty percent were age four and older. Within the last decade the figure has been 10 percent."

So far sportsmen are reacting favorably.

Alaska's Rush for the Gold

With a gleam in its eye, the state of Alaska trashes its river valleys

Audubon, November 1993

WHO CAN ARGUE with poet Robert Service that there are strange things done in the midnight sun by the men who moil for gold? But the strangest can't have been the postmortem capers of some roasting flatlander. It has to be the way miners rip out Alaskan river valleys, turn them inside out and toss them over their shoulder.

The procedure, called placer mining (pronounced with a short *a* and possibly derived from *platea*, Latin for "broad street," or *placer,* Spanish for "pleasure"), has been going on in Alaska since 1880, when gold was discovered near what is now Juneau. In those days a sourdough with a pick and shovel could move about five cubic yards of river valley a day. The idea was to dig down to the "pay gravel," the layer just above bedrock that had swept down from the gold-veined hills, then wash it through a narrow, ribbed sluice that would catch the heavier flecks of gold as they settled out.

Unfortunately for animals and fish, the pay gravel is spread out not just under streambeds but also under the lush, green fabric that sheathes rivers and nourishes wildlife in the cold, sterile uplands the way velvet nourishes caribou antler.

Alaska's wealth is its 365,000 miles of undammed, undefiled rivers, not the few flecks of gold beneath them. But don't try selling that to placer miners, most of whom fantasize that they're going to hit the mother lode when in reality they do well just to break even. Today, with about 200 active mines, Alaska is North America's biggest producer of placer gold. Still, the industry provides work for only 1,250 Alaskans. Strange indeed that the state would spend its wild rivers on them. "Maybe there are other motives," I suggested to Arctic Audubon Society president Larry Mayo as we orbited in his Cessna 180 over the mining community of Central, 100 miles northeast of Fairbanks.

It was harsh, lovely country, tucked up against the Arctic Circle. Even now, in high summer, snowdrifts persevered on the north faces of bald hilltops, deserted save for scattered caribou that tossed their heads and showed the whites of their eyes as we raced low over the summits. Then, in seconds, we'd be out into the high void, where the air was thin and the dirty green desert fell away to horse-whisker-sparse groves of white and black spruce. Way down in the notches the rich green of a few unmolested river corridors was flecked with the seasonal gold of birches and aspens already switching off their juices for another siege of cold and darkness.

The mined corridors, on the other hand, were gouged and bare for hundreds of yards on either side of their thin water veins. Old mine tailings—the big stuff shunted through the sluices—lined the banks like tipped-over stacks of Ritz crackers. Topsoil and overburden were being hacked out and strewn around floodplains. Banks were festooned with trash, trucks and metal shacks.

From our airspeed of two miles a minute I estimated the length of Porcupine Creek's bare, muddy carcass at 12 miles. The morbid remains of Fish Creek measured eight. In as bad shape or maybe worse were Eureka Creek, and Pioneer, Dome, Sourdough, Crooked, Harrison, Mammoth and Gold Dust, all killed within the past few months or years.

Placer operations had been pretty ugly even before miners started feeding their sluices with bulldozers and backhoes. The heavy equipment proliferated until World War II, when the government confiscated it for the war effort. Placer mining resumed in 1946 but was held down by the fixed price of gold. Then in 1972 President Richard Nixon deregulated gold, thereby permitting Americans to buy and hoard it for the first time in 40 years. The price per ounce shot from $35 that year to more than $600 in 1980, and the valley-eating machinery surged back into the wilderness.

Some of the claims I inspected are administered by the state, others by the US Bureau of Land Management. When I stopped in at the BLM's Steese/White Mountains headquarters, in Fairbanks, district manager Roger Bolstad told me what state and federal bureaucrats have been pronouncing for decades: "We're working with the miners, and things are getting better."

It's true, I suppose. Settling ponds were strung along the valleys. And tailing piles were being smoothed out, a procedure that has been happening consistently on state land since mandated by law in October 1991 and on federal land since May 1987, when the Sierra Club and the Northern Alaska Environmental Center prevailed in a lawsuit against the BLM. It's called reclamation, and it's about as effective as using the toe of your boot to clean up a gob of greasy sauce that squirts from a Big Mac onto an Oriental rug.

The pace of improvement is hard to track. Certainly it eluded Sylvia Ward, associate director of the Northern Alaska Environmental Center, and American Rivers attorney Tom Cassidy, who were with me in the plane and who had flown the same route the previous year. At Eagle Creek, for instance, an operation supposedly supervised by the BLM was discharging café au lait directly into the river, just as in 1992. On other streams, settling ponds that apparently had been working last year were leaking now.

All the ripped-up valleys funnel water to Birch Creek, a federally designated Wild and Scenic river that, at least along the stretch we flew, appeared healthy, save for the wide deposits of silt that held off the shading, stabilizing willows. Data collected from the watershed in 1984 by the Alaska Department of Fish and Game showed previously documented symptoms of placer mining such as "elimination of essentially all fish" from mined streams. But it also showed elimination of fish from *unmined* streams above placer activity; they couldn't swim through the silt plumes on their upstream migrations. With the advent of EPA-required settling ponds, however, water quality became less degraded. In 1984 fish—principally Arctic grayling—had been captured at six of 18 sites; in 1990 they were found at 12. So yes, the state and feds are working with the miners, and things *are* getting better.

Birch Creek's main stem looks healthy only if you're not a fish. The bottom gravel suffers from a mining-induced affliction that researchers call embeddedness—that is, it's cemented together by fine particles and therefore highly unfriendly to benthic organisms and developing fish eggs. Subsistence fishing by Athabascan Indians has been badly hurt.

Elsewhere in Alaska, placer operations have released toxic metals such as arsenic and silted lakes to the point that they no longer can support fish or waterfowl. The Tuluksak River, which provides salmon and drinking water to the Yup'ik Eskimo village of the same name, has been largely sacrificed to placer gold. "One miner cut into both banks to get his dredge across," reports Eric Smith, the lawyer for the Anchorage-based Rural Alaska Community Action Program. "It took him 10 days, and he just trashed the river. There was an unbelievable volume of pollution pouring down." While the water has cleared up, it seems to be making the villagers sick. "They've been told that it's giardia, but the symptoms don't look like it," says Smith. "They get bad diarrhea with a lot of blood."

Preserving the "placer-mining way of life" is one of the main missions of the Alaskan Independence Party, the party of governor Walter Hickel and lieutenant governor Jack Coghill, the party that advocates—as part of its official platform—secession from the union. If Hickel and his party get their way, the blessings of placer mining will be extended to 205 lakes and rivers, including 12 of 26 Wild and Scenic rivers, 26 rivers and lakes inside national parks, 74 rivers in national wildlife refuges and 20 rivers and lakes in national wilderness areas. No matter that these lie within national reserves. The state, with much legal precedent, claims mineral rights to the bottom of all "navigable waterways," and it is suing the federal government to establish such rights once and for all.

Of the countless quills festering the flesh of the Independence Party, the sharpest is the Alaska National Interest Lands Conservation Act of 1980, the law of the loathsome Georgia peanut farmer that finally settled which federal holdings would be protected from development; the law that derailed the state's manifest destiny of Lower-48-style, hack-and-gouge exploitation; the law that spawned the party itself. So there is indeed a motive other than gold lust for feeding Alaska's wild river valleys to a few penny-ante miners who mostly lose money. It is lust for sovereignty.

The BLM respects this lust. In fact, word inside the agency is that the last two Alaskan directors have been told by Washington to get along with the state. So for $100 a year the BLM lets placer miners "camp"—i.e., construct permanent, walled buildings with storage facilities for fuel—along the 90-mile navigable stretch of the Fortymile River, which is designated Wild and Scenic. Even below the high-water mark the BLM has a great deal of authority to manage mining, but it chooses not to. And the miners choose to live high and dry on federal land, frequently fouling it. A typical entry in the agency's Camp Abandonment Checklist states that on June 20, 1992, the inspector picked up two large bags of garbage; the pit toilet was filled with water, cardboard and cans; waste had been deposited along the trail; and junked gear was scattered behind the camp.

The Wild and Scenic Rivers Act of 1968 provides that designated river systems shall not be dammed or diverted, yet recent BLM-authorized dams and diversions for placer mines have obliterated entire channels of such Fortymile tributaries as Wade Creek (where Jack Wade found gold in 1895) and Franklin Creek (named for Howard Franklin, whose big strike in 1886 precipitated the rush into the Fortymile country).

In 1990 the BLM let miner David Likins introduce to the Fortymile and Alaska a giant "New Zealand floating dredge," which was capable of processing 2,000 cubic yards of river gravel a day and that would have violated noise-pollution standards even in New York City. This intrusive monstrosity prompted American Rivers to declare the Fortymile one of the nation's 15 most threatened rivers. "American Rivers, the Northern Alaska Environmental Center and EPA all worked together to run Likins out," laments Steve Borell, director of the Alaska Miners Association. True enough, but the point is that they shouldn't have had to. The BLM should have run him out.

According to the miners, however, the BLM is too strict. "The Fortymile is being managed as if it were a park," avers Jamie Cox, vice-chair of the Alaskan Independence Party's District 33, who, after working the claim for Likins, bought it with her husband in 1992. "You can't just mine anymore. You have to be a lawyer and wade a morass of bureaucratic jargon and paperwork. Most of us make just enough to get by; it's more the lifestyle. I don't know any rich miners. That's the really sad thing that's being lost. We don't hurt anything. We drink the water that we're running through our sluice boxes."

"As it comes out?" I inquired.

"No," she admitted, "as it goes in."

In 1990 the state pressed its claim to placer rights by declaring navigable passage on Moose Creek, which sustains the best grayling population in Denali National Park and is fed by Wonder Lake, whose beauty was shown to the world by Ansel Adams. As evidence that the creek was navigable, the state cited an alleged rubber-raft trip by a Mr. Cole, who reported a full six to eight inches of water. Accordingly, in 1991 and 1992 the state issued three mining permits and allowed the staking of 37 claims, all inside the park. Permittees received a gushy letter from the state Division of Mining, offering "congratulations," informing them they were undertaking "landmark" projects, and wishing them "good luck."

Again, there was a motive beyond gold lust. It was access to Denali—and the park-bound mining village of Kantishna—via new roads being ballyhooed by state officials such as Lieutenant Governor Coghill, who says that he wants the road map of Alaska "to look like a plate of spaghetti."

But the public, even the Alaskan public, was not enthusiastic about seeing Denali's river valleys turned inside out, some for the second time. Mining inside the park had ceased in 1985, when the Sierra Club and the Northern Alaska Environmental Center successfully sued to prohibit the National Park Service from dispersing mining permits in Denali without a thorough environmental review. American Rivers listed Moose Creek as threatened. And *The Anchorage Daily News* editorialized, "If Gov. Hickel would mine Denali, is there any place he *wouldn't* develop?" Thus chastened, Hickel backed off last May, withdrawing the claim of navigability pending further study and incurring the wrath of his own party, which now calls him a "federalist" and an "internationalist."

On July 4, 1993, the Alaska Reclamation Crew, a front for the Independence Party, organized a protest "picnic" on a placer claim along Moose Creek, vowing to choke off public access to Denali by blockading park buses and refusing to obtain the required permits for driving private vehicles on the narrow, precipitous Highway Three to Kantishna. Faced with a dangerous traffic jam on the busiest weekend of the year, the Park Service opted to lay low, videotaping the protesters and citing them later. "I was scared to the point of tears," says Jamie Cox, who is a member of the Reclamation Crew, "because there were about thirty G-men in their uniforms . . . . They were all around, on the roads, up in the hills, *and they had guns.*"

The brains behind the picnic were largely those of Alaskan Independence Party secretary, radio personality and third-generation miner Lynette Clark, 47, better known as Yukon Yonda. She met her husband, Dexter, 42, while they were both mining the upper Birch Creek watershed. He proposed to her standing on a bulldozer, threw her in the sluice, and hollered to all hands that he'd found the biggest gold nugget in Alaska. On the way into Moose Creek last Fourth of July Dexter had been at the wheel, so it was he who received the citation. Yukon Yonda says her man will go to jail before paying a fine to the federal government.

Those who don't take the Alaskan Independence Party seriously fail to understand Alaska and forget that the party runs the state in the persons of Hickel and Coghill. Like many members, Yukon Yonda joined because she was so taken with party chairman and founder Joe Vogler, 80, a placer miner whom she characterizes as "wonderful, intelligent, cranky and kind." If there is anything that Vogler hates more than the wolf, which he calls a "greedy, gut-ripping, son of a bitch, stinking, dirty, cowardly predator," it is the common critic of placer mining, whom he calls a "pantheistic follower of the Antichrist." Among the few things Vogler truly loves are roads. Once he horrified the Park Service by making one with his bulldozer in Yukon-Charley National Preserve, and he once advocated using atomic bombs to cut a highway through the glaciers sealing Fairbanks from Juneau.

But Chairman Vogler disappeared mysteriously on May 31; the search has been called off, and there has been a prayer service attended by Hickel. In Vogler's absence Yukon Yonda has been doing most of the talking for the party. I met her late on the night of August 14 as she worked the back bar at the Howling Dog saloon, in Fox, Alaska, where you can buy panties decorated with renderings of dogs in coitus. Yukon Yonda—a solid, tough-looking woman with brown hair pulled close to her scalp, long bead earrings and a black sweatshirt with the Alaskan flag on the back—popped me an Alaskan Pale Ale, lit a cigarette and dropped her elbows on the bar.

"I was shut down from mining in 1984," she intoned. "I would not get a permit. I don't believe as an American I need a permit to be productive, and the permit was so I could pollute. I don't pollute . . . . EPA had a hit list. There were 12 or 13 names on it, and those people are all shut down now. Joe Vogler's name was on top; I was fourth . . . . In 1982 there were shots fired outside my house. They didn't have the balls to come up and confront me."

Nothing the Alaskan Independence Party says or does surprises the Northern Alaska Environmental Center anymore. "The amazing thing," Sylvia Ward told me, "is that these people are *living;* they're not historical figures. We have Jurassic Park in Alaska."

The exception, of course, is Joe Vogler. He is not living, having been "murdered" last spring by the US Department of the Interior—or so claims Yukon Yonda. In fact, those "brown-shirt bastards out of the National Park Service" had tried to assassinate him back in 1981, she reveals. They'd ambushed him on a trail but had been driven off by a circling plane. Jamie Cox agrees: "I think everybody really knows that the feds are responsible for Joe's disappearance. The Park Service coveted his mining ground . . . . They're crazy if they think Joe's disappearance is going to tone the movement down."

Whatever application "crazy" has in Alaska, it is not an adjective I'd apply to the Park Service employees I encountered there, none of whom suggested that the Independence Party is about to tone down. Denali compliance officer Steve Carwile drove me to Moose Creek, an icy rill that hurries down from the Kantishna Hills. We found it eminently navigable—by truck. At half a dozen locations we forded with ease, barely dampening the hubcaps.

Where Moose gathers up Glen Creek I prospected for gold with a four-piece fly rod. I would have sworn that there were no fish in the shallow, transparent flow. Yet somehow Arctic grayling materialized under my bouncing dry flies, slicing the riffles with their golden flanks. They were hard, firm fish with black chin stripes and hand-size dorsal fins that glowed with neon shades of violet. They struck me as fish worth getting excited about, worth defending.

On Glen Creek, in an experiment designed to last at least a decade, the Park Service is trying to determine if genuine placer reclamation is possible. According to project leader Roseann Densmore, there's been impressive managed succession of plant life since work began in 1989. Along one stretch, bars of dead brush radiate out from the stream like fish vertebrae. They were placed there to hold the banks together until revegetation occurred. A few days after they went in, there was a flood. They worked.

Later, as Carwile and I helicoptered through the Kantishna Hills, I had to keep reminding myself that I was in a national park. Everywhere the tundra had been lacerated and bruised by heavy vehicles. Tailings curled like worm castings along wide, braided channels and grossly eroded banks. Abandoned buildings, fuel tanks, washing equipment, trucks, trailers and buses littered the uplands. Eventually, the junk that won't burn or isn't worth private salvage will be crushed and airlifted out by the Park Service.

The miners haven't given up the fight to mine Denali, but they are feeling dispirited and unloved. "Regulations continue to get stricter and stricter because people in places like Massachusetts and Maryland don't want placer mining in Alaska," Steve Borell, of the Alaska Miners Association, informed me. He spoke the truth. Alaska doesn't belong just to Alaskans. Unless and until the Independence Party pulls off secession, even state land is part of the United States of America. And Americans don't want their wild river valleys disemboweled to preserve a "way of life." Things are, as the bureaucrats say, "getting better," but they could scarcely get worse. And considering the importance of Alaskan rivers, are placer miners people who ought to be "worked with" or just kindly guided into more profitable, less destructive employment?

I tried hard to find a "good" placer operation. Just about everyone in Kantishna says that Sam Koppenberg, 60, is the best there is. He was "reclaiming" sites long before it was required. His new wife, Roberta, who runs the elegant Kantishna Roadhouse, acknowledges that the money he makes goes to pay his bills and that he'd like to quit mining. But after the Park Service ran him out of Caribou Creek he experienced a cash-flow problem and had to set up his equipment on Faith Creek, in the Central Mining District. I asked Arctic Audubon's Larry Mayo to fly me out there.

We circled for a long while, and neither of us could see how the state's best placer miner was being any kinder to wild Alaska than the competition. The ingenious mobile sluice box Koppenberg had devised left low tailing piles, and he'd made an obvious effort to recontour the topography. He had violated no regulation.

But outside the sparse turf of one reclamation site, no shred of vegetation survived; the valley had been moonscaped. A brace of bulldozers clutched at the hills and spread them around the floodplain like brown finger paint. Like the other mined river valleys I'd surveyed, this was a broken horror. And Faith Creek was running brown. There was a direct discharge into the river.

UPDATE

Placer mining is still a way of life in Alaska, its intensity a function of the price of gold.

The Northern Alaska Environmental Center sued EPA for letting dredgers operate without permits. In the settlement negotiations EPA had promised to research impacts of the suction dredges. But now, because of budget restrictions, the agency has had to withdraw that promise. Still, the suit has resulted in a revised permit process that the center's new director, Sylvia Ward, says, "will provide more safeguards for rivers, fish and water quality."

Now I need to write about the threat of the big gold mines operated by shell companies that will barge into sensitive areas on the state's fast-track permitting process, rip, tear, leach with cyanide, then walk.

Alaska isn't prepared for it. This kind of gold gouging is going to make environmentalists nostalgic for placer mining.

Joe Vogler's body has turned up! He was murdered just like Yukon Yonda told me, except not by a fed. Joe isn't around to confirm the story, but here's the version according to his killer, Manfred West—a fugitive from justice who had faced forgery charges in Fairbanks:

West stops by Joe's place to ask if it would be OK to hide out in one of his mines. Apparently, Joe said no because West visits him again, this time in an effort to sell him explosives. It is not clear what "pissed off" Joe, as State Trooper Jim McCann put it to the grand jury. (Joe was always pissed off about something, and possibly he was being protective of the gold he was hording in his house.) In any case, he calls West a "punk" and fires a bullet through his truck. West shoots Joe dead, pulls plastic bags over his head, wraps his body in a green tarp and mummifies him with duct tape. That done, he drives Joe out the Chena Hot Springs Road and buries him under four feet of gravel at Mile 25.

This is what is known for sure: When Trooper McCann came sniffing around West's cabin he dialed up the suspect on his cellular phone and chatted with him for three and a half hours about how he shot Joe, collecting all sorts of amazing anecdotes. After the conversation finally ended West set the cabin ablaze but was hauled from the smoldering rubble fit enough to stand trial.

Superior Court Judge Ralph Beistline sentenced West to 80 years in jail (75 years for killing Vogler and five years for burying his corpse in a gravel pit). "Murderers," the judge was quoted as saying by the *Fairbanks Daily News-Miner*, "should be discouraged from this kind of conduct."

How Green Was My Party

The dereliction of the Reagan Republicans

Fly Rod & Reel, May/June 1994

I REFUSE TO WEAR my Colby College necktie because the mules thereon bear such a resemblance to donkeys that I am commonly mistaken for a Democrat. Not that I am proud of being a Republican. In fact, the only Republican presidential candidate I have ever voted for was Nixon, who remains the closest thing we have had to a proven environmental president since Teddy Roosevelt.

As I recently wrote my friend and fellow GOP'er Nathaniel P. Reed, who served heroically as Nixon's Assistant Secretary for Fish, Wildlife and Parks: "My readers keep bludgeoning me for saying nasty things about Reagan and espousing 'liberal' causes such as making cowboys pay their way on public range. [The notion that environmentalists by definition are liberals] distresses me . . . I believe strongly in the Republican philosophy—no free lunch, the sanctity of the individual, etc. But I feel abandoned and betrayed by my party. Nat, what happened to us?" Reed wasn't quite sure. But, as always, he provided me with insights, and answers to questions I hadn't thought to ask.

But first, I need to jump to the Letters section of *Fly Rod & Reel*, wherein my family members sometimes are hard pressed to balance the nastygrams. Hell, I wasn't "attacking" one Canadian correspondent when I suggested that he might be less effusive about Reagan if he lived in the US. *I was giving him the benefit of the doubt!* Perhaps, from reading only foreign newspapers, he hadn't heard that Reagan defunded every fish and wildlife program possible, shut down environmental enforcement and turned resource and regulatory agencies over to felons, developers and property-rights wackos. Reagan enthusiasts have a right to call themselves either informed or committed to fish and wildlife, but not both at once.

The timidity of George Bush extended the Reagan years through 1992. But now that they are over, we should not just square our shoulders and look to the future. If we don't muck around in the past a bit and learn from it, we are likely to get Reagan back in the form of, say, Sen. Bob Dole (R-KS) or Sen. Phil Gramm (R-TX). In 1994 the Reagan Republicans are still leading the party away from its traditional values, still defiling the proud heritage of Teddy Roosevelt. Conservatives *conserve* resources; hence the name. Reagan Republicans squander them like Barnacle Bill on Saturday night. As TR declared in 1910, "Every man holds his property subject to the general right of the community to regulate its use to whatever degree the public welfare may require it." In his great campaign Roosevelt challenged and KO'ed the Me-Firsters (who keep congealing under all sorts of Orwellian monikers, the most recent being "the Wise Use Movement"). Reagan hired them.

Never has the influence of Reagan Republicans been more painfully apparent than in *Fly Rod & Reel*'s recent Dirty Dozens list, in April, comprised of legislators who voted against fish, wildlife and the environment at least 75 percent of the time. Of the 133 names we published, 128 were Republicans. This is a shocking, sickening statistic. It means that the Reagan Republicans who run the GOP control votes. And it means that, with a few notable exceptions, moderate Republicans are afflicted with flaccid spines and a warped sense of loyalty.

"Republican voters are being poorly served," comments Peter Kelley, of the League of Conservation Voters. "They back a candidate who says he will do good things for the environment. They propel that candidate into office, and then he turns around and votes against the environment." In 1991 the league conducted a poll in which it asked the following question: "When you hear a news story about how some local industry is in conflict with laws protecting a fish or bird or plant or animal, do you find your sympathies are usually more with protecting the wildlife or more with protecting local business and jobs?" Sixty-eight percent of the Democrats sided with wildlife; but you'd expect that, right? Guess what percentage of Republicans sided with wildlife. Five? Ten? Twenty? No, 68 percent also.

Surveyed again in 1994, the Republicans sided with wildlife by a margin of 47 percent to 30 percent, while the Democrats were 62 percent for wildlife, 22 percent for jobs. But this erosion may reflect the fact that in 1991 the Republicans' guy was in the White House, claiming to be the environmental president.

The dereliction of the Republican leadership has enabled the Democrats to prance around like Doris the Recyclasaurus at the throwaway-container lobby's annual "Keep America Beautiful" party. To hear it from some of our correspondents in Letters, one cannot be an environmental activist without also being a Democrat. But, as a group, the Democrats don't care about the earth either. On average they post environmental voting records of about 50 percent, a flunking grade in any school *I* ever attended. Congress is controlled by Democrats. Every committee, every subcommittee is chaired by a Democrat. So if the Democrats are, as they would have us believe, the party of the environment, how is it that in the face of critical fish and wildlife losses Congress keeps sitting on its hands? As we asked our readers in April, "Where do we *get* these people?"

During the course of my research for this piece, I pestered both the Republican and Democratic national committees by phone and fax, querying their chairmen about their environmental agenda. The only response I got was a one-page form letter from the Democrats—mostly white space—professing how green they are: "Introduced a wetlands plan to protect these prolific ecosystems. The Administration's package reflects the vital need for effective protection and restoration of the nation's wetlands, and advocates much needed reforms to increase the fairness and flexibility of federal regulatory programs." Yet the package reflects no such thing and, as you may recall from the bleatings of the Bush Administration, "fairness and flexibility" are doublespeak for continuing net loss. Essentially, the Democrats' wetlands plan is a bitter disappointment to anyone who cares about fish and wildlife.

"Developed a Forest Management Plan that finally broke the impasse on forest issues in the Pacific Northwest," the form letter continued. And yet the Democrats' forest plan sacrifices the headwaters of trout and salmon streams, gives loggers access to "reserves" and is, in general, so inadequate that it probably won't make it through the courts.

The Republicans have a point when they charge that the environmental community is dominated by big-city Democrats. Part of this is the Republicans' fault for not getting involved. But part of it is the refusal of environmentalists to associate with those Republicans who have the talent and commitment to make a contribution. Consider the experience of Mike Hayden, now president of the American Sportfishing Association and a promising yellow-perch jiggerman who takes his training at my New Hampshire fishing camp. You have to be a good man to be raised a Republican in Kansas (the state that produced Bob Dole), work your way through the legislature, serve as governor and all the while remain a strong environmentalist. But Hayden did it. Then, in the last year of the Bush Administration, the president turned to him for help after the Assistant Secretary for Fish, Wildlife and Parks—the conscientious, but not especially qualified, Connie Harriman—had been bullied into paralysis by Interior Secretary Manuel Lujan. Hayden (as far as he or I can determine, the first trained wildlife biologist ever to serve as Assistant Secretary) had excelled during his brief tenure—listening, learning and boosting morale in the Fish and Wildlife Service and the National Park Service to the point that in my open letter to Mr. Clinton, in the March '93 *Fly Rod & Reel*, I urged that he be kept on. Backed by a strong president, he might have been another Nat Reed; but politics are politics, and Hayden quickly found himself out on the street.

Seeking employment, he contacted the search firm hired by The Wilderness Society to replace its president, George Frampton, who had just left to take over Hayden's old post at Interior. Hayden announced that he had a serious interest in the job and wanted an interview with The Wilderness Society's board of directors. He was told he was wasting his time, because he was a Republican.

While Governor of Kansas, Hayden initiated an ecosystem-wide program to conserve and restore the Great Plains. He brought in all his fellow governors (and even their counterparts in Canada and Mexico) and he educated them about the need to look at total habitat instead of political boundaries—about why North Dakota, for instance, could best save its breeding birds by chipping in to protect their winter habitat along the mouth of the Colorado River. Hayden took his program with him to Interior, fighting for it, bringing it before the American people. After he left Washington, the Democrats sponsored a conference on the Great Plains ecosystem. Somehow Hayden's name wasn't included on the list of speakers. An oversight? His friends kept phoning him to ask why he wasn't going to participate, and he kept saying he hadn't been invited. Finally, to find out what was going on, he called a close friend at the Western Governors Association who had helped him get the program started. "Mike," she told him, " we got the word from Interior—no Republicans."

"Everywhere we turn we run into these partisan barriers," laments

Hayden. "People tell us, 'You can't possibly care about the environment, you're a *Republican*.' It's kind of a self-fulfilling prophesy. Every time we try to make contact with these folks, the first thing that comes up is party politics."

Nowhere is the perception of party politics a greater liability than at the League of Conservation Voters. Peter Kelley says he knows of but four Republicans on the 25-member board. This is because most members are taken from the big, Democrat-controlled environmental organizations like the National Audubon Society, Friends of the Earth, Environmental Defense Fund, Natural Resources Defense Council and The Sierra Club. While the league bends over backward to be non-partisan, and the legislation it uses to determine the National Environmental Scorecard has nothing to do with party politics, try selling this to a guy from Choctaw, Oklahoma, who wears BASS and NRA patches on his jumpsuit.

"So how come Mike Hayden's not on your board?" I asked Kelley, knowing that a year earlier Interior Secretary Bruce Babbitt had towed him into the office by the ear and said, "Here is a Republican who cares, take him." Kelley explained that Hayden was well respected at the league and had somehow just "fallen through the cracks." I believe it, because a week later LCV President Jim Maddy phoned Hayden to ask if it would be OK to submit his name to the nominating committee.

One of the best and most courageous environmentalists in Congress is Rep. Arthur Ravenel, a Republican from South Carolina now running for governor. He took on the powerful, ruthless shrimp lobby in his own state, scoffing at death threats, and forced shrimpers to fit their nets with the hugely effective turtle excluder devices that supposedly were going to put them out of business. He is a strong, articulate wetlands proponent, a stalwart defender of marine fish and mammals. "Ah reckon the Republicans have figured that the environment is the traditional Democrat area of endevah and just left it alone," he told me in his grand, Southern-colonel drawl. "*We got to get involved*. One of the reasons we're in the minority in districts that could swing either way is that lots of Republicans will vote for the Democrat if the Democrat is an environmentalist."

If Reagan's heirs succeed in preserving anti-environmentalism as a plank in the Republican platform, the party is going to self-destruct. According to a recent LCV-commissioned study, 88 percent of American voters consider themselves environmentalists, and 37 percent consider themselves "strong environmentalists." To understand just how out of touch Republicans are with the national will, one has only to vet the candidates they are grooming for the next presidential race. Leading the pack is perennial *FR&R* Dirty Dozener Phil Gramm, the crusty senator from Texas to whom the party has turned over the chairmanship of its Senatorial (campaign) Committee. Gramm, one of the louder members of the Congressional Sportsman's Caucus, was dishonored with *Fly Rod & Reel*'s J. Danforth Quayle Memorial Rotten Potatoe Award in 1993 and its Royal Nonesuch Award in 1994.

I'll confess that I am not Senator Gramm's favorite outdoor writer. He has publicly accused me of attempting to "smear" his reputation by writing articles "rooted in a rumor spread by a person whom [he has] never met." But the senator didn't need any help from me in smearing his reputation, and Nat Reed (the person Gramm never met) spread no rumor. What Reed told me and what I passed on to the public was that, according to "a little bird" who contacted Reed during the summer of 1988, Reagan's Fish and Wildlife Service Director Frank Dunkle had tipped Gramm off that the federal duck cops had his Maryland farm under surveillance.

The special agents hadn't been hunting senators; it was just that there was so much grain scattered around ponds belonging to Gramm and his neighbor that they could see it from their airplanes as they flew hither and yon. When the agents staked out the neighbor's farm, they observed Senator Gramm walking toward bait in hunting attire and carrying a shotgun. When Gramm saw he was being watched, he retreated. Dunkle, who allowed that he had tipped off Gramm "because he was a very useful senator," was dismissed from the Fish and Wildlife Service largely for this breach of public trust and largely to spare Reagan Republicans the embarrassment of yet another criminal prosecution.

At this writing, the other most-talked-about Republican presidential candidate is Senate Minority Leader Bob Dole of Kansas, also a perennial *FR&R* Dirty Dozener and also dishonored by their J. Danforth Quayle Rotten Potatoe and Royal Nonesuch awards. Both Gramm and Dole bootstrapped their environmental voting records from 0-percent in 1992 to 6-percent in 1993. If they keep improving at this rate, they'll be in tune with today's America by 2009.

"When I look at the leading candidates who wish to assume the Presidency and not one of them can spell the word 'environment,' I am sorry for my party," declares Reed. I suppose my question to him—

What happened to us?—was, in a sense, rhetorical. The process is ongoing, and no one can step back and take in the whole picture. Perhaps in the mid-21st Century a historian will answer it in a book called *The Demise of America's Two-Party System*. But, as I said, Reed provided me with insights and answers to questions I hadn't thought to ask.

"It would be an absolute tragedy for the Republican Party to give up the mantle of Teddy Roosevelt and all that has been done by good, strong Republican leaders," he said. Nat Reed speaks of the "Great Crisis"—air, water and land pollution and uncontrolled population growth. He saw it in 1960, tried to bring it to his party's attention when he went to Interior in May of 1971. For a while it looked as if he had succeeded. Backing Reed were strong, intelligent earth advocates like Bill Ruckelshaus, Bill Reilly, Russ Train.

"Have you ever heard of a predator poison the ranchers call Compound 1080?" President Nixon asked Reed just before his appointment. "Mr. President," said Reed. "Not only have I heard of it, I won't take the job unless you'll let me make a serious run at removing it from public land." Nixon did; Reed succeeded. The good Republicans stopped the Cross-Florida Barge Canal, banned DDT and its relatives. When Reed couldn't get action against the infamous eagle killers in Colorado and Wyoming, he went to see Attorney General Elliot Richardson, who snatched the phone, dialed the US attorneys and told them they'd be job hunting if they didn't get on the case in 30 days. They did; the United States won.

In his campaign to save Redwood Creek and its trophy steelhead from clearcutters, Reed asked the President to have his helicopter pilot swing out over the moonscaped headwaters. Nixon did; the next morning Reed found a note on his desk that said: "Full speed ahead on Redwood Creek!" Then Nixon left the White House, and gradually the good Republicans blew away like spinners on a night wind.

"I'm tired, Ted," Reed told me. "We all are. The Great Crisis is growing. Recognition that it is growing by the American people is going to make the issue of environment critical for the rest of our lives, and our children's and grandchildren's. There's no escaping it now, because we did not heed the clarion call 30 years ago. We were too slow, and then we lost the 12 years of Reagan/Bush. Anti-environmentalists, the kind of guys Teddy Roosevelt took on, were reassembled somehow by Ronald Reagan. And George Bush didn't have the confidence or courage to kick those bastards out. Like a bunch of leeches, they sat around Washington sucking away his few good thoughts and deeds."

Just before Bush lost the election, Reed attended an enormous think-tank session in California aimed at formatting initiatives over the next four years. It wasn't a Republican function as such, but it was dominated by Republicans, very rich, very well-known ones. "These Republicans had had it," says Reed. "They'd had 12 years of Reagan and Bush, and they were not going to vote again for that kind of sloppy environmental record." They held a secret ballot for who they wanted to see as the next President. Clinton won by 87 percent.

A Bully Interview

How, I wondered, *would Teddy Roosevelt have responded to what the Reagan Republicans were doing to his Grand Old Party?* What a kick it would be to interview him. The more I thought about it, the more determined I became to do just that. It wasn't going to be easy. TR, as you might imagine, is not an easy man to get hold of these days. Finally, however, I contacted a medium and arranged a Q&A session.

Both the medium and I were fully awake, and no candles, alcohol, incense or hovering tables were involved. I suppose at this point I ought to reveal that the medium was Mr. Roosevelt's secretary, and that this particular Roosevelt—TR IV—is the late President's great-grandson, a Republican leader in his own right. The old bull moose would be proud of his issue. Teddy IV, 51, is a Harvard grad, a former Navy Seal who fought in Vietnam, an ardent hunter and fly fisherman, an environmental activist and a successful executive with Lehmann Brothers in New York City. As a board member of Trout Unlimited, he was instrumental in bringing in President Charles Gauvin and rescuing the organization from financial mismanagement and directional chaos. More recently, he has been named to the board of the League of Conservation Voters. Herewith, our interview:

Where and how did the Republicans lose their way?
I'm born, bred and will die a Republican. The Republican Party, in my mind, has some strengths that are desperately needed. But we're abandoning them. During the Reagan Administration we walked away from our historical commitment to the environment and our historical commitment to fiscal prudence . . . . Republicans traditionally believed that you don't spend money if you don't have it, that, instead, you invest in the future. Well, the environment's the same thing. You don't destroy the environment today for a near-term gain and be left with nothing. One of the great strengths of the American

environmentalism is that, unlike the Wise Use Movement, it has genuine grass roots. I get very unhappy with my own party when we don't see what an enormously popular issue this is. We're giving up the opportunity to lead, but lead in a way that is entirely consistent with the real traditions of the party.

Why do Republicans dominate our Dirty Dozens list?
It's the Orange County Republicans having taken over from the Nelson Rockefeller Republicans. These guys are, I think, a little bit too selfish, are looking at the near-term and don't understand the lessons of history. If you consider the great Republican leaders going back to Lincoln, you had people who were strong but who represented the liberal wing of the party. The Republican Party seems bent on committing ideological suicide. If it were a business, you'd fire the people running it.

What can you do for your party as a board member of the League of Conservation Voters?
I feel that LCV offers a great opportunity for the good Republicans to get support. And I want to try to make sure that environmentally sensitive people who are running for the first time and people like Chafee [Senator, RI] and Jeffords [Senator, VT] get LCV support. Chafee and Jeffords are good, sensible leaders. And to my way of thinking, they are a lot better Republicans than, say, Mr. Dole [Senator, KS]. The Republican Party needs to get some ideological leadership that goes back to our roots.

You must have had reservations about joining LCV.
Absolutely. I was afraid it was another political action committee. Jim Maddy [LCV president] and John Watts [LCV board member] brought me around. I had my hands full, and I needed another board like a wind knot. The environmental organizations that I care about all depend to a great extent on what Congress does. And if Congress isn't going to renew the Endangered Species Act or the Clean Water [Act], all the work I do for TU goes down the drain. I figured I had to go into this organization—which is somewhat controversial—get my hands dirty, and probably take a few knocks. I knew I couldn't look at myself in the morning if I didn't try to meet that challenge. Maddy and Watts worked on my guilt.

UPDATE

Basically, the reason I'm still registered as a Republican is to tweak Mace. If you think the party tends to be short on substance when it comes to protecting the environment, you're right. A manual called *A Pro-Active, Pro-Environment Agenda for House Republicans* has been mailed to all GOP congressmen by the House Republican Conference. It reveals all manner of ingenious methods for legislators to paint themselves green. For instance, you can get your picture taken flouncing around with a borrowed shovel on Arbor Day. Herewith, a few excerpts from this astonishing document:

"As we all know, the environmentalist lobby and their extremist friends in the eco-terrorist underworld have been working overtime to define Republicans and their agenda as anti-environment, pro-polluter, and hostile to the survival of every cuddly critter roaming God's green earth . . . . The extremist environmental movement will stop at nothing to distort the facts, lie about our legislative agenda. The next time Bruce Babbit [*sic*] comes to your district and canoes down a river as a media stunt to tell the press how anti-environmental their congressman is, if reporters have been to [the representative's] adopt-a-highway clean-up, to his tree plantings, and his Congressional Task Force on Conservation hearings, they'll just laugh Babbit [*sic*] back to Washington . . . . Action Items: Tree Planting. This exercise provides members with excellent earned media opportunities. When participating in tree planting programs you should include both children and seniors."

Whose Woods Are These?

Saving the Northern Forest will take more

than task forces and studies

Audubon, May 1994

THE 26 MILLION ACRES stretching from Machias, Maine, across the top of New England to Syracuse, New York, is a land of contrasts—harsh and gentle, breathtakingly beautiful and hideously abused. It is a delicate, diverse zone of transition where northern evergreens intersperse with southern hardwoods; where moose, eagles and bears mingle with gray squirrels, starlings and house cats; where icy lakes reverberate with the yodeling of loons and the bleating of boom boxes. It is strewn with cedar swamps and maple ridges, spruce thickets and birch flats, blackflies and trout flies. It is fragrant with balsam and woodsmoke, rank with diesel breath and the rotten-cabbage stench of pulp mills.

The paper companies, the principal landlords, like to call it a working forest. To the public, which owns only 16 percent, it is the Northern Forest. A million people live in it; 70 million more can reach it by lunchtime if they start driving at daybreak. Within it are two dozen mountains more than 4,000 feet high, 5,000 ponds and lakes and almost 9,000 miles of large, clean rivers.

Most of the Northern Forest—15 million acres' worth—is in Maine. So are most of its problems. Here in the most forested state in the union, paper moguls and politicians have an alternate name for the "working forest." Just as frequently they call it an industrial forest.

Never has that name struck me as more apt than on February 8, when I flew over the top half of Maine with Rudy Engholm, who commands the New England wing of the Environmental Air Force, a nationwide group of 200 pilots who donate their time and often their money to provide journalists and resource managers with uncorrupted views of humanity's footprints. Industrial foresters chide the press for flying over clearcuts. You can't get a "feeling" for them that way, they say; you need to survey them from the ground. But I do both, and I see lots more from the air.

For instance, if you canoe the Allagash Wilderness Waterway, you get the impression of passing through Thoreau's Maine woods. But it's all a facade. From the air we saw the 400-foot-wide "beauty strip" of standing trees clinging to the bank like beaver hide, and beyond it a broken wasteland stretching to Canada. Engholm had punched the stopwatch as we passed over Brassua Lake's western beauty strip, blasted by a tailwind and slicing the thin, superchilled air at 200 miles per hour. The clearcut, recently photographed from space, finally petered out six and a half minutes later. Because the public sees clearcutting only from the ground, it believes those TV and magazine ads in which make-believe scientists in white smocks and yellow hard hats call it "forestry."

To feed their ravenous pulp mills, Maine paper companies have scalped an area the size of Delaware in the past decade. Slash is bull-dozed; native hardwood seedlings are frequently poisoned to make way for an unnatural softwood monoculture useful for producing paper but not wildlife. For the past three years a state Forest Practices Act has been in effect that supposedly "controls" clearcuts, restricting them to 250 acres.

Today just as much fiber is being removed from Maine as before 1991, but the cutting is spread out over a wider area. While some species of fish and wildlife may be doing better than they were before the Forest Practices Act (which isn't saying much), others—such as woodland-nesting neotropical birds—are probably doing worse.

Flying or walking over the Northern Forest—especially those parts where I have worked, camped, fished and hunted—is painful for me these days. Last summer, as I trudged the new logging roads east of Moosehead Lake, I looked for and couldn't find the mountain rills that used to blaze with cowslips, where trout fry would scatter like welding sparks whenever I stooped to drink. I couldn't find them because they had dried up. Their mixed-hardwood canopy had been skidded away, their wildness crushed under giant forest mowers called feller-bunchers. Now the brooks they used to feed run low, hot and chocolate brown.

Until the late 1980s a single thought sustained me: Despite the savaging the paper companies gave the land, at least they kept out the condo and second-home developers. If one tried hard, one could imagine the Northern Forest healing itself. After all, it had done so once before. In 1892 public outrage at the last round of clearcutting impelled the New York State legislature to start buying the stump fields that have since sprouted into Adirondack State Park. The federal Weeks Act of 1911, which authorized purchase of the New England stump fields now called the Green Mountain and White Mountain National Forests, was spawned by the same outrage. "I hate a man who would skin the land," boomed Theodore Roosevelt.

But paper companies, tripping through the Northern Forest via their computer consoles, have started flinging around the acronym HBU (Highest and Best Use), by which they mean nontraditional plans for their property. Now, instead of liquidating just the forest, they are liquidating the bare, churned-up land that used to nourish it and that may not be able to grow merchantable trees again anyway. They offer this land to condo and second-home developers. And because such developers basically seek river or lake frontage, HBU translates to suburbanization of remote watersheds. Who but paper-industry pooh-bahs and slap-dash developers could seriously call such use of wild woods and water "highest and best"? How Thoreau railed against such "poverty of nomenclature," as he called it.

Thoreau, however, was only the bard of the Northern Forest, not the hero of it. The hero, the man who did more than anyone to save it—albeit unwittingly—was developer Claude Rancourt. In 1988 Rancourt, aka New Hampshire's Trailer Park King, terrified the public, Congress and federal agencies into action by acquiring options on 92,000 HBU acres in Vermont and New Hampshire, including the wild, lovely Nash Stream watershed just north of White Mountain National Forest. Everyone had assumed that the land was safe—if not from abusive logging, at least from tacky development. After all, it had been owned by a giant forest-products company, Diamond Occidental. But Diamond had been seized in 1982 by British corporate raider James Goldsmith, who had dissolved the company and was hawking its holdings.

With the environmental community shaking state and federal legislators by the lapels, New Hampshire and the US Forest Service bought 46,000 acres of the watershed from Rancourt, leaving him with a sweet 25-percent profit and gravel-mining rights along Nash Stream. Then the real estate market went belly-up, he and other developers went bankrupt and the Northern Forest got a temporary reprieve.

Meanwhile the weighty mass of Congress had been set in motion. Led by senators Patrick Leahy (D-VT), Warren Rudman (R-NH) and George Mitchell (D-ME), it funded a study by the Forest Service on how best to preserve the Northern Forest, as it now was being called, from the Claude Rancourts of the world.

As part of the plan, the governors of Maine, New Hampshire, Vermont and New York appointed a task force to recommend revisions in the first draft of the study. The final draft, which was released in 1991, was a near-worthless vacuum bag of conservation strategies sucked from scores of hearings, workshops and conferences. Carl Reidel, who served on the Governors' Task Force and who directs the environmental program at the University of Vermont, called it "a dizzying array of schemes intended to find some common ground between calls for outright public acquisition and industry's fear of regulation."

The only practical way to save the Northern Forest is for the public to buy and set aside large wildland reserves and for the four states to agree on strict land-use regulations for the remaining private holdings. This last option, anathema to Wise Use activists and paper barons, entails "greenlining"—i.e., promulgating special regulations for the areas on a map encircled by a green line. The paper industry didn't mind talking about public land acquisition—provided the public remained under the table, begging for scraps—but the word "greenlining" set it foaming at the mouth. Every time members of the Governors' Task Force brought it up or talked about acquiring fish and wildlife habitat in ecologically significant blocks, the Maine contingent—Ed Meadows, commissioner of the state Department of Conservation, and Ted Johnston, president of an industrial coalition called the Maine Forest Products Council—stomped them down.

"In the interest of keeping Maine at the table, the task force simply ignored the tough decisions," recalls Reidel. "Maine held the baseball bat and gloves, and every time we tried to do something they said they'd go home. Then we'd crawl back in there and appease them. I felt like Chamberlain at Munich."

So the Governors' Task Force passed the buck to its successor, the Northern Forest Lands Council—consisting of four governor-appointed members from each state and a representative of the US Forest Service. Under congressional authorization the council has persevered in studying the Northern Forest. Last September it released a report called "Findings and Options," basically another vacuum bag of conservation strategies.

In selecting the council, the governors drew heavily from people with forest-products connections and sympathies. Therefore, the report didn't get into public land acquisition, greenlining or even forest practices. "It's as if a school blighted with teen pregnancy and venereal disease didn't allow any talk of sex," says environmental author Mitch Lansky, of Wytopitlock, Maine, who serves on the council's Citizens' Advisory Committee. Reidel has likened council activity to rearranging the deck chairs on the Titanic.

Still, the council hasn't been a total loss. In December 1992 it released a subcommittee report dispelling the industry-generated superstition that unreasonable environmental regulations are forcing the sale of large parcels in the Northern Forest. Among the real reasons, it revealed, was new investment strategies. And in its draft recommendations to Congress, published last March, the council opened the door for the creation of reserves and addressed the issue of abusive logging, recommending a process for better state control. Perhaps the council's greatest contribution is that it has gotten champions of the Northern Forest thinking and talking on a regional basis.

In the Northern Forest, as in so many biologically and politically sensitive regions, study has become the preferred alternative to action. Frustrated by the dawdling, the National Audubon Society and 23 other environmental groups have formed a Northern Forest Alliance to prod the council, the states and the federal government. One point all hands agree on is that a healthy forest depends on a healthy, sustainable forest-based economy. Of all strategies shaken from the vacuum bags of Northern Forest studiers, encouraging such an economy is the most frequently encountered.

To be truly healthy a forest-based economy needs to be diverse. Everyone agrees on this, too. But what no one seems to understand is that in Maine, which is programmed by the paper industry at every level of government, diversity is a nice idea that just won't happen. Moreover, the industry is in bad financial shape. Great Northern Paper, the state's biggest landholder, has eliminated 2,100 jobs since 1984. In roughly the same period, full-time logging jobs in Maine have declined 40 percent.

Much of what ails Maine paper companies is self-inflicted. Their nonsustainable, cut-out-and-get-out approach to forest management has reduced spruce and fir (the valuable species for paper) by 40 percent, and now about half of the pulp mix is hardwood. Using Northern

Forest hardwoods for paper instead of sawlogs is like making fish cakes out of salmon fillets. Not that the hardwoods are all that healthy these days. Throughout the Northern Forest, high-grading—the practice of taking the healthiest trees and leaving the genetic wrecks—has transformed prime saw timber to pulp, and pulp to fuel.

"Over the last 50 years Maine has been at the bottom of the nation in terms of employment and level of living," says Charles Fitzgerald, who serves on the board of a young, aggressive environmental group called Restore: The North Woods and who sustains a small wood-products mill in Dover-Foxcroft with his own well-managed timberland. "Small landowners can't get fair prices for their timber because the paper companies undercut them."

"What do you mean by a forest-products industry?" asks author Mitch Lansky. "Are you talking about a dominant paper industry that can control prices and that will accept a high-graded forest because it only wants pulp? Or are you talking about local sawmills, fishing and hunting guides, river-rafting companies, mushroom gatherers, maple syrup producers? There are lots of ways to make money from a forest. We need healthy communities, and healthy communities need to have some sort of stable economic base, not a destructive, exploitative base."

Now, with markets in the Pacific Northwest shutting down, Maine has taken to exporting raw logs and with them much of what little diversity its forest-based economy enjoyed. In 1993, 16.5 million board feet of unmilled timber was shipped overseas. Hemlock and white pine, bound for Turkey and China, are stacked in a half-mile-long pile in front of the docks in Portland, Maine.

Northern Forest advocates keep talking about how they are avoiding the nasty, resource-draining confrontations ripping apart the Northwest. But they are avoiding them only because they haven't taken on the paper industry. Yankee environmental organizations tend to be cautious and conservative, preferring to "work with" industry rather than control it; frequently there is forest-products influence on their boards. In Maine they have been beaten up by the paper companies so long and so savagely that such victories as the Forest Practices Act seem stunning, as if Oliver Twist had wangled a second serving of gruel.

Northern Forest advocates say they are lucky not to have a spotted owl. But they lack one only because they don't use or even understand the Endangered Species Act. The pine marten, a large, arboreal weasel vanishing with its old-growth habitat, is probably in no better shape than the marbled murrelet, another forest-nesting bird inconveniencing Northwest timber companies. The US population of Atlantic salmon—which breeds only in Maine—is just as likely to be lost as the spring-run chinooks of the Snake River. But it has taken Restore: The North Woods—a group based in Concord, Massachusetts—to successfully petition the US Fish and Wildlife Service to consider the Atlantic salmon for endangered or threatened status. I have it from quieter, more contented environmentalists that Restore's "real motive" is to lock the loggers out of Down East watersheds. If so, it's a pretty good one.

Now that the council's draft recommendations to Congress are out, the Wise Use movement has a big rubber snake to scare the public with. The wise-users are well organized in the Adirondacks, where they are reported to have slashed tires, cut off power, thrown skunk oil and shot at cars. Elsewhere in the Northern Forest they so far are neither well organized nor well funded.

Mary Adams, of the Maine Freedom Fighters, calls the Northern Forest initiative a tax plot by "extraterrestrials" who want to "sell us down the river and turn us into a neat and tidy Indian reservation where we can pick up sticks for our fires in designated areas and wait on tourists." Robert Voight, of the Maine Conservation Rights Institute, identifies the initiative as "the next great attempt by environmentalists to kick all rural citizens off their lands and make the region devoid of people." Thomas Morse, of the Vermont Property Rights Information Center, reveals that Northern Forest advocates are "cultlike" and, further, that they are "flatlanders from out of state."

The impending fight over the Northern Forest will likely make or break the Eastern irruption of the Wise Use movement, whose fortunes are linked to the conduct of the environmental groups it lies about. "The property-rights people have knocked themselves out of the council discussion by their own stupidity," comments veteran Northern Forest crusader Jamie Sayen, editor of Earth Island Institute's *Northern Forest Forum*. "They've taken the pressure off the council by saying, 'Whatever you want, we're against.' They've just launched a nasty, scurrilous attack in an attempt to get Maine to pull out. All it has done is piss off people on the council who were sympathetic to property rights. If we allow them to bully us, they can prevent the discussion from happening. If we stand up to them as we have in recent council sessions, they're powerless; they fall apart."

The one nice thing about clearcuts is that the land underneath them sells cheap. In Maine, which contains 58-percent of the Northern Forest and only 5-percent of its public land, there may be as many as two million acres that can be purchased at fair market value. They can be unloaded to other clearcutters, they can be subdivided and sold to developers or they can be bought by the public as the beginning of a wildlands reserve big enough for sustained, responsible logging; wildlife research; fishing; hunting; wolf, cougar and caribou recovery; and a future for creatures like the pine marten and the Atlantic salmon. A National Thoreau Reserve, perhaps, rising in Maine and flowing west—a reserve, as Thoreau wrote when he first proposed one, "in which the bear and panther, and some even of the hunter race, may still exist, and not be civilized off the face of the Earth."

"Look what we did in the Adirondacks," remarks Dave Miller, the National Audubon Society's vice-president for New England and New York. "We can do the same for the Maine woods, Vermont's Northeast Kingdom, and northern New Hampshire. We're at the real crest of something about to break here, if we can outnumber the Wise Use folks, make this the next generation of forestry issues in this country. It's a critical time in history. But if we walk away and Washington turns its back and the Lands Council report stays on the shelf, then it's back to the status quo."

One of the driving forces behind the Northern Forest initiative has been Mollie Beattie, now in charge of the US Fish and Wildlife Service. As director of Vermont's Richard Snelling Center for Government, she made the best statement on the initiative that I have heard before or since, a statement for which she got lambasted by champions of perpetual study. "Pretty soon," pronounced Beattie, "the time for comfortable data-gathering and mapping will be over. There will be only two choices. The first will be to buy up a couple of reserves and offer up a few standard economic-development programs; effectively, to declare victory and get out. The second will be to take a risk that is as big as the Northern Forest itself, that of truly conserving all of this special place before it is gone, without our old techniques, our old suspicions, and our territorial myopia. No more metaphors and maps. Think big. Trust each other. Do something bold."

Before Rudy Engholm set a course back to Lewiston, he swung me over Upper Enchanted Township—my woods, where I used to lie on my back beside wild trout water, listening to loon song and the banter of barred owls, watching the plumes of my campfires trailing into the brilliant Milky Way. Here, from the cliff that soars out of Big Enchanted Pond—where my bush pilot, George Young, once tipped his wing at an eastern cougar—you can gaze out over Maine's flat middle. Then you can turn and contemplate mountains the color of Yankee twilight and lakes that glitter, as Thoreau wrote, "like a mirror broken into a thousand fragments."

Much of the Northern Forest was still clad in virgin white pine when my late friend, the writer-poet Arthur McDougall, stood on a sidewalk in Bingham and listened to John Kelly reproduce the hideous caterwauling he and his logging crew had heard on their camp roof. With lanterns they had searched from Dead River landing for miles in all directions, never finding a human footprint in the new snow. It was the devil dancing on the roof, they concluded. They said the country was enchanted.

I hadn't been back to my enchanted forest since the mid-1980s. Now it was gone. Big Enchanted Pond lay amid the ruins. West of the cougar cliff the clearcuts merged in an endless moonscape, veined with logging roads and skidder trails. Over the past six years 50 percent of the township has been skinned. And now the beauty strips and the sterile, stump-flecked castings of feller-bunchers are on the market for second-home development.

UPDATE

There's a lot of BS being put out on what's happening to the Northern Forest. If you want to learn the truth subscribe to the *Northern Forest Forum*, a beautifully edited and written newspaper published by the Northern Appalachian Restoration Project of Earth Island Institute. Send $15 to Forum, Box 6, Lancaster, NH 03584.

The Northern Forest Alliance is spending big money without a whole lot to show for it, but I suppose the mere fact that it exists is good news.

Jym St. Pierre now works as the Maine director for Restore: The North Woods—the group loggers and sportsmen love to hate because it seems capable of actually effecting change, like getting the state to take care of America's only wild Atlantic salmon. He reports that Restore has formally withdrawn from being a member of the Northern Forest Alliance, but still works with it. Restore has launched a petition drive to create a 3.2-million-acre national park in northern Maine encompassing Baxter State Park, Moosehead Lake and the headwaters of the state's major inland rivers, including the St. John, Allagash, Penobscot and Kennebec. Property-rights zealots are horrified, but the plan makes economic sense for everyone, especially paper companies looking to unload scalped forestland.

The River Always Wins

Will we ever get the message?

Audubon, July 1994

IN THE SUMMER OF 1993 one of the earth's great rivers, a silt-laden colossus that drains 330,000 square miles of the North American continent and is navigable for most of its 2,000 miles, broke over its banks and raged through its sparsely wooded watershed. The river had withdrawn to the channel and was back to its normal color of wet concrete when I flew over it in mid-August, but evidence of the flood was readily apparent. Dirt banks had been blown apart, uprooted vegetation strewn hither and yon.

The river was the Yukon. And if you hadn't heard that it overflowed, it's because no one but the river wrote about it. Since people do not dare to live in it, which is to say on the regularly inundated floodplain, the media ignore its naturally fluctuating water levels. The Yukon just basks pythonlike in the thin Arctic sun, coiled between the Bering Sea and the alpine lakes of British Columbia, breathing in and breathing out.

From the swollen mouth of the Yukon southeast along the planet's hazy, silver-veined arch, other North American river systems were breathing, too—some faster and deeper than others, but all of them inhaling rain and snowmelt. Two-thirds of the way down the middle of the continent, the Mississippi—the biggest of them all—took a normal breath last summer, the sort of breath it has taken every few decades since ice sheets last chased it south.

But this time a phalanx of levees—earthen dikes paralleling both sides of the main stream and the major tributaries—compressed and elevated the flow. The alleged flood barrier was longer, higher and thicker than the Great Wall of China. It had been tailored by the US Army Corps of Engineers and fitted when the river was between breaths. Then, with every little exhalation, the barrier had been cinched tighter by farmers who built their own levee systems closer and closer to the banks, snatching sustenance from the fertile silt like sanderlings chasing a retreating wave.

When the river inhaled again, its new corset bulged, popped and flew apart. The media were agog, Congress frantic, the public stunned. The flood was widely reported to be a 500-year event, which seemed odd because records hadn't been kept for even 200 years and the Army didn't have a clue as to what a 500-year flood was really like. Soon the flood was downgraded to a 120-year event. This year's flood—happening as I write (in late April 1994)—might also have been a "120-year event" had the enormous snowpack not melted before the heavy rains.

While the 1993 flow of 1.03 million cubic feet per second, as recorded at St. Louis, was the highest since the 1.3-million-cfs reading in 1844, runoff of roughly the same magnitude—i.e., nearly one million cfs—was measured in 1883, 1892, 1903, 1908, 1909, 1927, 1944 and 1973. The river had been telling us something we weren't hearing.

In 1993 the river did not creep and seep back over its floodplain as it had done for thousands of years. Its fertile sediments did not, as of old, settle over the landscape like windless snow. Instead it blasted through and over a thousand dikes, killing 50 people, routing 62,000 families, wrecking 55 towns, destroying $12 billion worth of property, clawing out the lining of the world's breadbasket.

The levee system was supposed to have made it safe to live and work in the Mississippi and her tributaries. The US Army had promised. "This nation has a large and powerful adversary," the Corps of Engineers had explained in one of its early promotional films before its much-touted but little-evidenced environmental awakening. "We are fighting Mother Nature . . . . It's a battle we have to fight day by day, year by year; the health of our economy depends on victory." Soon thereafter, the Army engineers saw fit to declare victory over the Mississippi. "We harnessed it, straightened it, regularized it, shackled it," they bragged. When the river breathed again, reclaiming its old channel, exploding out of its pathetic dirt container and sweeping away the works of humanity, America called it an act of God.

One year later have we learned anything about manmade flood control? Some of us—but not Congress and not the Army—have learned that it isn't desirable or even possible. Some of us have learned that where river living is left to the creatures designed for it, floodwater can only renew, that it can no more damage a floodplain than fire can hurt a forest.

The sand that now covers so much riverside cropland, for example, did not displace it; cropland had displaced sand. When nature was doing the engineering, sand had been a vital part of the ecosystem, providing breeding habitat for sundry snakes and turtles, piping plovers, least terns and spadefoot toads. Now these creatures, some flirting with extinction, have a brighter future. Even the unnatural ponds called scour holes, drilled out of the loose earth by jets of water gushing through levee breaks, are filled with fish and lined with herons. Last winter the Missouri Department of Conservation counted 42 bald eagles hunched around just one.

Because so many flood-adapted species had record spawning years, we thought we learned that this human disaster was "good" for fish. But 1993 wasn't a "good" year for any life form that had evolved in the Mississippi; it was a normal year. All the others—before the massive failure of the levee system—had been bad years.

President Clinton had learned from the Bush administration's slow response to Hurricane Andrew how politically dangerous it is not to quickly douse disaster areas with pork. Accordingly, he shook loose a $5.33 billion relief package that facilitated the repair of most levees and enabled and encouraged most flood victims to rebuild in the river.

But the Clinton administration has also learned that wars on Mother Nature don't work. That may sound like a kindergarten lesson, but for our federal government it is a major awakening.

Here and there the river is being allowed to keep what it reclaimed. Farmers are getting $100 million to back away from 110,000 acres of reborn wetlands, and floodplain colonists weary of getting wet have received half a billion dollars to move out of the river.

Even the US Fish and Wildlife Service has started to learn a little of what its new director, Mollie Beattie, has been telling it—that single-species management is economically and biologically counterproductive. At last the service has second thoughts about its traditional approach of mass-producing ducks by sealing floodplains from rivers with Corps-style levees and manipulating fake wetlands for moist-soil plants. "The best thing we can do for waterfowl is have healthy, naturally flooding river systems," one of the new thinkers told me. "That way we'll have lots of ducks, lots of fish and lots of birds."

Strapped into the shotgun seat of the Missouri Department of Conservation's Cessna 182, I inspected the stone revetments that were supposed to have shackled the Mississippi River's biggest tributary, the Missouri. Now, on the ides of March 1994, they were under sand and under water. Everywhere the floodplain was cratered with scour holes, as if it had been saturation-bombed by B-52s. Some are 50 feet deep and 200 yards across; even the Army says it can't afford to fill them in.

Still, the Corps is trying to repair its flood-containment array, which, throughout the Mississippi Basin, includes 30 super levees it built itself and 1,500 private levees, most of which were engineered to its specifications and funded four-to-one with federal dollars. By the time you read this, all the federal levees and about half the private levees will be up again.

Three thousand feet below me, in a scene from an ant farm, bulldozers crawled over cropland reclaimed by the river, pushing silt into failed levees and making new ones around the upland shores of scour holes. Sand covered former corn, wheat and soybean fields up to four miles back from midchannel. It had drifted to 10-foot depths, burying boat ramps and silos, buckling the sad, broken husks of houses and barns where nothing lives now save lonely cottonwoods planted by families who thought the river had been defeated. There was sand in front of us, sand in back of us, sand as far as I could see.

On the ground at Grafton, Illinois, where the Mississippi collects the Illinois River coming down from Chicago, I stopped for lunch at Beasley's Fresh Fish. Jim Beasley nets the river; wife, Deborah, cooks. The water had lapped the bottom of their sign four feet above my head, but they'd gotten everything out in time, and the cement walls had held. Other people weren't so lucky. The road along the river was lined with abandoned houses water-stained to the eaves, some leaning with the flow. A piece of flotsam hung from a telephone wire.

Tired of rebuilding, the citizens of Grafton have voted to move a third of the town out of the river and up onto dry land. In all, about 200 Mississippi Basin communities from southern Missouri to Wisconsin will make major retreats from floodplain living, at a total cost to US taxpayers of $500 million. "If you know anything about the history of the Midwest, you know that people who came here were going to cling to the land regardless of what they could get out of it," says Scott Faber of American Rivers, a nonprofit conservation organization. "This is unheard of."

I stopped at the café in Hartsburg, Missouri, but it was closed and won't reopen. Lots of the residents aren't going to rebuild. The town was lonely and silent, save for the procession of dump trucks hauling dirt down to the ruptured levee. The four-foot-high banks of dry river mud along the streets had been plowed up like snow. Broken sandbags surrounded broken neighborhoods. Houses slumped windowless beside rubble-filled dumpsters. A tilted sign with two letters missing said: Hartsburg Thanks Ever on . Hell of a Try.

Standing in one of the levee breaks was levee-district president Orion Beckmeyer—hazel eyed, steel haired, leather skinned, a farmer since 1961. Now farmers in Hartsburg and elsewhere are considering pulling their operations out of the river. Under the Soil Conservation Service's $100 million Wetlands Reserve Program, they can convert qualifying acreage to wetlands by selling easements to the government. But if the farmers do that, they can't gouge dirt from the wetlands to fix their levees.

"It's taking a man's property use without paying for it," laments Beckmeyer, who is thinking about selling wetland easements on 30 of his own acres now covered with thigh-deep sand. "I don't know where that leaves this country. God gave us these resources, and we need to use them. We need to feed the world."

Three hundred miles north, in Louisa County, Iowa, ice lingered in the Mississippi's backwater puddles left from the big flood, and the red-winged blackbirds, old news in Grafton and Hartsburg, had just arrived. Now they were flashing their red epaulets and shouting from every snag. They were seeing a different sort of spring. The US Fish and Wildlife Service flew me over one of its metal water-inlet structures in the Mark Twain National Wildlife Refuge. The dike that used to be level with it wasn't broken—it was gone, sheared off at ground level. Now what remains just stands there, a monument to river power and human impotence.

Slightly downstream and a little way up the Iowa River, we orbited over 3,000-acre Levee District Eight while an adult bald eagle orbited below us. Maybe it was hunting fish in the recharged, reclaimed oxbow lakes. Sealed from the river by the levee, the oxbows had silted in, and their fish had died out. But now the river had returned, as it would return each spring through the hopelessly ventilated flood barrier, scouring out the silt, collecting young fish, spreading spawners. This is how rivers used to work before the engineers "improved" them, to use their word. Here, at least, the Mississippi and its ecosystem were breathing again.

Later that day I inspected the blown-out levee with Tom Bell, Wapello District manager for the Mark Twain Refuge. The sun was warm on our necks, the air cool and scented with old fish and new mud. Crows jeered at a red-tailed hawk. Shovelers cut V wakes on the oxbow lakes. Mallards burst out of flooded timber. Gulls caroused over gizzard shad stranded in a year-old puddle. A red-headed woodpecker played peekaboo with us from behind a pin oak. To our left the Iowa River had cleansed a field of corn, leaving driftwood and stubble sticking up through sand. New wetlands were everywhere; and the only sounds were made by wildlife.

The river at Levee District Eight had been trying to tell people something. Eighteen times over the past 66 years it had busted up the levee, and 18 times humans had fixed it. The 1990 repairs had taken so long that the farmers didn't get a crop the next year. Crop-insurance premiums were going up; payments, based on crop yield, were going down. Still, when the river busted up the levee in 1993, the Corps prepared to plod ahead in its war with Mother Nature. The big levees the Corps builds itself. But if you sign up for its private-levee program and do your bulldozing to government standards, you can chase the retreating water almost to the bank, and the Corps will pay 80 percent of the repair cost each time the river breaks your levee. The only catch is that the alleged benefits have to outweigh the costs, usually not a problem.

Had the farmers come up with their 20 percent ($160,000), the Corps would have replaced its Maginot Line around Levee District Eight yet again. But this time even the farmers had had enough, especially now that they had a chance to sell out to the Fish and Wildlife Service. The service couldn't put its hands on the cash, so it turned to the National Fish and Wildlife Foundation—an eight-year-old organization hatched and partly funded by Congress. The foundation put up a no-interest emergency loan of $250,000 and arranged a matching loan from a private group called the Conservation Fund. The Iowa Natural Heritage Foundation pledged $10,000 and agreed to do the actual land transactions, and the Soil Conservation Service provided $1.7 million. "This is the first time anything like this has been attempted," declares National Fish and Wildlife Foundation executive director Amos Eno, "and we're going to be doing a lot more of it."

The floodplain colonists I met along the river didn't like me. I was there to listen and learn, but having written about the false promise and environmental costs of flood control for 25 years, I had a few too many answers to their rhetorical questions. They could hear me thinking, "I told you so."

Clearer voices than mine had been telling them so since before the dams went in and the Corps started "channelizing" rivers—i.e., correcting their meanders, gouging out their magic, mystery and life, leaving in their places sterile, riprapped gutters straight as a forced march. Because these writers knew and loved natural, unruly rivers, they understood that the real costs of alleged flood control are not measured in money and property but in wildness and beauty. The rivers had spoken to them, and they had tried to pass the message on to the colonists and the Army. No one was listening.

"The military engineers of the [River] Commission have taken upon their shoulders the job of making the Mississippi over again, a job transcended in size by only the original job of creating it," wrote Mark Twain in 1882. "Ten thousand River Commissions, with the mines of the world at their back, cannot tame that lawless stream, cannot curb it or confine it, cannot say to it, Go here, or Go there, and make it obey; cannot save a shore which it has sentenced; cannot bar its path with an obstruction which it will not tear down, dance over, and laugh at."

The Army has never liked that kind of talk. In 1943 Colonel Lewis Pick—who commanded the Corps's Omaha regional office and who fired people for resting on Sunday—got mad at the Missouri River, which flows for 2,466 miles before its confluence with the Mississippi, at St. Louis. The Missouri had humiliated him, chased him out of his own city, which for a while was navigable only by boat. The river was too large for practical containment of minor floods, too swift for profitable navigation. But it was the only place left where you could build big dams, so Colonel Pick whipped together plans for five. Eager to make work for returning servicemen, Congress told him to go for it.

Since Twain penned his commentary, Army dams, channelization projects and levees on the Missouri River have eliminated 100,000 acres of sloughs, backwaters, side channels and seasonal wetlands. From Ponca, Nebraska, to St. Louis, bottomland and riparian forests were reduced 96 percent. On the entire Mississippi system above St. Louis, 19 million acres of wetlands—the only flood control that has ever really worked—were engineered to oblivion.

The Army's brand of flood control didn't save Bill Lay's family farm in Arrow Rock, Missouri. I stood on the bluff with him, looking out over his dead cropland—last March a black desert full of dirt, this

March a real desert full of sand. On this fine, gusty morning it blew over Lisbon Bottoms and Jameson Island like smoke from a prairie fire, catching in our nostrils and hair. Lay figures he might be able to plow some of it back into the soil and replant, but then he'd have to irrigate. Otherwise, most of the land won't grow anything save sycamore, white swamp oak, pin oak, cottonwood, black willow and silver maple, which now will steal back in from remnant patches of lush bottomland forest that Lewis and Clark saw when they stopped here on their way up the Missouri in 1804.

Lay is being courted and stroked by the Ecological Services branch of the Fish and Wildlife Service, which hopes to buy his ruined farm and the ruined farms of his neighbors in order to restore the Missouri River's natural flood cycle on 3,023 acres. This sort of ecosystem management is considered heresy by a large element of the service still committed to mass duck production.

Bill Lay is a shrewd businessman. He makes noises as if he's not so sure he likes the idea of unloading the carcass of his farm on the feds for something like $1,000 an acre. And he sounds bitter that this time US taxpayers won't kick in their usual 80 percent to fix his levees. So extensive was the damage to the soil and the levee system that the Corps can't justify levee repair even with its trick arithmetic. "They were private levees," complains Lay, "then we brought them up to Corps standards, and they said they'd repair the damage. Well, that's true except when the damage is too high. Now they ain't going to fix the damn things."

At a diner near Boonville we met Tom Sites of Blackwater. Lay is polite and friendly, so he laughed when he introduced me as "the enemy." Sites said: "The only people making any money off this thing are exporting it, like you writers."

I explained as tactfully as I knew how that some of the locals were doing OK, too. Deserving of empathy and thanks—not I-told-you-so lectures—are the destitute refugees, the tireless sandbag stuffers, the heroic volunteers who slogged through chemical poison and fecal filth, toting dogs, kids and grandmothers. But they have gotten a year's worth of ink, and now it is time to write about professional flood victims who make a business out of collecting relief. They cash their checks, do some token repairs in order to maintain government-subsidized flood insurance, then wait for the river's next inhalation.

If your home is 50-percent damaged, you have to prop it up on wooden stilts to keep collecting flood insurance. But this is so expensive that families are tempted to move out, thereby slashing the county's tax base. So damage assessments, which are made by the county assessors, have a way of hovering at 49 percent.

The National Flood Insurance Program was conceived 26 years ago as a means of steering development out of floodplains. Instead, it has ensured flood damage by encouraging people to remain in the river. One extended family, squatting on the floodplain in St. Charles County, Missouri, has collected flood insurance on 25 separate claims since 1979. But 87 percent of floodplain colonists victimized by the Mississippi hadn't bothered to buy flood insurance. Why should they have? They knew the government would give them relief checks and that they could pick up a quick insurance policy when the river was literally lapping at their doorsteps. A company in Chesterfield, Missouri, didn't purchase insurance until a week before the rising water caused it $1 million worth of damage.

Tom Sites is a tenant farmer with no floodplain land to dump on Uncle Sam. Most of his capital is tied up in equipment, and he really did get hurt by the flood. But other farmers are making out like toll collectors at a two-way rotary. When the Corps lined the river with stone revetments, rich sediments accrued behind them. The river got narrower, and the farmers moved closer, getting a gift of prime land. Next the government built them levees to protect that land. When the levees failed, the government cut the farmers relief checks. Now the government is buying back the land it gave them in the first place.

Buffalo was what I ordered at Beasley's Fresh Fish, in Grafton, Illinois. Not the mammal, the fish—a native sucker, growing to 50 pounds, that evolved to broadcast its eggs over flooded bottomland and whose young fatten on the rich plankton blooms that pour from saturated earth. Buffaloes used to fuel the local economy, but as the levees rose, sealing them off from the fields, they faded. In recent years they had steadily lost ground to exotic European carp, also floodplain spawners but which seem to be able to make it anywhere. In 1993, for the first time since the Illinois Natural History Survey began keeping records five years ago, buffaloes outproduced carp. "Why?" I inquired of Rob Maher, a fisheries biologist with the survey who was seated next to me, eating his own slab of buffalo. "Home-court advantage," he said.

As the flood crested, Maher and his colleagues began collecting young-of-the-year fish in unheard-of quantities and locations. Blue suckers, which are being considered for endangered status, were seen for the first time in the middle Mississippi between St. Louis and Cairo, Illinois. In the same area one survey team was unable to lift a fyke net because it contained 8,600 black crappies—fish not usually found in the main river.

FDR's New Deal wasn't a good deal if you evolved in the upper-Mississippi system. The dams, levees and other make-work "improvements" that went in during that period, together with even grander postwar boondoggles, have endangered some 15 fish species, in fact if not by government decree. These fish evolved in turbid flows, developing special adaptations like flat heads, external sensory organs called barbels, and small eyes that in some cases have over-grown with skin to reduce abrasion from moving sand. They have great difficulty dealing with the clear water that occurs when silt drops out of dam-slowed current, largely because their prey can see them coming. And they require floods to spawn.

"Big-river fishes typically migrate all over the place, looking for spe-cialized habitat," comments Larry Hesse of the Nebraska Game and Parks Commission. He uses the example of paddlefish, ancient plankton grazers that are being considered for endangered status. Paddlefish need rock-rubble substrates for spawning, hard to find in the Mississippi Basin. A big female carrying a couple of million eggs might find a good spot, but if she doesn't sense rising water or if the water's too cold—as it often is below a dam's outfall—she'll reabsorb her eggs.

The blue catfish, which can reach 300 pounds and was most likely the monster that exploring priest Jacques Marquette rammed with his canoe in 1673, is scarcely ever seen in the Missouri north of Kansas. When one does show up, it predates Colonel Pick and the New Deal. The ebony shell, once the dominant mussel in the upper Mississippi, needs to attach itself in larval form to the gills of skipjack herring. But when dams were built, cutting off the skipjack migration, ebony shells began fading away. As long ago as 1931, biologists were unable to find a single ebony in the upper Mississippi under nine years old. Today there is limited reproduction but only because a few skipjacks have been slipping over the dams during floods. Eleven other kinds of mussels have been lost.

At the National Biological Survey's fisheries lab, in Columbia, Missouri, I held a struggling two-year-old pallid sturgeon. It was bone hard, shark strong and about as long as my forearm. The two outer barbels above the sucker mouth were longer than the inner two, the tail skinny and trailing a whip, the eyes in the flat, pit viper head so small I had to look for them. This fish was from the first and only captive-reared year class, and its parents had been among the first pallid sturgeons ever seen by biologists. The DNA molecules that shaped the being twisting in my hands had organized themselves 250 million years ago—before the appearance of many dinosaurs; yet it had taken million-year-old man just four river breaths to almost erase them.

Six days before I'd arrived, Pallid Sturgeon Recovery Team member Kim Graham, of the Missouri Department of Conservation, had stocked 7,200 of this fish's siblings at three sites on the lower Missouri and five on the Mississippi below St. Louis. Like most of the Mississippi's troubled fish, pallids spawn when they sense rising, warming water. So the pallid sturgeon recovery plan recommends emulating the river's natural pulse by asking the Corps to release water from the dams in spring. But in 1994 the Corps' attitude doesn't seem a whole lot better than during the New Deal when it proclaimed, "We will not play nursemaid to the fish."

Even Twain's voice is young. For centuries people who know rivers have been questioning flood control. A thousand years before the birth of Christ the practice was outlawed by the Egyptians, who depended on the Nile's life-giving respiration. "Do not hinder the waters of the inundation," ordered the *Book of the Dead*. If the ancient Egyptians could learn from their big river, maybe modern Americans can learn from theirs. "Did we?" I asked Larry Hesse.

"I think we already have gone back to our habits," he told me. "The strategic planning team that was created by the White House was given the responsibility of coming up with some innovative floodplain-management ideas, such as levee removal, by the middle of March 1994. While that was going on, the levees got rebuilt. What kind of sense is that? That's not learning anything."

While American Rivers' Scott Faber is encouraged by some of the Clinton administration's revolutionary initiatives to move people away from floods instead of vice versa, he's not sure how much we've really learned. "Disaster assistance is still skewed in favor of relief and against long-term flood-loss reduction," he remarks. "Most people are deciding to rebuild in harm's way, and once again, flood-control policy is falling victim to small decisions."

The bits and pieces of floodplain the government is acquiring or converting to wetlands will help, but humanity needs to step out of the river altogether, leaving a continuous, uninhabited floodway. Such a floodway, winding over 275,899 acres, was actually authorized by Congress along with Colonel Pick's 1943 counterattack on the Missouri, but landowners nixed it as too expensive. Even at today's prices you could purchase the floodway for $232 million—about a quarter of what the Army spends for one of its superdams. But when Rick Hansen and his colleagues in Fish and Wildlife's Ecological Services branch suggested this approach, they were shouted down. "People just went ballistic," recalls Hansen. "That was too much money. So instead we spent $5 billion bailing out flood victims."

As a conduit for commerce, the Missouri River never had much potential. For example, 50 years after Colonel Pick's cost-benefit analysis proclaimed that the river would move 12 million tons of goods annually, it moves less than 2 million. Now, to meet a fantasized demand for navigation, the Corps proposes to further disrupt the flood cycle with renovations to its lock-and-dam system that could cost as much as $6 billion.

After last year's flood the Corps went right on ignoring fish and wildlife. "One thing it did that we feel was very destructive was to pull the river down in an attempt to drain flooded levee districts after the fish had gone into their [shallow] wintering areas," says Rip Sparks, director of river research laboratories for the Illinois Natural History Survey. "So we're fearful that the tremendous 1993 production may have been harmed. The interesting thing is that the engineers keep saying they can't pull the river down for environmental purposes because they have to maintain navigation, and yet here they did it to drain fields."

Low flow at the right time, however, is as important to a river's health as spring flooding. "That's one of the natural processes that I'm afraid won't be addressed," says Chuck Theiling, an Illinois Natural History Survey biologist. Mud flats are essential to shorebirds and seeds of cottonwood; the endangered false decurrent aster can germinate nowhere else. Low flows also expose sediments to the air, allowing them to compact. When this doesn't happen, unnaturally high sediment loads suspended by wave action in Corps reservoirs kill aquatic plants by cutting off their sunlight.

I met Theiling at his new office, in Wood River, Illinois. The Corps used to let him work in its building in West Alton, Missouri, but that got destroyed by the flood. After half a century the river was still humiliating the US Army. We drove out to four-year-old Locks and Dam 26—the Corps's pride and joy and the planet's biggest civil engineering project. Standing on the sand dunes that had reclaimed the parking lot at the Corps' Riverlands demonstration area, we watched shad splash in shallow water. Spring had arrived, but Locks and Dam 26 had reversed the Mississippi's flood cycle.

Farther upstream Theiling showed me woodland pools still full of 1993 floodwater, habitats that had been drained and leveed off from the river since the mid-1920s. Now they supported aquatic plants. The seeds had not been borne on the flood. They'd been ensconced in the soil all that time—waiting while the US Army played King Canute, while Earth wheeled 70 times around Sol, while humans lived out their allotted three-score years and 10. Waiting for the river to take a normal breath.

UPDATE

Much of the sand-covered cropland I inspected is now part of the Big Muddy National Fish and Wildlife Refuge, a floodplain corridor stretching from Kansas City to St. Louis, where the Missouri River can do its own thing. More than 100,000 acres has been enrolled in easement or acquisition programs.

"We're trying to facilitate processes where the river can reconnect itself with its floodplain," declares Big Muddy's manager, J.C. Bryant. "The sad thing about the Missouri is that it has been turned into a ditch. The ecosystem approach really boils down to what some of us old timers call integrated management. What we're saying is that when we make a management decision on a piece of land we want to do it with some ecological orientation." A similar project, targeting 50,000 acres, is underway along the Iowa River.

Scott Faber, of American Rivers—the single most knowledgeable person I have encountered on flood issues—reports three big improvements in our national mindset:

1) Now anyone in the commodities program has to purchase crop insurance. This will vastly reduce agricultural losses and force flood-plain farmers to bear costs of farming in risky areas.

2) Now lenders will be penalized if they don't make sure that mortgage holders have flood insurance.

3) Congress has decided that from now on it won't add to the deficit to pay for flood disasters.

When I talked with Faber for this update he'd just emerged from a 24-hour, closed-door session with flood-plain industry and agriculture. "Now they're thinking about long-term health of the Mississippi," he told me. "They want to increase flood-plain habitat. They're starting to see flooding as part of a river's natural cycle."

Even the Corps has learned something, says Faber. After the flood, its two-year study showed that raising levees would cause catastrophic damage in St. Louis—precisely what American Rivers had been arguing all along.

Can the Forest Service Heal Itself?

A morally corrupt federal agency may be on the mend

Wildlife Conservation, September/October 1994

GWYNN CREEK was a lovely, productive trout stream hurrying down from Oregon's Siuslaw National Forest when, one day in 1985, it disappeared under an estimated 100,000 truckloads of dirt. The landslide, which originated in a small clearcut high in the mostly unlogged watershed, negotiated the stream's four-mile course in minutes, crossed Highway 101 and merged with the Pacific Ocean. Standing on the highway bridge, an official of the US Forest Service who couldn't conceive of a landslide traveling all that distance was heard to exclaim, "Thank God this wasn't started by a clearcut."

As a casualty of Forest Service malfeasance, Gwynn Creek is hardly atypical. The Service, a 29,000-person bureaucracy within the US Department of Agriculture, spends $3.5 billion a year supposedly to ensure multiple use and to protect fish, wildlife and plant communities on 191 million acres of national forest lands.

Created by President Theodore Roosevelt, the Service was built to prominence by his friend Gifford Pinchot, its first chief and the first North American to approach forestry as a science and a form of husbandry. "It is the honorable distinction of the Forest Service," wrote Pinchot, "that it has been more constantly, more violently, and more bitterly attacked by the representatives of the special interests than any other government bureau. These attacks have increased in violence and bitterness in proportion as the Service has offered opposition to predatory wealth."

But somewhere, the Forest Service lost its way, degenerating into a handmaiden and broker for the timber industry, selling public trees at a loss and then trying to hide those losses with creative accounting, such as amortizing the cost of building haul roads over 240 years. These roads, along with the clearcuts the agency prescribes, prevent public recreation and destroy public ecosystems. Today virtually all support for the Forest Service comes from predatory wealth, while constant, violent and bitter attacks issue from the very people it used to represent.

One of the most experienced and most frustrated Forest Service critics is Brock Evans, of the National Audubon Society, who started trying to reform the agency in 1957 while serving as the Sierra Club's Northwest representative. He has given up. "Cutting trees is the holy mission, indeed the only mission," he declares. "I am no longer disappointed with the Forest Service . . . . I expect nothing. Twenty-five years of laws to guide the agency's actions into more balanced forms of multiple use, 25 years of wilderness bills, each one bitterly opposed by the agency if trees were included, 50 years of education in forestry schools, which teach that cathedral-like trees harkening back to the Middle Ages are really 'ugly and decadent' and should be 'harvested and put to good use,' have created today's 'forester.' These are the people who run the agency."

Ed Marston, publisher of the Western-oriented *High Country News*, perhaps the nation's most respected environmental newspaper, agrees. "The Forest Service is beyond redemption and should be abolished," he writes. "It would not be a huge loss. There is little institutional or human memory in the agency, given the frequency with which employees are transferred, given how the agency has isolated itself from the ground and from communities, and given its contempt for science."

The Forest Service, however, has started to mend itself from within, and it just may prove to its critics that it isn't hopeless. The healing became highly visible five years ago, when something snapped inside a quiet, nonconfrontational timber planner named Jeff DeBonis in Oregon's Willamette National Forest. Despite his tender age of 37, DeBonis had intimate knowledge of and deep loyalty for the Forest Service, having served it for 10 years in three regions. Earlier rainforest restoration work in El Salvador with the Peace Corps and in Ecuador with US Aid for International Development had given him a global perspective on resource conservation.

DeBonis had been repulsed by the land abuse he'd witnessed and helped facilitate in other national forests, but the destruction he saw in the Willamette incensed him. "The forest was in horrible shape," he recalls. "Road-induced slide areas, streams accumulating lots of gravel—obvious cumulative effects." So, in January 1989, DeBonis sat down at his desk and pounded out an internal memo to his colleagues via computer mail: "We, as an agency, are perceived by the conservation community as being an advocate of the timber industry's agenda. Based on my 10 years with the Forest Service, I believe this charge is true. I also believe, along with many others, that this agency needs to retake the moral 'high ground,' i.e., we need to be advocates for many of the policies, goals, and solutions proposed by the conservation community."

It all seemed quite innocent—except to the old-guard timber beasts who ran the Forest Service and who gasped, spluttered and frantically powwowed about how best to squash the insurrection. The memo found its way to Troy Reinhart, CEO of Douglas Timber Operations, of Roseburg, Oregon, who demanded that DeBonis be formally reprimanded, telling DeBonis's superiors that "the only moral high ground the preservationist community wishes to reclaim is putting the forest products industry managers six feet under."

The acting district ranger issued a formal gag order after DeBonis wrote back to Reinhart that forests "would be well-served if the type of information I distributed in my memo, i.e. the truth, was the basis of our resource management decisions, instead of the short sighted, politically expedient decision-making we seem to be plagued with now." Two weeks later DeBonis was informed that he'd be terminated if he continued to speak out.

DeBonis had to make a choice: follow the agency's ancient, mob-style directive and shut up; or exercise his First Amendment rights in such loud, flamboyant fashion that his bosses wouldn't dare fire him. He chose the latter course, siring an internal organization he called the Association of Forest Service Employees for Environmental Ethics (AFSEEE) and inundating the Service, the media and the environmental community with 20,000 first-issue copies of the group's newspaper, *The Inner Voice.*

"I've been told that writing in favor of preserving old growth, or stating that we, as an agency, ought to forge an alliance with the environmental community (our natural allies) is a conflict of interest," DeBonis wrote. "Whose interest? It is not considered a conflict of interest to promote the timber industry's agenda . . . . In the past we have been silent, perhaps out of a misguided loyalty . . . . However, we must always remember that our loyalty belongs to our nation and to the public trust."

The response was overwhelming—crashing applause from the rank and file, withering condemnation from Forest Service leadership as a whole. Today AFSEEE has 1,100 Forest Service members and 9,000 nonagency supporters in eight local chapters, and an $800,000 annual budget, 60 percent of which is derived from dues ($20 a year per member), the rest from private grants. DeBonis, who has moved on to hatch and head a similar organization for all state and federal agencies called Public Employees for Environmental Responsibility (PEER) says AFSEEE hasn't changed the Forest Service or anything happening on the ground. "It's a long-term process," he remarks. "We're in the process of making changes; we haven't made them yet."

But Forest Service employees who have been punished for doing their jobs and who have turned to AFSEEE for support aren't so sure. "AFSEEE is my savior," proclaims Cindy Reichelt, a public affairs officer based in northeast Washington State. What Reichelt doesn't say, however, is that it was AFSEEE, or at least her association with it, that got her in trouble in the first place. Her unpardonable sin was to invite DeBonis and a fire-and-brimstone, wise-use zealot to debate management issues at a forest resources conference. "It sent the [Colville National] Forest supervisor off the deep end," she reports. "He told me that none of his staff officers were going to have anything to do with AFSEEE. He gave me a 'marginal' job appraisal, about which I filed a grievance and won."

Reichelt's job was eliminated, and she was detailed out to projects in which she had no interest. Her office was moved 12 times. She was forbidden to use the phone, go to meetings, speak at outside engagements or involve herself with outside organizations—apparent reprisals that the Forest Service either calls coincidences, or refuses to comment on because there's some sort of investigation.

Rich Fairbanks, timber sales manager in the Willamette Forest, suffered a similar fate and received the same kind of support from AFSEEE. His rank offense, committed on August 26, 1992, was appearing with his wife, Terry (also a Forest Service employee) on "Eye on America"—a report CBS-TV tacks onto the end of its news broadcasts. The Fairbankses said nothing incorrect or even very controversial—that the export of raw logs to foreign countries has more to do with job loss in the Northwest than does the controversy around the spotted owl, that the way to rise through the ranks of the agency is not so much to do good work as to "get the cut out" and that clearcuts aren't replaced with forests but with ecologically sterile monocultures. No one who has ever worked for the Forest Service would disagree with these statements.

Adding fuel to what the Fairbankses said on the show was who they sat next to: Jeff DeBonis. Forest Service officials flew into a rage. The Willamette supervisor sent a memo to all employees castigating the Fairbankses' statements as "misleading." From Washington, DC, the couple was dressed down by public affairs boss Christopher Holmes, who professed to be "offended and disappointed" and who accused them of allowing themselves "to be used by Jeff, AFSEEE and CBS for their purposes" and of doing "a disservice to your fellow employees." From the rank and file, however, came such warm support as: "I appreciate and admire your courage for speaking your mind"; "Bravo to you for providing honest factual statements instead of the usual political BS we often hear."

Two weeks later, after a distinguished 20-year career, Rich Fairbanks was "surplussed"; that is, his job was put on the list of positions to be eliminated. Training opportunities, work details and countless little perks that are part of Forest Service life started to dry up. "I was put to work investigating timber theft—a real hostile work environment, just trouble from the get-go. The one thing I asked was to not be put under this one fellow who had had lots of problems. Sure enough, I was assigned to him. He has since been fired."

After filing a grievance with the National Federation of Federal Employees, Fairbanks got his job back. "The federation saved my butt," he says, "but if I hadn't been a member of AFSEEE and spoken out like that, I'd be gone. AFSEEE has done a tremendous amount for . . . this agency; we've made it hard for the Forest Service to step on people. . . . I'm working for a guy who believes in the First Amendment. He's given me administrative leave to go and speak at a Forest Service conference about what AFSEEE thinks needs to change."

One change sought by AFSEEE is genuine commitment to the restoration of fish and wildlife, resources to which the Forest Service has no less legal obligation than to timber. Consider the case of Bill Shoaf. Throughout his 15-year career with the Forest Service, Shoaf had received nothing but "fully successful" and "outstanding" performance evaluations. As a result, the Tongass National Forest in southeast Alaska fetched him from Washington, DC, to conduct the required environmental impact study for the nation's largest timber sale. What Shoaf's team found was not at all to the liking of the timber beasts who run the Tongass. Sensitive populations of fish and other wildlife, fragile soils, limestone caves and simple economics made 66 percent of the land said to be "harvestable" under the forest plan legally off-limits. The team also found that Tongass managers had violated the National Environmental Policy Act by permitting logging on 5,047 acres of mostly old-growth forest without environmental or public review, and by surveying logging roads and laying out harvest units in advance of timber-sale planning, thus making the environmental assessment process an idle exercise aimed at justifying existing decisions.

Shoaf was surplussed and reassigned to a make-believe position, which consists of waiting for work that doesn't come. He says he has been bullied, harassed, "gagged" and instructed in writing to suppress his team's findings. The Forest Service refuses comment, claiming there's an ongoing investigation into Shoaf's charges. Twenty-two of the nation's top scientists, including the renowned Paul Ehrlich, professor of population studies at Stanford University, have signed a letter to Vice-President Gore, advising that "such attempts by Forest Service administrators to pervert science-based approaches to resource management create an air of intimidation, discouraging the conscientious performance of duty. This air of intimidation permeates much of the agency."

AFSEEE identifies the case as "the most blatant attempt by the agency to violate the public trust" it has ever seen. And Shoaf says, "Without AFSEEE I wouldn't have known how to put myself in the daylight. It's a lot more difficult to shoot someone at noon than at midnight . . . . AFSEEE has stood by me, providing emotional and free legal support . . . . I still love the Forest Service. I'm not a tattletale; it has really ripped my heart out to have to do this. I'm not looking for any glitz; all I've done is get beat up. But I won't back off."

Has Shoaf's AFSEEE-supported stand translated into improvement on the ground? In a sense it has. It has prevented the Forest Service from finalizing an illegal plan for the Tongass, convinced the timber beasts that business as usual is politically infeasible and provided ammunition to the environmental community so that it can sue if the plan is approved.

In 1993, in Idaho's Clearwater National Forest, AFSEEE took a more direct role in facilitating change, publishing its own research after the Forest Service canceled a study exposing improper timber sales over a huge area of fragile, highly erodible soils. "The Clearwater National Forest has been seriously degraded by logging activities and the road-building that supports this logging," reported AFSEEE. "Streams have been seriously smothered by silt; important species are on the threshold of extinction; and essential old-growth habitat is withering . . . . AFSEEE concludes that the Regional Management Review was a political device meant to appease local timber interests and to set the stage for action against qualified and competent professionals."

According to Craig Gehrke, of the Wilderness Society, the Clearwater report is "a very powerful tool" because AFSEEE is comprised not of environmentalists but Forest Service professionals. "That made the report newsworthy, gave it credibility," he declares. "We—the conservation groups—threatened to take the Forest Service to court. AFSEEE gave us the documentation we needed. We reached a settlement." The cut had been set at 173 million board feet; now it's at 80 million.

All the people AFSEEE protects are, in one sense or another, whistle-blowers. And therein lies a great danger, because whistle-blowers are by nature very different. To quote Cheri Brooks, editor of AFSEEE's *Inner Voice*, "They tend to be weird . . . . Furthermore, a lot of them are cranks with axes to grind. But that doesn't necessarily mean they aren't real whistle-blowers . . . . Sometimes there's a really fine line. You just have to decide if the issue is real."

To make its decisions, AFSEEE conducts an exhaustive screening process. Buzz Williams, Southeast program coordinator, explains, "There are two phases. The first takes place in our Eugene, Oregon, headquarters through a lawyer who determines if a grievance is genuine. The second level is with the Government Accountability Project (GAP), which we retain as legal counsel and which decides if there's merit to a case. We have people call us who obviously hate their supervisors; they didn't get what they wanted and it has nothing to do with environmental ethics. Realistically, one case out of 10 has merit."

In 1992, AFSEEE helped organize a hearing before the House Subcommittee on Post Office and Civil Service in which John McCormick, formerly in charge of the Forest Service's whistle-blower protection program, testified that the program was "designed to fail." McCormick, who had been a special agent with the Forest Service law enforcement branch, knew whereof he spoke: He had been a whistle-blower himself. "To illustrate the low priority placed on whistle-blower charges," he told the subcommittee, he was exiled to "the slot for handling those allegations."

The sin for which McCormick was exiled had been to catch timber beasts in the Tongass National Forest building a $160 million road through a wilderness prior to timber-sale planning—exactly the sort of violation Shoaf later uncovered. "I was ordered not to investigate," he says. "I told them, 'You put that in writing because I'm going to take it up to the US Attorney in Anchorage and ask that you be indicted for obstruction of justice.' They didn't care for that."

McCormick, who has left the Forest Service, filed an appeal and won a substantial cash settlement. But he paid a price. His workday became "a living hell." One of his bosses spent more than an hour one day reading him a list of derogatory terms and explaining why they all applied to him. He suffered blackouts. He was hospitalized for stress. His marriage broke up. Was it worth it?

It was for fish and wildlife, for other special agents and for the American public. Thanks largely to McCormick and AFSEEE, enforcement procedures have been revised so that, beginning in 1994, special agents report directly to the chief of the Forest Service instead of the bureaucrats who run the particular forests the agents are investigating.

A survey of the Forest Service by the University of Idaho at Moscow indicates that 46 percent of general staffers believe AFSEEE is a catalyst for positive change compared with only 23 percent who see that change as negative. According to survey leader Greg Brown, the data suggest that AFSEEE may be as much a result of change within the Forest Service as a cause of it. He says AFSEEE appears to be an "accelerator" and "a good reflector of new values and attitudes." Brown sees a "greening of the Forest Service. But at the same time it's politics as usual in Washington."

Those politics have been slightly disinfected by AFSEEE. Since AFSEEE's inception, one of its major goals had been to replace F. Dale Robertson, the old-guard timber beast Reagan picked to run the Forest Service, with someone committed to looking at forests as ecosystems instead of standing board feet. Last October Robertson resigned under pressure and a month later President Clinton appointed one of three candidates backed by AFSEEE. The new chief is Jack Ward Thomas, 59, a 27-year veteran of the agency and the first wildlife biologist ever to hold the post. When President Bush asked Thomas to conduct a genuine spotted owl study—as opposed to the industry-approved, make-believe versions that had so agitated the public—Thomas accepted on condition there'd be no political meddling and that he could pick the interagency scientific team. To the horror of the Bush administration, Thomas's report confirmed what environmentalists had been saying all along: saving the spotted owl meant saving at least four million acres of old-growth forest. Thomas, so the story goes, had the following dialogue with a Bush official several weeks before the release of his final report:

Bush official: "This is The White House calling. Can you please send over an advance copy of your report?"

Thomas: "No."

Bush official: "I don't think you understand. This is The White House."

Thomas: "The White House will have to wait like everyone else."

Thomas has Pinchot's integrity, and he has something Pinchot lacked: a profound understanding of and commitment to Earth as man did not make it. On December 9, 1993, the new chief danced upon 75 years of tradition by firing off this directive to agency brass: "We will: Obey the law. Tell the truth. Implement ecosystem management." When asked at a press conference what he thought of AFSEEE, Thomas said it was a great concept—as far as it went.

"AFSEEE used to have a very hard time getting through the front door of Forest Service offices to engage in dialogue with leadership," comments Andy Stahl, who left the Sierra Club Legal Defense Fund early in January to become AFSEEE's new director. "Now the doors have been thrown open."

Reichelt and Fairbanks serve on the AFSEEE board, and both are pumped up about the appointment of Chief Thomas. "People see that my association with AFSEEE is not as bad as they thought," says Reichelt. Fairbanks reports that the Forest Service has done a "180" on how it views AFSEEE, from "classic denial to general acceptance."

Still, it is doubtful that AFSEEE and Thomas, by themselves, can reform the Forest Service. A more realistic goal might be to convince the rest of us that it isn't hopeless and that the nontimber aspects of its multiple-use mission ought not to be reassigned to another agency. Traditions and old allegiances die hard. Everywhere pockets of fascism fester, abetting industry as it mobilizes for the counterattack. The timber beasts may be quieter, but many have gone to the bunker to wait for a new president named Quayle or Dole.

UPDATE

The Forest Service hasn't healed itself as much as I had thought it would by this time. Cindy Reichelt is being surplussed, supposedly because of "downsizing." But she's the only one on the Colville

National Forest's hit list, so the motive is pretty obvious. PEER is helping her mount a legal challenge. "Since I've been on this forest they've moved me 23 times," she told me. "I speak up, and they don't want me to."

When the Forest Service—in what AFSEEE called the most "blatant attempt by the agency to violate the public trust" it had ever seen—punished Bill Shoaf for daring to do his job, 70 (or about a third) of his fellow employees signed a letter supporting him. In December 1994 the Forest Service, chastened and sued by environmentalists, decided to prepare a new EIS for the Central Prince of Wales Timber Sale. But by this time Shoaf had soured on the agency, and on February 28 he announced his retirement.

In April 1995 I returned to Prince of Wales Island after a 10-year hiatus. The island—which didn't look that good in 1985—had been draped with new clearcuts, laid out like plowed fields in cotton country. Rains in October 1993 had caused more than 300 landslides. Now there were 3,500 miles of logging roads, and the 16-year-old forest plan called for 8,500 more. The good news was the Forest Service's new Alaska boss, Phil Janik, is committed to an enlightened forest plan. The first wildlife biologist to serve as regional forester in Alaska, Janik had been an architect of a bold and brilliant strategy to save salmon and steelhead habitat called PACFISH (not an acronym). He had left lots of bootprints in Alaska; and he was an old hand at writing plans to protect threatened and endangered species, especially wolves and grizzlies. He's trying to do right by the Tongass, but the Alaska Congressional delegation—Representative Don Young and senators Ted Stevens and Frank Murkowski—is undercutting him at every turn and trying to give away the Tongass to the forests-products industry from their heel-scuffed desks in Washington, DC.

The Forest Service's Timber Theft Task Force, which Jeff DeBonis's PEER group and the Government Accountability Project helped set up, had been finding all sorts of major fraud and theft by the biggest timber corporations in the Northwest. "So," says DeBonis, "the Forest Service abolished it. What the task force had been finding out was just too damn embarrassing. We're about to sue."

County
Supremacy

Just another Wise Use Ruse

Fly Rod & Reel, March 1995

"It is entirely appropriate that the major commercial, mythic figure for the Southwest is Billy the Kid, a reckless, marauding, gun-slinging juvenile delinquent who died early without any significant accomplishments to his name other than a number of unmotivated murders. This reckless punk lacked even the social affability to lead or participate in a gang, yet he idealized rebellion, albeit without a cause. The promoters of the county supremacy movement sought, as all myth-makers must, to find and claim deep historical roots."
—Scott Reed, in *The Idaho Law Review*

WITH DUST IN MY NOSE and grit in my socks, I trudged up into a clutter of plywood casinos strewn between piles of silver-mine tailings in the badlands of southwestern Nevada. It was mid-September 1992, and I'd come to the remote town of Tonapah, the seat of Nye County, to document what overgrazing is doing to fish and wildlife and to interview a mob of shrill welfare ranchers who lease public rangeland at less than a quarter fair-market value and who are trying to depose the United States Forest Service.

Leading the federal government in this confrontation is Jim Nelson, 54, the smart, tough supervisor of the Toiyabe National Forest who won *FR&R*'s Stickleback Award in 1992 for defending America's fish and wildlife against me-first privatizers from a pseudo-popular movement that has changed its name with each defeat, from "Sagebrush Rebellion" to "Wise Use Movement" to "Home Rule" and, most recently, to "County Supremacy."

"We could have another Waco out here," says Nelson. "Some of these guys are talking about killing us. If the counties did have this land, they'd hammer the hell out of it, and the public wouldn't have access, much less anything else. Riparian areas are the arteries of the planet and they're getting destroyed all over the West. *We're just not going to let that keep happening.* We've had an ecology team working on riparian for the last five field seasons, and we're getting the science behind us to really support what we're trying to do."

Three years ago Tonapah rancher Wayne Hage, who is suing the Forest Service for grazing regulations that he says amount to a wrongful "taking" of private property, repeatedly defied orders to get his stock off sensitive public land. Finally, Nelson's patience ran out and he rounded up Hage's cows and sold them at auction. This sort of bold enforcement action just plain wasn't done by federal resource managers, and for once the me-firsters were speechless, if only for a day or two. Soon, however, they were screaming for Nelson's blood. They got not a drop because he had taken the precaution of briefing Forest Service brass and even the US Congress.

The Toiyabe's Tonapah Ranger District is everything the town is not—big and lovely (though sometimes the beauty is the sterile, lunar sort of Keats' riparian zone where "the sedge has withered from the lake, and no birds sing"). At 1.2 million acres, it is larger than many national forests and it contains a third of all designated wilderness in Nevada. District Ranger Dave Grider—one of Nelson's equally resolute understudies—figures this cold, fragile desert country can safely support about one cow per square mile. In comparison, some parts of the Midwest can support ten per *acre*.

Standing between aspen-clad Table Mountain and the bald Toquima Range, Grider and I looked out over 25 miles of Monitor Valley. Now, where Great Basin wild rye once lapped the stirrups of the pioneers, dust devils dance over a dead sea of purple sage. "You can't blame all this on the ranchers," Grider declared. "The Forest Service hasn't always done its job."

Throughout Hage's allotment Grider and I encountered hideous erosion, an invasion of rabbit bush, wire grass and sage, hoof-hardened earth that shed rain like oiled canvas and blown-out carcasses of trout streams whose dry channels were 20 feet across and 15 feet deep.

When streamside vegetation is healthy it cools and stabilizes trout habitat. It slows and spreads runoff over the floodplain so that rich, renewing sediments settle around stems and roots. But when riparian cover is ripped out and beaten down by bovine teeth and hooves, rain and smowmelt blast away streambanks, setting off "headcuts" that race along narrow channels, unzipping them like overstuffed duffel bags. The rapids that form at the mouths of feeder creeks set off more headcuts, and soon a delicate vascular system transporting the West's lifeblood opens into one gaping wound. Surface water warms, stagnates, evaporates. Groundwater drops. Streams and wetlands cease to exist and the land takes on a new, stable, hopeless condition called "ephemeral wash."

Cow-induced desertification of Monitor Valley got underway long before Nelson, Grider or even Hage arrived on the scene. As bad as it is, however, the disease is not terminal on Forest Service land. I wasn't so sure about the prognosis for Hage's private holdings. Displayed here was the national, cow-pie-in-the-sky promise of County Supremacy— scarcely a five o'clock shadow of grass roots, just a dusty rodeo-scape of compacted dirt and encrusted dung under obscene, fish-spangled signs that shouted: "Member Private Land Wildlife Stronghold. A nationwide project. This landowner cares! He has committed his property to a significant conservation and wildlife program benefiting YOU."

All modern maps show that 87 percent of Nevada is federally owned, but Nye County Commissioner Dick Carver says this is just a superstition. "There is no such thing as a national forest," he proclaims. Carver and his fellow county commissioners have passed a resolution "recognizing that the State of Nevada owns all public lands within the borders of the State." In addition to annexing the Toiyabe National Forest, the Nye County Commission has announced that "all ways, pathways, trails, roads, county highways, and similar public travel corridors . . . on public lands in Nye County are hereby declared Nye County public roads." Jim Nelson, however, has no plans to deed over the forest because, as a condition of being admitted to the Union, Nevada voluntarily relinquished this and other territorial lands to the federal government in 1864.

Last summer Nye County revealed that it would celebrate the Fourth of July by constructing an unauthorized road through Forest Service land in Jefferson Canyon. When the commission so informed Dave Grider, he advised it that such a project would amount to criminal activity. But County Commissioner Carver claimed it was the feds who were the scofflaws. Stepping briskly to the grandstand, he issued this statement to the press on July 3, 1994: "I have asked the Nye County Sheriff's Department to have a deputy here tomorrow, and if anybody obstructs us putting in this road, I want them hauled to the slammer."

The morning of the Fourth found Carver mounted on a county bull-dozer at Jefferson Canyon, pontificating about the vile, ubiquitous feds to an enthusiastic rabble of several hundred county supremacists, some of whom wore sidearms. When Carver at last commenced hacking out the road, Grider declined to provide the hoped-for fireworks. Instead, Special Agent Dave Young vainly held up a sign that read: "Stop Disturbance. Not Authorized." At this writing (mid-November) no charges have been filed, but Grider says: "We are completing a detailed investigation, and it's our intention to turn over the factual account to the US Attorneys and let them decide about citations." Meanwhile, Carver has filed a complaint with the Nye County District Attorney, charging Young and Grider with "obstructing a public official in performance of his duties." Comments Grider: "If the Toiyabe really belongs to Nevada, read me where it says a county commissioner's duties involve climbing on a county cat and bulldozing across state lands."

On the Humboldt National Forest, which Nelson has been looking after as acting supervisor since last June, me-first ranchers in the guise of county government are even more defiant. In 1994—the eighth year of a severe drought cycle—they bawled like branded calves when the Forest Service sent their stock home early. "We're not trying to eliminate grazing," declares Humboldt resource staff officer Ben Siminoe. "We're just saying, if we're going to have grazing out there, it's going to be in conjunction with the other resources and in compliance with our forest plan."

The Humboldt is a beautiful, delicate forest with important habitat for redband trout (a state species of special concern), bull trout and Bonneville cutthroat (designated as "sensitive" by the Forest Service) and Lahontan cutthroat (a federally threatened species). "I was just out there on the ground," says Jim Nelson, "and in every case [cattle] utilization in riparian zones was between 80 and 100 percent. The riparian areas are just *plowed*. I understand why this has happened— we've never really dealt with that issue in an aggressive way over there. But I told everyone on the forest that I don't want to see those kind of conditions again. I want the land administered according to the standards. Next July when the cows go on and we start administering those standards, the scat's really going to hit the fan."

Apparently impressed by all the flap about national forests being make believe, Elko County rancher Don Duval drove his backhoe onto the Humboldt and installed a collection box in a natural spring used by mule deer and other wildlife. That done, he ran 350 feet of pipe down to his cattle, thereby eliminating the riparian zone. The Forest Service was not amused. It hauled him into federal court, where Magistrate Phyllis Atkins sentenced him to one year's probation and a fine of $2,000, $1,800 of it to be suspended if he restored the spring "to the satisfaction of the Forest Service."

Duval had packed gravel around the spring box and left the surplus on the ground. Rather than make him pick it up, the range conservationist who wrote the rehabilitation plan said he could just spread it around and cover it with sufficient topsoil to allow revegetation. Rummaging about for a means of distorting the facts, county supremacists seized upon the topsoil option. The "dirt," they said, would "destroy" the spring. State Assemblyman John Carpenter (R-Elko) filed a petition for declaratory relief, alleging that the removal of Duval's unauthorized development would cause irreparable damage to land and wildlife. The sycophantic *Elko Daily Free Press* rhapsodized about Duval's "improvement" and, using the Elko County Commission as a Greek chorus, whipped local ranchers to prayer-meeting frenzy. A phone-a-thon to "save" Kelley Spring was organized by a group calling itself the "Kelley Spring Protective Association." There were meetings, rallies and demonstrations. Children were made to stand beside the spring and sing the national anthem.

On September 24, 1994, in what the *Free Press* called the "Ruby Valley Tea Party," perhaps 300 county supremacists assembled at Kelley Spring and erected a fence, thereby preventing deer and other wildlife, supposedly flourishing because of Duval's "improvement," from drinking. The Elko County Commission, which had voted to endorse the fencing, donated a metal stake. Another stake bore the name of Nye County. Signs were posted around the perimeter: "No Trespassing for the purpose of destroying this spring." And: "The land inside this enclosure, and the water, belong to the people of the great state of Nevada as well as all other public lands within the external borders of the State of Nevada."

Rancher Duval rose eagerly to the role of abused child. "I morally cannot force myself to throw dirt on top of clear water and make a mud bog that will destroy the resource," he sniffed in a letter to Magistrate Atkins—a letter she read first in the *Free Press*. Nelson and Atkins, however, weren't messing around and, as Duval himself cannily prognosticated, it was either return the water and replace the riparian zone or "be thrown in jail." So on October 4, he backed down and took out his development.

The next day about 40 county supremacists put it back in. "The citizens of Elko County have shown they have the guts to take matters into their own hands and they will continue to fight small battles here and there to improve their own lives," oozed the *Free Press*. At this writing, box and diversion pipe remain in place and Kelley Spring is still fenced. The Forest Service vows to act, but—to avoid the confrontation and media circus the ranchers want—after things have "cooled down."

Another Elko County resident who has taken matters into his own hands is Cliff Gardner, an aspiring guru of County Supremacy who thinks John Carpenter is soft on federal intervention and last November lost to him in a bitter campaign for state assemblyman. In late August 1992 a major range fire swept across a Humboldt Forest allotment where Gardner was allowed to graze his cattle. To protect Gardner's ranch from flood damage, the Forest Service spent $33,700, not counting labor, planting grass, forbs and shrubs; to rehabilitate 1,000 acres of prime winter deer range, the Nevada Department of Wildlife contributed labor and $5,200; and to be a good neighbor, Placer Dome (a mining company) kicked in $1,800.

Because the forest plan required that the area be rested from cattle for at least two years, Gardner was informed that he wouldn't be permitted to run his cows on the burned area in 1994. He could, however, graze the rest of the allotment if he'd erect a fence around the burned part—a project the Forest Service said it would be pleased to help him with. Gardner agreed, but when district personnel came out to help him with the fence, he changed his mind. Then, on May 18, he defied the feds by turning out 100 head of cattle. The Forest Service revoked all his grazing privileges in June, but at this writing he has 160 head trespassing on the burned area. "We chose not to round them up and auction them off," says a Humboldt Forest spokesman, "because we think his strategy is the same as Wayne Hage's, that he wants another 'takings' court case . . . . The criminal investigation is ongoing and appropriate action *will* be taken."

The burned area sustained not only deer but, in Dawley Creek, wild brook trout. Was it really wise to sprinkle unauthorized cows among the ashes, I asked Gardner? Absolutely! "Cattle," he averred, "are a boon to fish and wildlife. It's a complete fallacy that grazing is destructive. Picture your yard. You go out there every week and cut that grass back." I then asked Gardner if he thought the National Fish and Wildlife Foundation had chosen wisely when it recently presented its coveted Chuck Yeager Award, for valor in defense of fish and wildlife, to Jim Nelson. No, he did not. "Jim Nelson," he cried, "is one of the leading socialists within the Forest Service. He has done more to run key ranchers off the range than any other forest official." But Nelson, who calls himself "the best friend the ranchers have," points out that it's not in the ranchers' interests to destroy the earth's capacity to produce forage. "I want to keep cattle on the public range," he says. "It's a way of life; it's important for local economics. But *we have to have good management.*"

Will Gardner continue to flout grazing regulations in 1995? You bet! "I'll just put my cattle out because those permits were only issued in recognition of my underlying right that existed before the Forest Service existed. It's just eliminating their management of the land, is all it's doing. My sovereignty still exists out there."

Hage, Carver, Carpenter, Duval and Gardner had shown me what County Supremacy promises for wild things and wild places. Three hundred miles northwest of Tonapah, in the Toiyabe's Carson-Iceberg Wilderness, District Ranger Guy Pence showed me the promise of enlightened stewardship. As we trotted our horses up along the East Branch of the Carson River, grasshoppers clattered underneath us and ferruginous hawks orbited beside mountaintop aspens that glowed neon yellow in the low morning sun. Soon we were up and into the open woods, threading between thick-trunked Jeffrey pines on the rough river-side trail to a big, wet meadow acquired by the Forest Service three years earlier. A black bear watched from a pine-cone-littered slope. A bald eagle sailed out of a cottonwood. Little Lahontan cutthroat held in green, graveled pools.

Pence, who had decided that the meadow needed a chance to heal, had kicked the cows off three years earlier. It was still in dreadful shape, but now willows, alders and aspens were growing back. Now the raw banks were closing and stabilizing and unpalatable plants like cheat grass and iris were retreating toward the uplands. At marked reference points we dismounted and Pence held up photos he'd taken when the cows were on. Only three years and the difference was stunning. Given half a chance, nature can fix almost anything we do to fish and wildlife habitat.

Each spring now, more vegetation will slow the floods. More fertile sediments will settle out, encouraging more growth. Bars will build to the top of headcuts. The canopy will close and the stream channel will zip itself up. The East Branch of the Carson will cool and deepen. Benthic organisms will flourish. Lahontan cutthroat will proliferate and grow larger.

Maybe one day soon you will float a dry fly down a dark, wild, deep glide and watch a two-pounder turn and follow and drift up to intercept it. Maybe Jim Nelson will still be running the Toiyabe and Humboldt National Forests. Maybe the county supremacists will be calling themselves something else. Maybe they'll be venting even more gas and wind. Maybe no one will be listening.

The Birth of County Supremacy

The County Supremacy movement pupated in New Mexico's Catron County—a 6,900-square-mile chunk of arid forest and high desert in the southern part of the state—when a few loud, obnoxious Wise Users got their backs up about new grazing and timbering restrictions on the Gila National Forest. In their capacity as members of the Catron County Commission, they ordained a series of outlandish, grossly unconstitutional laws that supposedly require federal agencies to ask county permission to manage federal resources on federal land. Recently the commission officially resolved that the feds' "unabashed, open arrogance and disregard for our constitutional form of government has given rise to public anger, and if left unchallenged will undoubtedly lead to much physical violence."

In 1994, county supremacists frightened officials of the Gila National Forest and the New Mexico Department of Game and Fish into indefinitely postponing reintroduction of Gila trout in two Catron County streams critical to recovery of this federally endangered species. Restoration had been about to get underway when the Gila Fish and Gun Club gushed crocodile tears about imagined environmental dangers of antimycin—the eminently safe, utterly dependable rotenone replacement by which the recovery team had planned to clean out the Gila trout's alien competition. In a statement released to the press, club president Manuel T. Serna warned against commitment to wild, self-sustaining populations of Gila trout, explaining that "fish hatcheries are a better alternative."

Clyde Brown, of Catron County, resents the business inconveniences caused by the endangered Gila trout, the southwestern willow flycatcher (proposed for endangered status), the threatened loach minnow and spikedace and all the other silly, insignificant specks of genetic jetsam floating into oblivion. "Tell me, what earthly good are these 'blessed' minnows anyway?" he recently demanded of the US Fish and Wildlife Service. "Just give me one good reason why they benefit mankind . . . . I think you bureaucrats had better back off before someone gets seriously hurt. Who among you would want to lose your life for a bird, even if he can sing, or a nearly microscopic-size minnow?"

On August 2, 1994, Catron County passed a resolution stipulating that the heads of all households should own guns. Swaggering around the hearing with a pistol strapped to his protruding chest was one Skip Price, a county supremacist who titillates the local press by flying the American flag upside down at his Double Heart Ranch outside Apache Creek. "Our country's sliding into the same thing Hitler had," the *Albuquerque Tribune* quotes him as saying. "He had brown shirts. They're green shirts and black shirts now—Forest Service and your SWAT teams, ATF. I've told them that if they come out here to fence off my streams, they're meeting bullets." Now Price tells me that, while those were indeed his words, he hadn't meant to imply he'd be knocking off any feds. He's not really sure what brand of pistol he was packing: "Maybe a Ruger." And so far the only thing he's shot is his truck, whose starter and manifold he took out with an accidental discharge through the floorboards.

Cows Trample Nevada's Rare Fish

The Nevada Department of Wildlife has been looking for and not finding populations of federally threatened Lahontan cutthroat trout in major tributaries of the Marys River, part of which flows through the Humboldt National Forest. "The places [on BLM land] that have been overgrazed have been demolished," fisheries biologist Brian Nokes told *FR&R*. "There are no more trout. You can't blame it solely on grazing because the drought has had an impact, but once cows start tromping around and beating up habitat, the water heats up and sediments cover spawning gravel. We're finding 70-degree water in prior Lahontan habitat. I can only describe the damage as total devastation." In 1979 Hanks Creek and Conners Creek had, respectively, 135.9 and 237.6 Lahontans per mile. Today they have none.

Relict dace, which the US Fish and Wildlife Service is considering for endangered species status, are beautiful, thumb-size cyprinids—with skinny caudal peduncles and iridescent purple flanks—that hover at mid-current and feed on the surface like trout. They are relics of extinct pluvial lakes that lay between the Humboldt and Bonneville drainages for almost five million years before drying up after the last glaciation. As the lakes receded, the dace retreated into springs where they evolved enormous breeding capacity. Now, when it rains heavily and the ancient lake basins fill up a little, the dace move out of the springs and explode into the temporary habitat.

"I've found springheads that are just hammered by cattle and horses," remarks project leader Jerry Stein. "They're mud holes. But stick a dip net in, and it's full of relict dace. They're incredible little fish; you put them in a bucket of water and leave it in the hot sun all day and they'll be alive when you come back. What the cattle grazing does, though, is create hummocking, and dace like a little bit of flowing water. That's why they can survive in these hammered springheads. But with hummocking the water gets stagnant; it can't flow."

The Wildlife Department is trying to census relict-dace populations, but one publicly subsidized county supremacist has just kicked the survey crew off his ranch. "The cattlemen don't like us," says a government official who asked not to be identified. "They'll want to go out and poison all the shrubs so they can have more grass for cows. They call us up and we say, 'No you can't do that; we need that habitat for deer.' So they get puffy and won't let us onto their land."

UPDATE

When Jim Nelson ordered Guy Pence and the other district rangers to control grazing in sensitive riparian areas, property-rights zealots threatened to assassinate them. "Someone's going to get hurt," Nelson told me on March 23, 1995.

A week later he was nearly proven correct. Herewith, my report from the January 1996 *Sierra* Magazine:

On March 30, 1995, at about 7:30 PM a bomb blew apart Pence's office in Carson City. Often he and some of his people are working at that hour; but on this evening nobody happened to be around. Shortly thereafter the phone rang in Jim Nelson's office. "You're next," declared the anonymous caller.

Then, at 9:50 PM on August 5, Pence's car and part of his house were blown up. It was a Friday, and he'd just left for one of his frequent working weekends, taking congressional aides out onto the land to show them what good range management is all about. His wife Linda and one of their daughters were sitting on the sofa in the front room a few feet from the van when they heard footsteps in the driveway. Linda opened the door, started out, and thought better of it. Just then the timer on the stove went off, and the two women went into the kitchen. Luckily for them, that's when the bomb exploded. It demolished the van, excavated an enormous hole in the concrete parking slab, destroyed the garage door and the siding of the house, and blew out all the windows in the front room, sending glass shrapnel into the walls and ripping apart the Sheetrock. When I phoned Pence at his office on Tuesday, August 8, I asked him if he'd gone to work Monday morning. "You better believe it," he said. But in October the Regional office (which Nelson answers to) transferred him to the Boise National Forest in Idaho, supposedly for his own safety. He's not happy about it.

Still, there are a lot of Guy-Pence types who work for Jim Nelson; in fact, that's the only kind he hires. Whatever the future holds for these brave resource managers, the future for the Lahontan cutthroat appears bright—at least on the Toiyabe and Humboldt National Forests (both of which Nelson supervises). Even before the bombings there had been an outpouring of national support for Nelson's revolutionary land stewardship. Now people stop Pence on the street and say, "We're behind you; we believe in what you're trying to do." With some exceptions—most notably the *Elko Daily Free Press*—regional newspapers have been reasonably fair.

County supremacists vainly tried to get Nelson fired for "setting up" my *Fly Rod & Reel* article. In supremacist-speak "setting up" means providing truthful answers to a journalist's questions.

Cliff Gardner has filed three suits against the Forest Service and lost all of them. The Forest Service has sued him and won. So if Gardner puts his cows back on the burned portion of his allotment, he'll be in contempt of court.

Dick Carver is still a Nye County Commissioner, and Nelson is still waiting for a decision on a suit filed by the Justice Department against the county for unlawful use of public land. So far neither Carver nor Duval has been criminally prosecuted.

A Plague Upon
Your Cutthroats

"An appalling act of environmental vandalism"

Fly Rod & Reel, July/October 1995

SPREADING THROUGH the biggest intact temperate ecosystem
on earth was an alien more hideous than any monster that ever slimed
a Hollywood spaceship. But I still had three more days of blissful
ignorance. It was July 27, 1994. My business in Mammoth, Wyoming,
was finished. The sun was still high in the azure sky and now, free as
a June freshman, I was headed for my favorite place on the planet—
Hayden Valley and the long, curling tail of the greatest inland cutthroat refuge in the world. "Hemingway," I noted in my fishing journal for that day, "had it right. Happiness is a trout stream all to yourself."

Well, not quite all to myself, because Buffalo Ford gets lots of pressure. But I like to wade across the Yellowstone River and fish the east
bank all the way to the falls at Sulphur Caldron. There's a little island
halfway up where I can almost always be alone. The water is green
and clean. You can see the big Yellowstone cutts cruising the shallows
or sipping insects in the swirling eddies. At this time of year their gill
plates and flanks are sunrise-red, but they have recovered from
spawning and are in fine flesh—wild, robust fish mostly 17 inches and
better. You have to see this place to believe how many there are.
Scores of bird and mammal species depend on them.

This river, the 87,000-acre lake that feeds it and the 59 trout-spawning
streams that feed the lake comprise the vast ecosystem based on
Yellowstone cutthroats—the interior West's analog of the sockeye-
based food chain of southwestern Alaska. The watershed and its

evolving fauna have endured dredging by major hydrothermal explosions, damming and rerouting by earthquakes and volcanoes, the clutch and crumble of glaciers, and colossal fires that sweep out old growth on 200- to 400-year cycles. It's all a beautiful, complicated, self-mending machine, impervious to every insult in the universe save human tinkering.

Anyone who says Yellowstone cutts are not selective is wrong. Anyone who says they aren't as strong as rainbows is missing the point. My purpose is not to fight them but to join them, to watch their tail-waggling riseforms at the end of my cast or their raindrop dimples as I fish down to them in the quiet coves, to feel them against a wisp of graphite, to cradle them in the coolness of their river while it piles against my ribs.

I come here to fish with my friends the otters and minks, to be part of the energy flow that rises with the pungent stream of sulphur vents, cycles down around my shoulders with dancing caddis and falling spinners, rises again with the bald eagles and ospreys whose shadows sweep along the green and golden banks, recedes seaward with the migratory white pelicans who cruise stealthily through feeding trout with their heads tucked way back into their folded wings, gathers strength in the continent's biggest alpine lake, explodes into gravel redds and grizzly gullets high in the ragged Absarokas. I come here also to watch the bison cross at dusk, the calves white-eyed and pumping hard to stay abreast of their mothers; to listen to the raucous shouts of Clark's nutcrackers and the discordant croaks of high, distant ravens; to hike in whisky-jack silence through wildflowers and fragrant lodgepole forests new and old; to feel proud of being an American; to rejoice in the world's best example of wildlife management gone right.

On July 30 a lure fisherman, plying Yellowstone Lake just south of Stevenson Island, took a 17-inch, five-year-old lake trout. Knowing it didn't belong, his guide turned it over to park rangers. On August 5 another five-year-old lake trout of about the same size was taken between Breeze Point and Wolf Point. In September US Fish and Wildlife Service gillnets turned up two smaller specimens, aged four years and two. Multiple year classes. Apparently these alien, highly piscivorous charr were reproducing in the high lake.

It wasn't an accident or an act of God. If the lake had been infected without human assistance, lake trout would have had to negotiate headwater streams (something they almost never do), swimming up the Snake River, crossing Two Ocean Pass and dropping down the upper Yellowstone. Or these deep-water residents, rarely taken by avian predators, twice would have had to survive brutal, six-mile flights via osprey, eagle or pelican from Shoshone, Lewis or Heart Lakes—where they had been unleashed in the 19th Century, when it was *de rigueur* for managers to play musical chairs with fish species. The Park Service has offered a $10,000 reward for information leading to the arrest and conviction of the perpetrator(s), whose work it calls "an appalling act of environmental vandalism."

Such vandalism is "disgustingly simple," remarks fisheries biologist Robert Gresswell, formerly of the Park Service and now with Oregon State University. "We've had other illegal introductions in the park, and it happens in state waters all the time." In May 1985 Gresswell and his associates were doing routine spawning surveys in a Yellowstone Lake tributary called Arnica Creek when, to their horror, they encountered brook trout. That August the Park Service treated the stream with antimycin, a modern toxicant safer than rotenone and more effective in that fish can't smell it. As a precaution, treatment was repeated 12 months later.

If ever you get an urge to thank the people who braved vicious opposition to show the nation what no-kill fishing can do for trout populations, who restored Yellowstone cutts from a state of collapse to a main course in the greater Yellowstone food chain, I suggest you start with John Varley, the park's head resource manager. Varley is a professional conservator of wildness, a new-order biologist who never accepted the conventional wisdom that passionate advocacy of nature is somehow unscientific. Hanging from his office wall is a watercolor of a human index finger metamorphosing into an exquisitely-rendered Yellowstone cutthroat. Once, when there was room, it was on his desk pointing at him. He created it as a nameplate with the idea of showing—instead of spelling out—who he was and what he did. But I think the Park Service should commission him to paint it bigger and on the ceiling of the administration building.

To me, the painting symbolizes the finger of enlightened, let-it-be management transferring the spark of life to an ecosystem killed by tinkerers. When I look at it, I see Superintendent Jack Anderson—refusing to be intimidated by a frenzied mob of concessionaires, politicians and dump-stadia gogglers—daring to make a real bear of Yogi by weaning him from garbage to cutthroats, carrion and white-bark pine seeds. I see Superintendent Robert Barbee defending natural-fire policy to chanting followers of Guru Smokey—"Barbecue Bob," the sagebrush rebels and know-nothing press called him. I see Park Service Director Bill Mott standing up to an ignorant, superstitious Reagan White House in defense of wolf recovery and habitat acquisition. And I see John Varley defending his beloved cutts against incensed minions of fillet-and-release and brainwashed fishing literati who kept saying, "You can't stockpile harvestable surpluses."

When Varley heard about the first lake trout he was physically ill. He didn't throw up, but it was close. The day before—July 29—he'd been briefing the new superintendent on resource issues. "We were in the backcountry, overlooking Yellowstone Lake," Varley told me, "and, man, I was giving him the business about how well we had protected this ecosystem and how pleased we should be. 'We've got a lot of problems; but there's something that's museum pure.' And 24 hours later I hear about the lake trout. I just can't think of worse news. They could have said brook trout—well, that's bad news, but we can get around that. They could have said brown trout; they could have said almost anything, but not lake trout."

The lake sustains 80 percent of all remaining Yellowstone cutthroats (*Oncorhynchus clarki bouvieri*) and 90 percent of the park's river fish winter there. For their first several years of life, the juveniles can't be found and, because they haven't shown up anywhere else, it's assumed they go out and down—to precisely where the lake trout lurk. The question is not what the lake trout will do to the natives, but when. Wherever the species has been superimposed on wild cutthroat populations, it has virtually eliminated them.

For example, in 2,200-acre Heart Lake, tucked between West Thumb and South Arm on the other side of the Continental Divide, lake trout have severely depressed a large, piscivorous strain of cutthroat that evolved with six other indigenous fish. Yellowstone cutthroats are smaller and even more defenseless. During their time in Yellowstone Lake, they graze on scuds, Chironomids and plankton; they evolved with only the longnose dace, which inhabits shallow, weedy bays and which they generally ignore. Longnose suckers, redside shiners and lake chubs—none of which are major cutthroat competitors—were introduced long ago by bait fishermen or possibly by professional tinkerers in an authorized effort to establish trout forage.

"If we don't do anything, everybody agrees that there's going to be a horrendous collapse," declares the park's resource naturalist, Paul Schullery. "Within 20 years the cutthroats probably will be reduced by 50 to 80 percent and somewhere out beyond that they will be essentially gone. There's this big subset of the grizzly population that keys in on these trout. When the Craighead brothers were studying grizzlies in the 1960s they never once saw a bear take a fish." By 1975, when the effect of catch-and-release started kicking in, bear activity was being observed on 17 of 59 cutthroat spawning streams. Now bears work at least 55, and one research team observed a sow with cubs averaging 100 fish a day for 10 days.

While in the park, white pelicans get almost all their nourishment from cutthroats, consuming an estimated 300,000 pounds a season. In 1924 the tinkerers looked upon these huge, ungainly birds and saw that they were "bad." Not only did they eat trout, they served as vectors for trout tapeworms. So for the next eight years the Park Service squashed pelican eggs. In a 1931 experiment to ascertain if trout tapeworms could be transferred to a mammalian host, a dedicated scientist named Lowell Woodbury swallowed 14 live ones; the study subjects perished in his digestive tract. Today the tapeworms still prefer pelicans and trout, and now the pelicans have rebounded along with the cutthroats.

Ospreys underwent a similar resurgence after the tinkerers quit using pesticides, after the conservators of wildness banned camping within a kilometer of active nests and after the cutthroat population increased by a factor of 10. In 1988 there were 66 nesting pairs in the park; last year there were 100. The park's bald eagles have fledged an average of 10 young a season for the past 12 years, with 17 in 1993 and 13 in 1994.

In 1973—the year Varley and his colleagues required that most trout caught in the park be released—they predicted the population shakedown would occur over the next seven years and that the effects of catch-and-release fishing would then be fully evident. They were wrong! Data collected on the Yellowstone River during the 1994 season revealed that the average size and the average age were still increasing.

But now, if the Park Service doesn't declare all-out war on lake trout, cutthroats are finished. Even if it does declare war, neither the cutthroat population nor the trout-based ecosystem can ever attain their natural potentials. Lake trout are there to stay.

Might the lake trout be the progeny of fish unleashed in the golden age of tinkering that have just percolated along ever since? After all, unsuccessful introductions of rainbows and Atlantic salmon were made back then, and while there aren't any records of lake-trout stocking, record-keeping in those days was a notoriously casual business. Fishers of the lake—generally novices who don't excel at species identification—constantly report catching things like hornpout and bluegills, and park officials have been conditioned to just nod politely. Maybe the tourists were right when they said they'd caught lake trout 20, 30, 40 years ago and more. It's a cheery thought, because it would mean that something is holding the invaders back, but I fear it's also wishful thinking. When I put my dream hypothesis to Bob Behnke, of Colorado State University, he said, "No, I don't think so. When I used to work for the Fish and Wildlife Service in the late '60s, we'd set gillnets all over that lake, some very deep. And we only got cutthroats. I think they've been in there 20 years max."

The most likely scenario is that some ecological illiterate who worshipped lake trout or someone who hated let-it-be managers (and there are plenty of both) caught some fish in Lewis Lake, popped them in a cooler and drove the 30-minute trip to West Thumb. The lake trout planted more than a century ago in Lewis and Shoshone Lakes came from Lake Michigan, and when lake-trout restoration got underway there, managers came to the park to collect eggs of the native stock. In the mid-1980s—just about the time biologists think the introduction was made—lake trout eggs were being stripped, fertilized and shipped back to Michigan. Maybe somebody borrowed a few.

Solving the case is going to be tough. One wag advisor to the Park Service has suggested that it host a Lake Trout Derby/Celebration, then arrest the first two guys who show up. Investigators are analyzing tissue samples from the fish caught last summer to compare DNA fingerprints with specimens from hatcheries and regional lakes. And Gresswell is hoping to do some chemical analysis of the otoliths to see if he can find a sudden shift in ratios of oxygen isotopes. If he does, it will indicate that the fish switched environments, something you wouldn't expect lake trout to do on their own. If, on the other hand, he fails to detect such a shift, it would indicate what most biologists expect and fear—that the fish hatched in the lake.

During my research, I came across a fictional account of illegal lake-trout introduction in Yellowstone Lake in the Summer 1991 *Gray's Sporting Journal*. A ranger drowns and a maintenance crew at Grant Village looks for his body with sonar. (This happened in real life, too.) During the search, big 30-pound-plus targets show up way down. They can't be cutts. Out comes the deep-sea tackle. Eventually, there's a hook-up and a prodigious tug of war until the head maintenance guy whips out a knife and lances the line. He then confesses that 28 years earlier he and the ranger had transplanted them: "A bucket plumb full of little ones, two buckets of six inchers, and eight or ten monsters. Took canoes up to Heart Lake, and we stayed for three days. Used nets . . . . We wanted some lake trout out the back door, don't you see?" For some reason these noble beasts are not reproducing, and the boss wants them left alone.

The more I dug, the more I was convinced I was onto something. *Gray's* had only the author's old address, and his last name, "Parks," struck me as fishy. The post office in his former town didn't have a forwarding address, and such a person was unknown to local guides, tackle dealers, newspapers, hook-and-bullet magazines, even an outdoor writer who lived on his old street. Finally, an insurance agent gave me the current address from a policy he had written on a boat—registered on Yellowstone Lake. Alas, Mr. Parks turned out to be a real, 37-year-old English professor who had guided for a concessionaire at Grant Village from 1979 through 1985, who hadn't heard about last summer's horrible news and who never once tripped my sensitive BS alarm. "Did you ever hear anyone saying they had put lake trout in Yellowstone Lake? I asked him.

After a long pause, Parks said, "I have to think about that. Something makes we want to say yes. No, I don't think so in Yellowstone Lake." Still, he allowed that he might have heard some talk, nothing too specific. He seemed genuinely upset about the threat to the ecosystem and eager to help in the investigation. He said he'd check with friends and get back to me.

How might an all-out war on lake trout be waged? Some of the nation's best fish scientists, convening in a voluntary emergency workshop, have kicked around ideas. There was talk of stocking triploid (sterile) sea lampreys, which in fertile, diploid form invaded the Great Lakes and proved so effective in ridding them of their native lake-trout stocks. You make triploid fish by shocking their eggs with chemicals, thereby giving them three sets of chromosomes rather than the normal two; but technology for producing triploids and achieving a 100-percent success rate doesn't exist. All you need is two mistakes and you've got double trouble.

Another interesting suggestion was to run bottom sediments through a big boat-mounted pump, spreading them over spawning beds. It takes just a dusting of silt to smother eggs. The trouble is, there's not much lake bottom that doesn't look like super spawning habitat.

Workshop member Bob Behnke thinks angling might be the most effective control. "Lake trout," he says, "are pretty vulnerable. If you can radio-tag a few and find where they congregate, you can put fishermen on them. Fishing pressure on [desired] lake-trout populations is a big problem in places like Flaming Gorge Reservoir. Fishermen with fish locators really slaughter them. Gillnets would work well too."

Chemical reclamation is out of the question. Antimycin is ruinously expensive, and there isn't enough rotenone on the planet. Five years ago the Utah Division of Wildlife Resources exhausted the world's supply of rotenone when it cleansed 13,000-acre Strawberry Reservoir of trout mongrels and exotic rough fish in order to make way for Bonneville cutthroats—the then-rare, salmon-size survivors of an extinct 50,170-square-mile glacial lake. Not only is Yellowstone Lake much deeper than Strawberry Reservoir, it has a surface area nearly seven times as large.

The Great Lakes contingent of the workshop knew a lot about knocking the bejesus out of lake trout because they'd seen how the Indians do it. The good news is that they feel confident the Park Service can keep ahead of the aliens, saving perhaps 80 percent of the cutthroat population, if it commits to expensive, labor-intensive "industrial-strength gillnetting." Robert Gresswell, a member of the workshop, says this: "I think you can overfish any species, and if you put in a concerted effort on lake trout, you can keep those numbers way low. We have a good chance of maintaining the ecosystem at a level that will allow most of the processes to continue pretty much like they are now."

The big problem will be money. If the cutthroat population is allowed to collapse, all the magical places like Buffalo Ford just become cold, sterile scenery bereft of fishermen and fish-eating wildlife. Park visitation even by non-anglers will plummet. The new lake-trout fishery won't recover five cents on the dollar, and the torrent of money that sustains local tackle shops, motels, restaurants and guide services, the money that built Jackson Hole and West Yellowstone, is going to dry up like tobacco juice on a stoked woodstove.

As Varley says, it's pretty hard to think of worse park news than lake trout among the cutts. But even as he was telling me the gory details, he was reporting the best park news that he or I could ever have imagined. Wolves were on the ground in Yellowstone and they'd be released in 72 hours. It had taken the conservators of wildness 20 years to pull this off, and no other initiative—not even no-kill trout fishing—had been more contentious. If Varley and his allies can restore what the tinkerers worked so hard to eliminate, they certainly can prevail in a perpetual campaign of lake-trout suppression.

Yellowstone may have a few extra and therefore ugly parts, but at least now it has all its original ones. You can't say that about any other sub-Alaskan area of the United States. Returning wolves to America's oldest and best-loved park is "a profoundly symbolic act," to borrow the words of Renee Askins, of The Wolf Fund—a private, single-mission group whose doors closed March 21, 1995, the instant the wolf-release-pen doors swung open. Despite the constant background noise from tinkerers, wolf restoration means that the nation is now behind let-it-be management, that the conservators of wildness have finally prevailed. And if there could be better news for native trout than that, I can't guess what.

UPDATE
In order to design a lake-trout-control program for the Park Service, a Fish and Wildlife Service team led by Lynn Kaeding conducted experimental netting during the summer of 1995. The panel of experts had identified 12 prime areas for netting. The team set gill-nets at nine of these, taking 153 lake trout ranging between six and 22 inches in length. Anglers reported catching 42 additional fish ranging in length from 16 to 24 inches; most of these were given to Kaeding's team.

Stomach analyses of captured lake trout indicated that they had been feeding heavily on fish. All the fish that could be identified were cutthroats.

The Ugly Trade in Gorgeous Feathers

So what's wrong with substitutes?

Atlantic Salmon Journal, Winter 1995

DRIFTS THERE A FLY more hideous than, say, the Green Machine, aka "Green Lowlander"—a clump of deer hair that flatters a cigarette butt flipped onto asphalt by a hooker wearing chartreuse lipstick—and which catches half the salmon taken on the Miramichi because that's what they use up there? Yes!

It is any classic tied with "authentic" material from bird and mammal species whose wild populations have been critically depressed, and which may or may not be protected by international laws like the Convention on International Trade in Endangered Species (CITES) and the Migratory Bird Treaty, or US statutes like the Endangered Species and Marine Mammal acts. Many classic feathers now come from birds legally raised in captivity—jungle cock, for instance, of which a single neck sells for about $150. Such enterprise, it might reasonably be argued, takes the pressure off wild birds.

On the other hand, commercialization of wildlife never has a happy ending for the species being trafficked in. Legal trade in exotic feathers from pen-raised birds, museum mounts and collections that predate protective laws can drive up the price on contraband, putting a contract out on vanishing species. The tiers and feather merchants I know care about all fish and wildlife and try to obey the law. And yet when they legally buy and sell, say, Indian crow, any of the macaws, flourican bustard, speckled bustard, toucan, and such cotingas as blue chatterer and cock of the rock, they fuel a growing illegal trade that further depresses the species in their native habitats.

The prices that the salmon-fly trade places on the heads of rare birds and on polar bears make a black market inevitable. For example, a pair of speckled bustard feathers can fetch $250, a pair of flourican bustard feathers $70, a center tail from a scarlet macaw $40, feathers from a blue chatterer or Indian crow $12 each. A classic salmon fly tied with these feathers can sell for $800, and I know of one that sold for $1,900. "With that kind of monetary demand, people *are* going to kill these species," declares Louisiana State University's Dr. James V. Remsen, an authority on neotropical birds. "The market really ought to be cut off. The insatiable hunger for exotica among North Americans is disturbing. People have got to start developing a conscience. If a campesino [the politically correct name for a Latin American peasant] made only $7 on a blue chatterer, that's still a day's wage."

The oldest salmon flies are somber, concocted with partridge, bittern, snipe and the like, but in 1658 a soldier in Cromwell's army named Richard Frank discovered that the salmon "delights in the most gaudy and Orient colors you can choose." By the middle of the 19th Century two basic patterns had emerged—dull when salmon were feeding (as anglers still believed they did) and gaudy when their bellies were supposedly full.

Colorful flies were slow to be embraced in England where, for years, traditionalists disdained them as "the Irish fly" and even went so far as to ban them on the River Tweed on grounds they were a "bugbear to the fish, scaring them from their accustomed haunts and resting spots." In North America they weren't much sought even by collectors until 1978, when master tier Poul Jorgensen published *Salmon Flies: Their Character, Style and Dressing.*

The book created an obsession for classics tied with traditional materials, sending prices off the page and horrifying bird advocates, especially Jorgensen. Ever since, he has been trying to atone for what he calls the "monster" he created. "This craze wasn't meant to be," he told me. "I researched and wrote up a lot of substitutes for these feathers—turkey, chicken, duck. That was the idea. But some of the guys just went wild, and started hunting down these rare feathers — tried to get them any way they could. They're corrupting these young tiers I'm trying to teach."

The craze has now spread to the Far East, especially Japan. "There are probably 20 tiers for every fisherman over there," says Phil Castleman, of Springfield, Massachusetts, a breeder of rare birds and the largest of all feather merchants. "It's just outrageous. Any American breeder could sell most of his feathers in the Far East with very little problem. Some of the Asian countries aren't members of CITES, so I don't buy anything from the Far East. People there have a great deal of trouble getting paperwork out of their governments and, even though the birds might be legal, I just don't want to fool around with them because I need paperwork. Birds are coming in without papers, and you'll see them around. My best advice for a salmon-fly tier is know who you're doing business with."

Unfortunately, conscientious feather merchants like Castleman can't begin to sate the demand. So there is plenty of room for the other sort. One tier in eastern Canada confided to me that he has a contact in Saudi Arabia (a nation that has not signed onto CITES) who has a contact in the US, and the material is "just channeled back and forth. The fellow from the states sends it over to my buddy in Saudi Arabia, and he sends it over to me."

In undercover operations special agents of the US Fish and Wildlife Service's Division of Law Enforcement have checked more than a dozen prominent fly shops and found at least six to be knowingly dealing in black-market materials for classic salmon flies. Two agents spoke to me on the record for this article, but I'll call them "Agent A" and "Agent B" to avoid spooking the criminals they're investigating. The division wants to take down the shop owners, of course, but its real quarry is their suppliers.

"When we talked to these shop owners about Atlantic salmon flies," Agent A told me this past August, "there was a tendency for them to reduce the volume of their voices and start telling us how they beat the system. The big thing that's generating this, especially in polar bear [legal in Canada but not in the US] and endangered species is the interest in Atlantic salmon flies . . . . A successful shop owner with very good materials admitted to us in two or three undercover contacts that he was smuggling in polar bear and seal, was getting heron [a migratory bird]. Any kind of endangered bird feathers you needed, he knew somebody. He even mentioned golden eagles [not endangered, but protected under US law]. He sold us polar bear; he sold us seal. He was ready to sell us herons, and he was interested in buying various other migratory birds. Another shop owner had a big thing about having goat, then winked at us and said it was really polar bear.

We got that from another shop, too. At still another shop we bought the skin of a Wilson's phalarope [a migratory bird]. What I find in the wildlife trade is an awful lot of lowlifes. Even in these fly shops—even with the yuppie cast to them—you're dealing with people who are talking about how they beat this law and that law. Criminals are criminals."

As a spin-off of this operation, the Division of Law Enforcement is prosecuting an influential fly dealer who is alleged to have smuggled polar bear hides from Alaska that had been illegally sold to him by Native Americans. While polar bear isn't used in Victorian flies, it is an important material in early-20th-Century hairwing patterns. The case will go to trial about the time you read this.

Agent B, the main operative on the polar bear investigation, has this to say: "We have to make the assumption that 99 percent of the people dealing in flies [for all fish] are doing it legitimately, carrying on legal business. It's a small percentage of folks who just can't do with the synthetics. They've just got to have the real McCoy. The closer we get to the Atlantic salmon fly tiers and the people who provide them with raw materials, the more illegal activity we see . . . . The shop owners say their polar bear is pre-Marine Mammals Act, and maybe it is. But let me tell you there is one hell of a non-ending, never-ending supply of pre-act polar bear. I know there is a lot of pre-act polar bear they're doling out to keep the price at four or five bucks a square inch. But we're talking 1972 [the year the act was passed]. That's a lot of years ago. The arithmetic just doesn't figure."

All the peddlers of authentic feathers that I talk to tell me they obtained their stuff from molts, dead pelts, museums or someone's pre-act estate, and maybe they did. But there is also one hell of a non-ending, never-ending supply of pre-Endangered Species Act and pre-CITES feathers out there. Both these laws were passed in 1973, and that's a lot of years, too.

"I know for a fact that some of the guys get stuff from South America," Poul Jorgensen says. "A black-market speckled bustard feather can be obtained for around $300, and toucan breast feathers for $6 each, of which six are needed to dress a Jock Scott. I ask people, 'Where do you get the feathers from?' Oh, they get them from the zoo and from people who have pets that die. I don't believe very much of that. Nobody has six birds of the same kind that suddenly die of a heart attack."

Another well-known tier who spoke to me on condition he not be identified offered this: "I've tied flies for 25 years and met a lot of nice people. But lately there's this cult—this whole thing of owner-ship of rare materials. You go to any antique show or sportsman's show, it's like a nightclub. You whisper and you can get the stuff, just like you can get cocaine. Chatterer, Indian crow, toucan, macaw . . . . There's lots of muffled talk, deals going down all the time . . . . We posture ourselves as righteous sportsmen and go into fits if we see a spin fisherman squeeze a six-inch brook trout. But we can put the kill order on birds in Venezuela."

One of the most talented and respected of all salmon fly tiers is Paul Schmookler, of Millis, Massachusetts. He invents his own patterns, fashioning them after butterflies. Sometimes he mixes feathers, alter-nating individual fibers by locking their zippers together. According to *Sports Illustrated* he uses up to 150 materials in a single fly—from polar bear to golden pheasant to speckled bustard to blue chatterer. When I interviewed Schmookler four years ago for a piece I was doing for *Fly Rod & Reel*, he was conducting a brisk trade in original mate-rials, offering 100-feather packages of blue chatterer and Indian crow for $700 and $500 respectively. When I interviewed him this past August, however, he said he had gotten out of the feather business.

"How come?" I inquired.

"Because of you," he said. "You scared the hell out of me and my wife with that article. She thought the feds were going to come after us like they did to [a famous tier who learned his lesson and doesn't deserve to be mentioned here]. They knocked his door down and came in with guns and threatened his wife because he had a jungle cock neck in his store which predated the act. I'm being chased out, hounded, witch-hunted . . . . Here I am stuck with materials, and I'm being used as a target and a whipping post. I don't need it. I've given 20 or 30 thousand dollars to Theodore Gordon Flyfishers. I donate year after year to all these conservation funds. I did it quietly and hon-orably, and I never ask for any money or pats on the back."

I told Schmookler I didn't doubt anything he said—except for the alleged conduct of the feds, because I was familiar with the bust and knew that the case agent conducted himself with restraint and pro-fessionalism, and that jungle cock wasn't involved—and explained to him that it had not been my intent to criticize him in any way or to imply that he has ever engaged in any illegal activity.

I then attempted, unsuccessfully, to contact another well-known merchant of authentic feathers who is said to have quit for the same reason. Finally, I phoned Sol Shamilzadeh, of New York City, who in

1991 had been offering what he reported and I believed to be legally acquired flourican bustard feathers for $150 a pair, breast patches (clusters of small feathers) from sundry macaws for $32.50 each, and Indian crow feathers for $150 per pack of 20. He immediately hung up on me.

Back in 1991, feather merchants tried to get my piece for *Fly Rod & Reel* killed before I had even submitted it to the editor. One declared, "It's an unwritten kind of thing with our little hobby—don't show a large profile or the government is going to come down on you with a hammer." In August 1995 the same individual phoned *Atlantic Salmon Journal* editor Harry Bruce and bent his ear for the better part of an hour about my being, among other things, a practitioner of "yellow journalism" whose work the magazine should not stoop to publish. In light of this communication, I now offer two lessons I've picked up during my life as an investigative reporter: First, the surest indication an issue needs light is when the special interests involved start telling you it can't stand any; and second, if you throw a stick into a pack of dogs and one yelps, that's the one you hit.

No word more infuriates master fly tier Ron Alcott than "authentic" as applied to feathers. He objects even to the word "substitute," arguing that "alternate" is more accurate. Alternate materials, he observes, were freely used by tiers of the 19th and early 20th Centuries. In fact, making do is a tradition in itself. "Damn it," he told me. "If they did it, we can do it."

What we now call "authentic" materials were frequently used because what we now call "substitutes" weren't available. For example, in the 19th Century, when the sun didn't set on the British Empire, tiers had to get along with blue chatterer when Eurasian kingfisher became depleted. Now, with kingfisher cheap and abundant, cultists blindly insist on blue chatterer. To prove how phony the "authentic" salmon fly craze is, *American Angler & Fly Tyer* Magazine commissioned Alcott to tie two Jock Scotts for its cover, one with legally obtained original materials, the other with modern alternates. Nary a fly snob could tell which was which.

In November 1995 Countryman Press, of Woodstock, Vermont, published Alcott's new book, *Building Classic Salmon Flies*. In it, he makes a compelling case for forgetting about rare original materials. "My intent," he writes, "is to convince contemporary tiers to 'make peace with the past' and realize that beautiful flies can be built using alternate feathers, and that in some patterns alternate feathers indeed make a much better-looking fly. Also, the present-day unavailability of some exotic feathers, import restrictions and exorbitant prices for what is available are themselves justification for using alternatives."

As a salmon fisherman and a bird watcher, I find it painful to report that, on occasion, both fraternities can be unendurably pompous and self-absorbed. We attend expensive fund-raising dinners, the better to fight such threats to the objects of our affection as drift-netters (who kill birds as well as fish), clearcutters, poachers, pesticide spewers and black-market traffickers. We rail against any enterprise that would further deplete our fragile, beautiful resource. But the other guy's fragile, beautiful resource? Well, that's a different story. We have not noticed, to borrow John Muir's words, that "when one tugs on a single brick in nature one finds that it is attached to the rest of the world."

Now consider the following report, published in a leading sporting magazine: "With all the other pressures on Atlantic salmon the relatively new demand for their smooth, pearl-like otoliths (ear bones) [is] abominable. Wealthy bird watchers, predominantly Latin Americans, have taken a fancy to camera and binocular straps studded and/or strung with as many as 400 otoliths from *Salmo salar* (each fish has but two). Otoliths from the coarse and ever-abundant freshwater drum, which are virtually indistinguishable, would serve equally well. But purists insist on 'authentic' material. At this point most traffic appears legal, but a healthy little black market exists, and prices portend a larger one. For instance, some of the swankier shops, such as *Me Eche Espanol*, in Buenos Aires, are getting up to $2,000 for a single strap." That was the lead paragraph of a piece entitled "The Highlander Hatch," which appeared in the March 1992 *Fly Rod & Reel*. It was, of course, a dirty trick to play on my readers because, as I explained to them in the next sentence, not a word of it was true. But it pushed their buttons. If it pushed yours, too, hang on to that feeling.

UPDATE

What I can't figure out is why so many fly tiers are mad at me. I carefully reported that only *a few* are crooks. They keep saying that this kind of negative publicity is "bad for fly-tying" as if fly-tying had a life of its own, as if it were an institution or a person. It's like when the pro bassers say that Ray Scott has been "good for bass fishing."

Look where Nixon and his staff got by telling the press not to ask questions.